C000235002

A Bit on the Side

A Bit on the Side

Politicians – Who pays them?
An Insider's Guide

PAUL HALLORAN
and
MARK HOLLINGSWORTH

SIMON & SCHUSTER

LONDON·SYDNEY·NEW YORK·TOKYO·SINGAPORE·TORONTO

First published in Great Britain by
Simon & Schuster Ltd 1994
A Paramount Communications Company

Copyright © Paul Halloran and Mark Hollingsworth, 1994

This book is copyright under the Berne Convention
No reproduction without permission
All rights reserved

The right of Paul Halloran and Mark Hollingsworth be identified
as authors of this work has been asserted in accordance
with sections 77 and 78 of the Copyright, Designs and Patents Act 1988.

Simon & Schuster Ltd
West Garden Place
Kendal Street
London W2 2AQ

Simon & Schuster of Australia Pty Ltd
Sydney

A CIP catalogue record for this book is
available from the British Library

ISBN 0-671-71350-7

Typeset in Sabon by Hewer Text Composition Services, Edinburgh
Printed and bound in Great Britain by
Butler & Tanner Ltd, Frome and London

Contents

Section One

Reader's Guide to MPs' Profiles

The profiles in this section contain all published information about MPs' commercial and financial interests. It also includes directorships the authors have discovered at Companies House which do not appear in the official Register of Members' Interests.

Information about their parliamentary activities is restricted to whether they are members of important Select Committees, Ministers, Parliamentary Private Secretaries and all Opposition front-bench spokespersons. Membership of more obscure Select Committees like Statutory Instruments, all-party groups and back-bench committees is not sufficiently influential, in the authors' view, to warrant inclusion.

The 'Declared Interests' section includes consultancies, clients, directorships, shareholdings, foreign payments, trade union sponsorship, professions, membership of the Lloyd's insurance market, land and property and overseas visits. Where it states 'advisor', this is essentially the same as 'consultancy'. The only arbitrary category is 'land and property'. An entry is only included if an MP owns a substantial amount of land or a property development company.

Where categories are omitted, this simply means the MP has no financial or business interests, does not hold any important parliamentary position or has decided not to declare it.

The 'Comments' section has two purposes. Firstly, to list directorships not declared in the official Register. This data was obtained by directorship searches at Companies House. Secondly, to provide some unusual background profile information – political and business – on prominent MPs, particularly on their commercial and financial interests.

MPs and their Financial Interests

In October 1993, James Couchman, a Conservative MP who has a directorship and three consultancies, was asked by a Channel 4 programme whether he should declare how much he earns from his outside business interests. 'That's a matter between me and the Inland Revenue,' he replied dismissively.[1]

This response is indicative of MPs' desire to keep details about their financial 'bits on the side' hidden from the public. Parliament has consistently voted against mandating Members to disclose comprehensive information about their commercial interests. Their defence is that MPs have a 'right to privacy' on these matters.

But do they? As Paddy Ashdown, leader of the Liberal Democrats, said in a Commons debate: 'When a person joins this House he is involved in the business of public affairs and must therefore relinquish some of that privacy. . . . Privacy often leads to secrecy, and secrecy is the blanket behind which corruption can take place. I therefore believe that there is a need to declare all sources [of cash] over and above parliamentary salaries. . . . There is only one loyalty that Members of this House have, and that loyalty is derived from the vote cast in the ballot box.'[2]

It is this potential conflict of loyalties between an MP's private financial interests and his or her public duties that undermines confidence in our democracy. After all, as the political lobbyist Douglas Smith reflected, 'If you are being paid by someone outside parliament, it must in a sense influence your judgement at certain moments.'[3]

But there is surely a more fundamental democratic right for the electorate to know the business activities of their representatives. For them to have basic, detailed, accessible data about their MP is what this book is all about.

Although much is kept secret from the public, MPs are obliged to declare a certain amount of information. There is a Register of Members' Interests in which MPs have to 'provide information of any pecuniary interest or other material benefit which . . . might be thought to affect his conduct as a Member or influence his actions, speeches or vote in Parliament.'[4] There are ten categories under which MPs are required to register. They are:

1. Paid directorships of public and private companies.
2. Paid consultancies.
3. Professional occupations, trades and vocations.
4. Clients of companies with whom the MP is retained as a consultant or director which arise out of his or her membership of the House of Commons.

5. Financial sponsorship as a candidate and MP by any person or organisation. Most sponsorships are by trade unions but this section also includes gifts of more than £125.
6. Overseas visits which have been funded by private interests.
7. Payments from foreign governments, agencies or individuals.
8. Land and Property.
9. Companies in which the MP has, either by himself or with a spouse, shareholdings of more than one per cent.
10. Names of specific Lloyd's insurance syndicates in which the MP is a member.

The Register is updated regularly but only published once a year. The updated version is available for public inspection in the Committee Office of the House of Commons. But, bizarrely, photocopying of extracts is prohibited.

More importantly, the Register is inadequate in both its structure and application. Any voter reading the document will only see a blurred vision of their MP's interests. Here are some items missing from the Register:

1. Amount of money received by the MP.
2. Shareholdings of less than one per cent.
3. Value and size of the declared shareholdings.
4. Nature of services provided by MP to the client.
5. Clients of public relations and private consultancy companies set up by MPs themselves.

The Register's lack of credibility is illustrated by the fact that it is voluntary, based on guidelines rather than sanction. For many years Enoch Powell, the Conservative and then Ulster Unionist MP, refused to declare any interests and no action was taken against him.

To be fair, there have been inquiries in recent years involving John Browne, Sir Michael Grylls and Michael Mates (although largely due to media pressure). But the mechanism to police the system is inadequate. The Commons Select Committee on Members' Interests is made up of MPs (who often have commercial interests themselves!).

It has no research or investigative staff, apart from an overworked Registrar. In addition, the Committee will launch an inquiry *only* after a complaint by a member of the public or an MP. Anyone asking for an investigation is also expected to provide prima-facie evidence as to the accuracy of the allegation. This, of course, is designed to deter complaints from the public. Only well-informed journalists or MPs are able to avoid the procedural elephant traps.

Apart from the voluntary Register, MPs are also exempt from legal prosecution for corruption. They can only be charged if the alleged offences take place *outside* Parliament. If a corruption offence is committed inside the Commons, then they are are immune from the criminal law. This is despite the fact that the financial interests of county, district and city councillors are governed by tough legal sanctions. They are required by law to declare all their financial interests in a statutory register. Any breach of the regulations is a criminal offence and councillors can, and are, jailed or fined in a court of law.

The legal exemption for MPs has remained the case despite repeated calls for reform. The most recent attempt was in 1990 but the then Prime Minister, Margaret Thatcher, responded: 'We would consider bringing forward legislation to make the corruption of Members a criminal offence only if there was clear evidence that the present arrangements were ineffective and the House agreed.'[5]

In the House of Commons chamber and in correspondence with Ministers and officials, MPs are obliged to declare their interests – but only when making a speech during a debate or in committee proceedings. Again there are loopholes and omissions in the rules. Here are the occasions when an MP does *not* have to declare his or her interests.

1. When asking oral questions.
2. When submitting written questions.
3. When making 'brief' interventions during debates.
4. When sponsoring Commons motions.

MPs are also allowed to vote for legislation which may benefit a company or organisation that is paying him or her. This was not always the case. In the nineteenth century Speakers of the House often ruled that MPs could not vote on matters in which they had a direct pecuniary interest. This has been neglected to such an extent over the years that it now only covers privately sponsored Bills. As the overwhelming majority of legislation are public Bills, MPs are allowed to vote and lobby to their hearts' content – even if they have a financial stake in doing so.

Essentially, MPs can vote, ask questions, lobby, speak and write letters to Ministers and civil servants on behalf of private clients with whom they have a business relationship.

Clearly, most companies do not pay MPs just to decorate their notepaper (although some do for PR purposes). They are looking for a return for their investment. After Patrick Nicholls lost his job as an Environment Minister in 1990, he was hired as a consultant to MinOtels Europe. 'We took on Patrick Nicholls and he's worked very hard for us,' said a MinOtels Executive. 'We consider he gives us very good value for money. He'll have to prove that as years go by. Nobody pays out money for nothing. He has been a great help to us so far and I'm quite sure will continue to do so and will earn the money that we pay him.'[6]

MPs can earn substantial extra cash from companies who 'need some help'. On average each consultancy brings in about £10,000 a year and a directorship about £15,000, but this fluctuates. Some consultancies can yield up to £60,000 and most directorships are combined with potentially lucrative shareholdings and share options. There are also commission fees for introducing clients to merchant banks, stockbrokers, investment firms and PR and lobbying companies.

This is all on top of their parliamentary annual salary of £31,687. MPs also receive an allowance of £40,380 for 'office costs', plus travel expenses (calculated per mile and dependent on size of the engine) and also a London supplement of £11,000 per year if the Member has a constituency outside Inner London. Consequently, an MP from the provinces will receive £82,000 a year from the public purse. Admittedly, this includes all expenses, notably the employment of office staff. But even then some MPs use their wives as secretaries.

Compared to his or her own constituents, an MP is more than adequately paid (the average wage is about £12,000 per year). Even on cautious estimates, an MP who has a few consultancies and directorships is raking in an extra £40,000 a year. And a large proportion of the money he or she receives from outside interests is paid purely and solely because they are MPs.

Then there are the moonlighters. During the Thatcher years of large Commons majorities, some back-benchers spent as much time on their private finances as on their public duties. According to Edwina Currie, Tory MP and a former junior Health Minister: 'There was a colleague who told the Whips he was in his constituency and he told his constituency that he was in London. In fact, he was in the Channel Islands, running a business. Another colleague lives in California and only comes to Westminster about six times a year.'[7]

But this book is not just an analysis of the morality of MPs and their financial bits on the side. It is a factual, accessible guide to the ordinary voter so that he or she can make an informed democratic decision. The existing sources of information are deficient and shot through with omissions. Hopefully, this book will, at least in part, fill in the gaps.

Sources:

1. 'Checkout' programme, current affairs documentary made by Diverse Productions, 26 October 1993.
2. House of Commons *Hansard*, 17 December 1985, col. 240.
3. 'An MP's Business', *World In Action*, Granada TV, 30 March 1992.
4. Register of Members' Interests, 1 December 1992, page iii, HC-325.
5. House of Commons *Hansard*, 2 April 1990.
6. 'Checkout' programme, Diverse Productions, 26 October 1993.
7. *New Woman* magazine, April 1991.

ABBOT, Diane

Constituency: Labour, Hackney North and Stoke Newington
Parliamentary Activities:
Select Committee Membership: Treasury and Civil Service
Declared Interests: Occasional broadcasting, journalism and lecturing.

ADAMS, Irene

Constituency: Labour, Paisley North
Parliamentary Activities:
Select Committee Memberships: None
Declared Interests: None listed.

AINGER, Nicholas

Constituency: Labour, Pembroke
Parliamentary Activities:
Select Committee Membership: Commons Services (Broadcasting); Welsh Affairs
Declared Interests: None Listed.

AINSWORTH, Peter

Constituency: Conservative, East Surrey
Parliamentary Activities:
Select Committee Memberships: Environment
Declared Interests: Non-executive director of JLI Group, plc; Consultant to S.G. Warburg Group

Comments: According to records at Companies House, Ainsworth is a director of Battersea Community Arts Centre Trust Ltd.

AINSWORTH, Robert

Constituency: Labour, Coventry North East
Parliamentary Activities:
Select Committee Memberships: None
Declared Interests:
Trades or Professions: Councillor, Coventry City Council
Overseas Visits: 10–11 November 1993, to France, to look at Eurotunnel terminal, paid for by Eurotunnel.

AITKEN, Jonathan

Constituency: Conservative, South Thanet
Parliamentary Activities: Minister for Defence Procurement
Declared Interests: Occasional author

Comments: Aitken's appointment as Minister for Defence Procurement in 1992 was greeted with surprise and some concern, given his long-standing business links with Saudi Arabia. He was a director of Al-Bilhad UK Ltd which received payments from contracts with the Saudi-Arabian Royal Family and government agencies. He was also deputy chairman of Aitken Hume, a financial services group which was used to channel £2.1 million of Saudi royal funds to buy a stake in TV-AM plc.

ALEXANDER, Richard

Constituency: Conservative, Newark
Parliamentary Activities:
Select Committee Memberships: Agriculture
Declared Interests:
Employment or Office: Advisor to Ancient Order of Foresters Friendly Society
Trades or Professions: Solicitor

Overseas Visits: 14–23 September 1992, to Northern Cyprus with a delegation from the All Party Parliamentary Group for Northern Cyprus, as guests of the Minister of Foreign Affairs and Defence of the Turkish Republic of Northern Cyprus

Comments: Alexander became notorious for placing a remarkable advertisement in the 'Situations Wanted' column of the parliamentary *House Magazine* in the summer of 1989. It stated: 'Hard-working back-bench Tory MP of ten years' standing seeks consultancy in order to widen his range of activities. Please contact Richard Alexander on 01–2194207.' Sadly, although he received three offers, he was unsuccessful.

ALISON, Rt.Hon. Michael

Constituency: Conservative, Selby
Parliamentary Activities:
Select Committee Memberships: None
Declared Interests: None listed.

ALLASON, Rupert

Constituency: Conservative, Torbay
Parliamentary Activities:
Select Committee Memberships: None
Declared Interests: Director of Westintel (Research) Ltd
Employment or Office: European Editor, Intelligence Quarterly
Trades or Professions: Underwriting member of Lloyd's; Author
Declarable shareholdings: Alfred Allason Trust.
Comments: Allason writes books on Security and Intelligence matters using the pseudonym Nigel West. Westintel is a company used to channel his royalties and expenses.

ALLEN, Graham

Constituency: Labour, Nottingham North
Parliamentary Activities: An Opposition spokesperson on Home Affairs
Declared Interests:
Financial Sponsorships, Gifts, etc.: He occasionally assists the Communication Managers Association on parliamentary matters. His constituency is sponsored by the Transport and General Workers' Union; no personal payment is made to him.
Declarable shareholdings: He owns one share in the Greater Nottingham Co-op.

ALTON, David

Constituency: Liberal Democrat, Liverpool, Mossley Hill
Parliamentary Activities:
Select Committee Memberships: None
Declared Interests: Occasional articles, lectures, book royalties, broadcasting; Occasional research assistance provided by the Movement for Christian Democracy.

AMESS, David

Constituency: Conservative, Basildon
Parliamentary Activities: Parliamentary Private Secretary to Michael Portillo, Chief

Secretary to the Treasury
Declared Interests: Director of: Accountancy Ltd, trading as Accountancy Aims; Westminster Recruitment Consultants (both unremunerated)

ANCRAM, Michael

Constituency: Conservative, Devizes
Parliamentary Activities: Parliamentary Under-Secretary for Northern Ireland
Declared Interests: Director of Portzim Ltd
Trades or Professions: Occasional freelance journalism
Land and Property: A small tenanted estate in Scotland and a partnership in a tenanted farm
Declarable Shareholdings: Portzim Ltd.

Comments: In 1984, while a junior Scottish Office Minister, Ancram owned 1,491 shares in Grand Metropolitan plc, whose subsidiary Grand Net Catering Services was seeking privatised contracts in catering and refuse collection.

ANDERSON, Donald

Constituency: Labour, Swansea East
Parliamentary Activities:
Select Committee Membership: Home Affairs
Declared Interests:
Employment or Office: Consultant to the Royal Society of Chemistry (no personal financial benefit)
Trades or Professions: Barrister-at-Law
Financial Sponsorships, Gifts, etc.: Sponsored by the National Union of Rail, Transport and Maritime Workers on the usual terms.

ANDERSON, Janet

Constituency: Labour, Rossendale and Darwen
Parliamentary Activities:
Select Committee Membership: None
Declared Interests: Member of the Royal College of Nursing Parliamentary Panel.

ARBUTHNOT, James

Constituency: Conservative, Wanstead and Woodford
Parliamentary Activities: Assistant Government Whip
Declared Interests:
Trades or Professions: Member of Lloyd's; Barrister (non-practising)
Overseas Visits: 19–21 September 1992, to Cadenabbia, Italy, to a conference of British and German Members of Parliament, as the guest of the Konrad Adenauer Stiftung.

ARMSTRONG, Hilary

Constituency: Labour, Durham North West
Parliamentary Activities: Parliamentary Private Secretary to John Smith, Leader of the Opposition
Declared Interests: Director of Project Genesis Limited (examining feasibility of redevelopment of steelworks site, Consett – no remuneration involved); Vice-President, N.C.H. (National Childrens Homes) (no

remuneration involved); Treasurer: Methodist Church Division of Education and Youth (no remuneration involved)

Financial Sponsorships Gifts, etc.: Sponsored by MSF (formerly ASTMS). North West Durham Constituency Labour Party receives £600 per annum

Overseas Visits: December 1992, three nights accommodation at the Inter-Continental Hotel, Nairobi, provided by the Ministry of Foreign Affairs of the Government of Kenya in the course of an otherwise private visit

Comments: From declarations made to Companies House in London, Armstrong lists addition interests as director of Rowanmist Ltd.

ARNOLD, Jacques

Constituency: Conservative, Gravesham
Parliamentary Activities: Parliamentary Private Secretary to David Maclean, Minister of State at the Home Office
Declared Interests:

Employment or Office: Consultant to the Norwich and Peterborough Building Society; Consultant to the Thomas Cook Group Ltd

Overseas Visits: 18–21 September 1992, to Cadenabbia, Italy, for discussions with German Parliamentarians as a guest of the Konrad Adenauer Foundation.

ARNOLD, Sir Thomas

Constituency: Conservative, Hazel Grove
Parliamentary Activities:

Select Committee Membership: Treasury and Civil Service

Declared Interests: Director of Tom Arnold Ltd; Tom Arnold Associates Ltd; Manrows Ltd; Pector Ltd; Primaver Ltd

Employment or Office: Consultant to Quay Consultants Ltd

Trades or Professions: Owner of musical and dramatic copyrights under the will of the late Ivor Novello

Declarable Shareholdings: Tom Arnold Ltd; Tom Arnold Associates Ltd; Pector Ltd; Primaver Ltd

Comments: Sir Tom was a powerful force in the Conservative Party as Vice-Chairman in charge of candidates, personnel and administration. More interestingly, his companies are a vehicle for Sir Tom's career as a theatrical impressario. Tom Arnold Ltd, for example, is the family production company for *The King and I*.

ASHBY, David

Constituency: Conservative, North West Leicestershire
Parliamentary Activities:

Select Committee Membership: Home Affairs

Declared Interests: Chairman of Drimount Ltd and of its subsidiaries, A & P Tools and Products Ltd, GPM Ltd, and GPM (Displays) Ltd; Barrister-at-law; Member of Lloyd's

Declarable Shareholdings: Drimount Ltd

Overseas Visits: 12–19 July 1992, to New York for Democrat Convention, sponsored by the British–American Parliamentary Group and the United States Information Agency.

ASHDOWN Rt.Hon. Paddy

Constituency: Liberal Democrat, Yeovil
Parliamentary Activities: Leader of the Liberal Democrat Party
Declared Interests:
Trades or Professions: Occasional payment received for newspaper and magazine articles, television appearances, and for talks given to companies and other bodies
Financial Sponsorships, Gifts, etc: Use of a car on loan from Peugeot Talbot plc
Declarable Shareholdings: He owns shares in Westland plc, whose value is less than £100
Overseas Visits: 8–12 August 1992, to Bosnia at the invitation of the Bosnian Serbs; 12–17 December 1992, to Bosnia; assistance with travel expenses from Croatian Government.

ASHTON Joe

Constituency: Labour, Bassetlaw
Parliamentary Activities:
Select Committee Membership: National Heritage
Declared Interests: Director of Sheffield Wednesday Football Club (unremunerated) (from March 1990); Occasional broadcasting and journalism
Financial Sponsorship, Gifts etc: By the Manufacturing, Financial and Scientific Union. No personal payment but help towards constituency party expenses of £850 per year and approximately 25 per cent of election costs.

ASPINWALL, Jack

Constituency: Conservative, Wansdyke
Parliamentary Activities:
Select Committee Membership: None
Declared Interests: Director of Sacrum Investments Ltd; Consultant to Rentokil plc; Consultant to BAA plc; Consultant to British Gas plc
Land and Property: 1 Lambridge Buildings, Bath, Avon
Overseas Visits: 22–26 May 1992, to USA, to Orlando Aviation Matters, for four days as a guest of Smith Industries, Martin Marietta and BA; 12–16 October 1992, to Washington D.C. and Pittsburgh, hosted by British Airways.

ATKINS, Robert

Constituency: Conservative, South Ribble
Parliamentary Activities: Minister of State for Northern Ireland
Declared Interests: None listed.

ATKINSON, David

Constituency: Conservative, Bournemouth East
Parliamentary Activities:
Select Committee Membership: None
Declared Interests:
Overseas Visits: 10–13 Febuary 1992, to Angola to observe Peace Process – Leader of Parliamentary Delegation sponsored by Strategy Network International; 29 July–4 August 1992, to Nagorno Karabahk, to deliver humanitarian aid, sponsored by Christian Solidarity International (CSI)

Comments: From declarations made to

Companies House in London, Atkinson is also a director of Christian Solidarity International.

ATKINSON, Peter

Constituency: Conservative, Hexham
Parliamentary Activities:
Select Committee Membership: Scottish Affairs, European Legislation
Declared Interests:
Employment or Office: General Consultant.

AUSTIN-WALKER, John

Constituency: Labour, Woolwich
Parliamentary Activities:
Select Committee Membership: None
Declared Interests: None Listed
Overseas Visits: 14–18 September 1992, to Libya at the invitation and expense of the Libyan Ministry of Foreign Affairs; 22–27 October 1992, to Slovenia. He paid travel expenses himself and accommodation and other facilities provided in part by the Government of Slovenia and the municipality of Maribor; 28–29 November 1992, to Dominica, to attend the annual conference of Dominica Labour Party. Travel and accommodation paid for by the Dominica Labour Party; 30 May 1993–2 June 1993, to Jordan and the occupied territories of Gaza and the West Bank, at the invitation and expense of Labour Middle East Committee. Additional hospitality and internal transport was provided by the PLO and Jordanian Government; 4–8 July 1993, to Tirana, Albania, for a seminar on 'Parliamentary Practice' at invitation and expense of the European Co-operation Fund with support from the European Bank for Reconstruction and Development.

BAKER, Rt.Hon. Kenneth

Constituency: Conservative, Mole Valley
Parliamentary Activities:
Select Committee Membership: None
Declared Interests: Director of Hanson plc (non-executive); Torrey Investments Inc. (non-executive); UK–Japan 2000 Group (honorary); Videotron Holdings Ltd (non-executive)
Employment or Office: Advisor to ICL plc; Advisor to Cable and Wireless plc
Trades or Professions: Writer
Overseas Visits: 18–20 March 1993, to Germany as a guest speaker for British Chamber of Commerce and 64 Business Club. Ev. Frankfurt main branch

Comments: Baker was Minister for Information Technology and Industry, 1981–84, Minister for Local Government 1984–85, Environment Secretary 1985–86, Education Secretary 1986–89 and Home Secretary 1990–92.

BAKER, Nicholas

Constituency: Conservative, North Dorset
Parliamentary Activities: Government Whip
Declared Interests:
Trades or Professions: Partner in Frere Cholmeley, Solicitors; Member of Lloyd's.

BALDRY, Tony

Constituency: Conservative, Banbury
Parliamentary Activities: Parliamentary Under Secretary at Department of Environment
Declared Interests: None listed.

BANKS, Matthew

Constituency: Conservative, Southport
Parliamentary Activities:
Select Committee Membership: Transport
Declared Interests: Director of LBJ Ltd; Clients of LBJ Ltd: Leigh Interests plc, Johnson Fry Ltd, Johnson Fry Property Ltd, HH Sheikh Ahmed Bin Saeed Al-Maktoum Emirates Airlines
Overseas Visits: June 1992, three day visit to Jakarta as a guest of BA on their inaugural flight; September 1992, four day visit to Dubai as a guest of Emirates Airlines in his capacity as a member of the Conservative backbench Tourism Committee; 12–14 March 1993, visit to Elveden Forest Holiday Village, with Conservative back bench Tourism Committee, as a guest of Centre Parcs.

BANKS, Robert

Constituency: Conservative, Harrogate
Parliamentary Activities:
Select Committee Membership: None
Declared Interests:
Trades or Professions: Member of Lloyd's, resigned 1989
Land and Property: Small farm and some property freeholds
Overseas Visits: 24–27 Febuary 1992, with parliamentary delegation to the Sudan, paid for by the Government of Sudan; 3–10 April 1993, to Sudan, under auspices of the British Council for Refugees

Comments: From declarations made to Companies House in London, Banks is also a director of Harrogate International Festival Ltd.

BANKS, Tony

Constituency: Labour, Newham North West
Parliamentary Activities:
Select Committee Membership: Procedure
Declared Interests: Parliamentary advisor to the Broadcasting, Entertainment, Cinematograph and Theatre Union (BECTU); Parliamentary advisor to the Musicians' Union; Parliamentary advisor to the London Beekeepers Association (no remuneration but occasional gifts of honey)
Trades or professions, etc.: Occasional broadcasting and writing
Financial sponsorships, Gifts etc.: Sponsored by the Transport and General Workers' Union. No payments made personally to him; Finance for research assistant provided by International Fund for Animal Welfare
Overseas Visits: 12–16 October 1992, to Cincinnati and Seattle to visit General Electric and Boeing. Costs borne by companies and British Airways
Comments: From Declarations made to Companies House in London, Banks is also a director of London Marathon Trust Ltd; Chelsea Pitch Owners plc.

BARNES, Harry

Constituency: Labour, North East Derbyshire
Parliamentary Activities:
Select Committee Membership: European Legislation
Declared Interests:
Financial Sponsorships and Gifts, etc.: Research services provided by a student of the Politics Department, Hull University.

BARRON, Kevin

Constituency: Labour, Rother Valley
Parliamentary Activities:
Select Committee Membership: Environment
Declared Interests:
Financial Sponsorships, Gifts, etc.: Sponsored by the Amalgamated Engineering and Electricians Union (AEEU)

Comments: From declarations made to Companies House in London, Barron is also a director of Rotherham Chamber of Commerce and Industry Ltd; Maltby Rainbow Projects.

BATES, Michael

Constituency: Conservative, Langbaurgh
Parliamentary Activities: Parliamentary Private Secretary to Nicholas Scott, Secretary of State for Social Security
Declared Interests: None listed
Overseas Visits: 3–11 January 1993, to Israel with Conservative Friends of Israel.

BATISTE, Spencer

Constituency: Conservative, Elmet
Parliamentary Activities:
Select Committee Membership: Science and Technology
Declared Interests:
Employment or Office: Law Clerk, Sheffield Assay Office; Member of British Hallmarking Council; Member of the Council of Sheffield University; Consultant to Music Industries Association; Consultant to Magellan Medical Communications Ltd
Trades or Professions: Partner in Dibb Lupton Broomhead (Solicitors); Member of Lloyd's; Occasional writing and broadcasting; Clients of Magellan Medical Communications Ltd: Pharmaceutical Contraceptive Group, Parke-Davis Ltd, Elan Pharma Ltd
Financial Sponsorships, Gifts, etc.: Provision of research facilities etc. by Magellen Medical Communications Ltd

Comments: From declarations made to Companies House in London, Batiste is also a director of Riverside Maintenance Ltd.

BATTLE, John

Constituency: Labour, Leeds West
Parliamentary Activities: Shadow Housing Minister
Declared Interests: None listed.

BAYLEY, Hugh

Constituency: Labour, York
Parliamentary Activities:
Select Committee Membership: Health

Declared Interests: Occasional fees for writing and lecturing; Member of the political opinion panel of Market Access International Ltd

Financial Sponsorships, Gifts, etc.: Sponsored by the National Union of Rail, Maritime and Transport Workers in accordance with the Hastings Agreement (all payments to York Constituency Labour Party – none to him)

Overseas Visits: 13–26 September 1992, to United States with the British–American Parliamentary Group, partly funded by the Group and partly by the US Information Service; 19–20 December 1992, to Serbia to observe the Serbian elections. The Socialist International paid for travel to Serbia and the hotel bill, the British Embassy in Belgrade provided a car and driver

Comments: From declarations made to Companies House in London, Bayley is also a director of The Foundation for Traditional Chinese Medicine Ltd.

BECKETT, Margaret

Constituency: Labour, Derby South
Parliamentary Activities: Deputy Leader of the Opposition
Declared Interests: Occasional broadcasting and lecturing

Financial Sponsorships, Gifts, etc.: Transport and General Workers' Union (as per Hastings Agreement). Room provided by T&GWU in Derby as an office.

BEGGS, Roy

Constituency: Ulster Unionist, East Antrim
Parliamentary Activities:

Select Committee Membership: None

Declared Interests: Director of Larne Enterprise Development Company (LEDCOM) (not remunerated)

Employment or Office: Councillor, Larne Borough Council; Member of the North Eastern Education and Library Board

Land and Property: Small farms, approximately 60 acres, Co. Antrim

Overseas Visits: September 1992, to Turkish Northern Cyprus, as a guest of the Government of Northern Cyprus; January 1993, to Gibraltar, as a guest of the Government of Gibraltar.

BEITH, Rt. Hon. Alan

Constituency: Liberal Democrat, Berwick-upon-Tweed
Parliamentary Activities:

Select Committee Membership: Treasury and Civil Service, House of Commons Commission

Declared Interests:

Employment or Office: Parliamentary Advisor to the Association of University Teachers; Consultant to Magellan Medical Communications Ltd; Consultant to Bourne Leisure Group Ltd; Clients of Magellan Medical Communications: Pharmaceutical Contraceptive Group; Schering Healthcare; Wyeth Laboratories; Organon; Cilag; Parke-Davis

Trades or Professions: Occasional broadcasting, lecturing and writing.

BELL, Stuart

Constituency: Labour, Middlesbrough
Parliamentary Activities: Opposition spokesperson on Trade and Industry (Corporate Affairs)
Declared Interests:

Employment or Office: Parliamentary advisor to Merck, Sharp and Dohme
Trades or Professions: Barrister; Writer.

BELLINGHAM, Henry

Constituency: Conservative, North West Norfolk
Parliamentary Activities: Parliamentary Private Secretary to Malcolm Rifkind, Secretary of State for Defence
Declared Interests: Director of Lothian plc (from July 1990)
Employment or Office: Parliamentary Advisor to National Association of Waste Disposal Contractors (NAWDC)
Trades or Professions: Barrister-at-Law; Member of Lloyd's
Land and Property: Farmland and woodland in Norfolk
Declarable Shareholdings: Glencara Stud Company; Lothian plc

Comments: During the passage of the 1990 Environment Protection Bill, Bellingham was a member of its Standing Committee. At the same time he was a consultant to the National Association of Waste Disposal Contractors which was affected by the Bill. According to records at Companies House, Bellingham is a director of Responsive Recycling Ltd.

BENDALL, Vivian

Constituency: Conservative, Ilford North
Parliamentary Activities:
Select Committee Membership: None
Declared Interests:
Employment or Office: Licensed Taxi Drivers' Association
Trades or Professions: Sole Principal of Bendall's; Surveyor and valuer.
Financial Sponsorships, Gifts, etc.: Vivian Bendall Parliamentary Dinner Club, functions sometimes held at the House of Commons, the financial benefits from which go to the Ilford North Conservative Association
Land and Property: Office building of Bendall's and two adjacent properties. Numerous other houses and commercial properties in the Croydon area
Declarable Shareholdings: Bendall Featherby & Co.

BENN, Rt.Hon. Tony

Constituency: Labour, Chesterfield
Parliamentary Activities:
Select Committee Membership: None
Declared Interests: Writer and broadcaster
Overseas Visits: Febuary 1992, to lecture in Zurich. Fare and hotel paid by *Woz*, a Zurich newspaper.

BENNETT, Andrew F.

Constituency: Labour, Denton and Reddish
Parliamentary Activities:
Select Committee Membership: Environment
Declared Interests:
Employment or Office: A Trustee of the Tameside Community Care Trust, a charitable trust, which is majority shareholder in Tameside Enterprise Ltd which provides residential care for the elderly and housing accommodation – no financial benefit to him

Land and Property: Part share in holiday cottage
Overseas Visits: September 1993, to Germany, participating in an all-party visit to look at environmental legislation in Germany and its impact on the chemical industry, as a guest of BASF.

BENTON, Joseph

Constituency: Labour, Bootle
Parliamentary Activities:
Select Committee Membership: Chairman's Panel
Declared Interests: None listed
Financial Sponsorships, Gifts, etc.: Sponsored as a parliamentary candidate by National Communications Union. Election expenses only – no personal benefit received.

BERESFORD, Sir Paul

Constituency: Conservative, Croydon Central
Parliamentary Activities:
Select Committee Membership: Education
Declared Interests: Dental Surgeon; Occasional fees for speeches or articles.
Financial Sponsorships, Gifts etc.: Laptop computer from Compaq

BERMINGHAM, Gerald

Constituency: Labour, St Helens South
Parliamentary Activities:
Select Committee Membership: Home Affairs
Declared Interests: Barrister-at-Law; Occasional articles, radio/television programmes
Financial Sponsorships, Gifts, etc.: Sponsored by General, Municipal and Boilermakers Union. £300 a year to constituency party and small contribution to election expenses; He has the loan of a satellite dish, etc. from Sky Television
Overseas Vistis: 2–5 December 1992, to Siracusa, Sicily, to attend a conference organised by International Parliamentarians for Global Action under the aegis of the UN, concerning the establishment of an international criminal court.

BERRY, Dr Roger

Constituency: Labour, Kingswood
Parliamentary Activities:
Select Committee Membership: None
Declared Interests: Member of Avon County Council.

BETTS, Clive

Constituency: Labour, Sheffield, Attercliffe
Parliamentary Activities:
Select Committee Membership: None
Declared Interests: Director of Hallamshire Investment (Sheffield) (unremunerated)
Financial Sponsorships, Gifts, etc.: Sponsored as a Parliamentary candidate by the Transport and General Workers' Union; Office provided rent and rate free from Sheffield City Council.

BIFFEN, Rt.Hon. John

Constituency: Conservative, North Shropshire
Parliamentary Activities:
Select Committee Membership: None
Declared Interests: Director of Glynwed International plc (non-executive); J. Bibby & Sons plc (currently a subsidiary of Barlow Rand) (non-executive from 3.8.1988)
Employment or Office: Member of the International Advisory Board of the International Association for Cooperation and Development in Southern Africa (unpaid); Advisor to the Euro–Turkish Corporation (unpaid)
Trades or Professions: Occasional paid contributions to radio, television and newspaper, and also occasional talks; Author of *Inside the House of Commons*
Overseas Visits: 17–20 September 1992, to Durban, South Africa, to attend the Britain–South Africa Conference. Fares and hotel accommodation paid for by the Conference; 3–10 April 1993, to the Turkish Republic of Northern Cyprus, as a guest of the Government of the Republic

Comments: Biffen was Chief Secretary to the Treasury 1979–81, Trade Secretary 1981–82 and Leader of the House of Commons 1982–87.

BLACKBURN, Dr John

Constituency: Conservative, Dudley West
Parliamentary Activities:
Select Committee Membership: National Heritage, Chairman's Panel
Declared Interests: Group Executive Chairman of the Kudos Group of Companies (from October 1990); Chairman of Kudos Inns Ltd (from 1 July 1991)
Declarable Shareholdings: Of the 36 shares issued on Shoalway Engineering Ltd he holds one share and a Directorship for which he receives no payment or expenses.

BLAIR, Tony

Constituency: Labour, Sedgefield
Parliamentary Activities: Shadow Home Secretary
Declared Interests:
Trades or Professions: Barrister (no longer practising); Occasional writing, broadcasting and lecturing
Financial Sponsorship, Gifts, etc.: Sponsored by Transport and General Workers' Union, but no money received personally; some research into training funded by trade unions, and the Rowntree Trust
Overseas Visits: 2–6 Febuary 1992, to Bonn and Brussels, as a guest of Friedrich Ebert Stiftung, with some funding from Rowntree Trust (visit in capacity as a Member of the Shadow Cabinet).

BLUNKETT, David

Constituency: Labour, Sheffield, Brightside
Parliamentary Activities: Shadow Health Secretary
Declared Interests:
Employment or Office: Parliamentary advisor to the Chartered Society of Physiotherapists – no direct financial benefit
Financial Sponsorships, Gifts, etc.: UNISON, no direct financial benefit; Sheffield City Council provides him with premises in Sheffield to use as a

parliamentary office, for which he pays no rent. Staff, furniture, services and running costs (excluding rates) are paid for him; Financial contribution from NALGO and IRSF towards office equipment, travel costs, etc. – no direct financial benefit

Comments: From declarations made to Companies House in London, Blunkett is also a director of Sheffield Lyceum Theatre Trust Ltd.

BOATENG, Paul

Constituency: Labour, Brent South
Parliamentary Activities: Opposition Spokesperson on Legal Affairs
Declared Interests:
Trades or Professions: Barrister-at-Law; Occasional lecturer and broadcaster
Financial Sponsorships, Gifts, etc.: Sponsored by the General, Municipal, Boilermakers & Allied Trades Union, under which the union will meet up to 80 per cent of authorised election expenditure plus an annual payment of £600 to the constituency Labour Party
Overseas Visits: 17–20 September 1992, to attend the Britain–South Africa Conference. Fares and hotel accommodation paid for by the conference

Comments: From declarations made to Companies House in London, Boateng is also a director of Defence Aid Fund Ltd.

BODY, Sir Richard

Constituency: Conservative, Holland with Boston
Parliamentary Activities:
Select Committee Membership: None
Declared Interests: Director of New European Publications Ltd
Trades and Professions: Underwriting member of Lloyd's; Author
Declarable Shareholdings: New European Publications Ltd

Comments: From declarations made to Companies House in London, Body is also a director of New European Publications Ltd.

BONSOR, Sir Nicholas

Constituency: Conservative, Upminster
Parliamentary Acticities:
Select Committee Membership: Chairman, Defence
Declared Interests: Director of Food Hygiene Bureau Ltd; Select Cellars Ltd
Employment or Office: Chairman (unpaid) British Field Sports Society
Trades or Professions: Barrister (Inner Temple) (non-practising); Farmer; Underwriting member of Lloyd's.
Land and Property: Farmland and property
Declarable Shareholdings: Food Hygiene Bureau Ltd; Select Cellars Ltd

Comments: From declarations made to Companies House in London, Bonsor is also a director of Medical Cyclotron Ltd.

BOOTH, Hartley

Constituency: Conservative, Finchley
Parliamentary Activities: Parliamentary Private Secretary to Douglas Hogg, Minister of State at Foreign Office
Declared Interests: Director of Canford

Auto plc; Consultant to Berwin Leighton, Solicitors; Underwriting member of Lloyd's; Miscellaneous fees and royalties for broadcasting and writing.

BOOTHROYD, Rt.Hon. Betty

Constituency: West Bromwich West
Parliamentary Activities: Speaker of the House of Commons
Declared Interests:
Financial Sponsorships, Gifts, etc.: Sandwell Metropolitan District Council provide her with the use of an office to see constituents on two occasions per month
Overseas Visits: September 1993, return ticket and four nights' accommodation in Cyprus provided by Calypso Hotels Ltd.

BOSWELL, Tim

Constituency: Conservative, Daventry
Parliamentary Activities: Parliamentary Under-Secretary at Education
Declared Interests: Self-employed partner in family farming business
Land and Property: Lower Aynho Grounds Farm, and also a small quantity of let land
Overseas Visits: Occasional special assignments abroad on behalf of the Conservative Party (and paid for by them or the European Democratic Union); An annual study visit to Europe under the auspices of the Konrad Adenauer Foundation.

BOTTOMLEY, Peter

Constituency: Conservative, Eltham
Parliamentary Activities:
Select Committee Membership: Transport
Declared Interests:
Employment or Office: Income from speaking, script and other reading, and writing; International advisor to International Fund for Animal Welfare and to Brian Davies
Trades and Professions: Economist

Comments: From declarations made to Companies House in London, Bottomley is also a director of The Water Companies Association.

BOTTOMLEY, Rt.Hon. Virginia

Constituency: Conservative, South West Surrey
Parliamentary Activities: Health Secretary
Declared Interests: None listed

Comments: From declarations made to Companies House in London,
Mrs Bottomley is also a director of London School of Economics and Political Science; Godalming Museum Trust.

BOWDEN, Andrew

Constituency: Conservative, Brighton, Kemptown
Parliamentary Activities:
Select Committee Membership: Selection
Declared Interests:
Employment or Office: Parliamentary and Public Affairs Consultant to American Express Ltd; Parliamentary Consultant to Southern Water plc; Parliamentary

Consultant to Wyncote Group plc
Trades and Professions: Personnel Consultant; Lecturing and broadcasting
Overseas Visits: Periodic visits abroad on behalf of People to People International

Comments: From declarations made to Companies House in London, Bowden is also a director of Woodward Schools (Southern Division) Ltd; Ardis.

BOWIS John

Constituency: Conservative, Battersea
Parliamentary Activities: Parliamentary Under-Secretary of Health
Declared Interests: Director of London Actors' Theatre Company (unpaid) (from September 1989); Battersea Arts Centre (unpaid) (from September 1990); Royal National Theatre (unpaid); The South Bank Centre (unpaid)
Employment or Office: Advisor to the Association of Colleges of Further and Higher Education; Parliamentary advisor to the Association of College Management; Joint Parliamentary consultant to the Assistant Masters and Mistresses Association
Trades or Professions: Occasional journalism
Overseas Visits: 12–24 September 1992, to the US with the British–American Parliamentary Group, partly funded by the Group and partly by the US Information Service.

BOYES, Roland

Constituency: Labour, Houghton and Washington
Parliamentary Activities:
Select Committee Membership: Environment
Declared Interests: Parliamentary advisor to the Retail Motor Industry.
Financial Sponsorships, Gifts etc.: Sponsored as an MP by the GMB Union

BOYSON, Rt. Hon. Sir Rhodes

Constituency: Conservative, Brent North
Parliamentary Activities:
Select Committee Membership: None
Declared Interests: Director of Blacks Leisure plc (non-executive); Audiogard International (GB) plc (non-executive)
Employment or Office: Consultant, ARC International Advertising
Trades or Professions: Royalties from books, printed articles, etc.
Declarable Shareholdings: Audiogard International (GB) plc
Overseas Visits: June 1992, to Israel and Jerusalem for three days to speak at an aniversary dinner. The expenses were paid by the Herut Movement of Great Britain

Comments: From declarations made to Companies House in London, Sir Rhodes is also a director of London School of Economics and Political Science.

BRADLEY, Keith

Constituency: Labour, Manchester Withington
Parliamentary Activities: Opposition

spokesperson on Social Security
Declared Interests: Very occasional payments for TV appearances
Overseas Visits: 6 June 1993, to Israel, paid for by Labour Friends of Israel

Comments: From declarations made to Companies House in London, Bradley is also a director of Parrs Wood Rural Trust.

BRANDRETH, Gyles

Constituency: Conservative, City of Chester
Parliamentary Activities: Parliamentary Private Secretary to Stephen Dorrell, Financial Secretary to the Treasury
Declared Interests: Director of J.W. Spear & Sons plc; Author and broadcaster

Comments: From declarations made to Companies House in London, Brandreth is also a director of the Shipgate Management Company Ltd.

BRAY, Dr Jeremy

Constituency: Labour, Motherwell South
Parliamentary Activities:
Select Committee Membership: Science and Technology
Declared Interests: Consultant to the Society of Telecom Executives; Occasional journalism
Overseas Visits: October 1992, to China with a parliamentary delegation as a guest of the Chinese government. He paid his own air fare

Comments: From declarations made to Companies House in London, Bray is also a director of the Science Policy Support Group.

BRAZIER, Julian

Constituency: Conservative, Canterbury
Parliamentary Activities: Parliamentary Private Secretary to Gillian Shephard, Agriculture Secretary
Declared Interests:
Employment or Office: Serving officer in 5 (HSF) Company, 10th Battalion of the Parachute Regiment
Trades or Professions: Freelance journalism and lecturing; writes articles, broadcasts and gives lectures on a freelance basis only.

BRIGHT, Graham

Constituency: Conservative, Luton South
Parliamentary Activities: Parliamentary Private Secretary to John Major, Prime Minister
Declared Interests: Chairman and Managing Director of Dietary Foods Ltd; Chairman, Cumberland Packing Corp. Ltd; Chairman, Cumberland Foods Ltd; Chairman, Mother Nature Ltd; Member of the board of International Sweeteners Association (unpaid)
Employment or Office: Parliamentary and Public Affairs Advisor to Safeway Food Stores Ltd
Declarable Shareholdings: Dietary Foods Ltd; Mother Nature Ltd

Comments: Bright's consultancy with Safeways Supermarkets caused potential embarrassment in 1991 when his client was found to have broken the law on Sunday trading. This was while Bright was PPS to the Prime Minister. He denied there was a conflict of interests. 'I have never discussed any matter relating to Safeways with the Prime Minister,' Bright told *World In*

Action. 'Their decision to open on Sunday and my advising them are separate issues. One should not break the law. I am not going to say how much they pay me.' From declarations made to Companies House in London, Bright is also a director of the Small Business Bureau Ltd.

BROOKE, Rt.Hon. Peter

Constituency: Conservative, City of London and Westminster South
Parliamentary Activities: Secretary of State for National Heritage
Declared Interests: Member of Lloyd's
Declarable Shareholdings: Ecole St George S.A.

BROWN, Gordon

Constituency: Labour, Dunfermline East
Parliamentary Activities: Shadow Chancellor of Exchequer
Declared Interests: Occasional journalism
Financial Sponsorships, Gifts, etc.: Transport and General Workers' Union (under Hastings Agreement).

BROWN, Michael

Constituency: Conservative, Brigg and Cleethorpes
Parliamentary Activities: Assistant Whip
Declared Interests: None listed.

BROWN, Nicholas

Constituency: Labour, Newcastle upon Tyne, East
Parliamentary Activities: Shadow Financial Secretary to Treasury
Declared Interests:
Financial Sponsorships, Gifts, etc.: The General Municipal Boilermakers and Allied Trades Union (GMBATU) financially sponsor his candidature as per the Hastings Agreement (arrangement commenced December 1988). This does not involve any payment to him
Overseas Visits: 24 January–17 February 1992, to Australia as a guest of the government of Australia.

BROWNING, Angela

Constituency: Conservative, Tiverton
Parliamentary Activities: Parliamentary Private Secretary to Michael Forsyth, Minister of State for Employment
Declared Interests:
Employment or Office: Parliamentary Advisor to the Institute of Sales and Marketing Management
Trades or Professions: Management Consultant (self employed); Occasional fees from market research and journalism
Financial Sponsorships, Gifts, etc.: Visit to Elvedon Country Forest Holiday Village as a guest of Centre Parcs, for three days in March 1993
Overseas Visits: 27 September–2 October 1992, to the United Arab Emirates with the back bench Tourism Committee, as the guest of Emirates Airlines; April 1993, one week in Kenya as a guest of the Kenyan Government and Lonrho Hotels
Comments: From declarations made to Companies House in London, Browning is

also a director and secretary of the Small Business Bureau Ltd.

BRUCE, Ian

Constituency: Conservative, South Dorset
Parliamentary Activities: Parliamentary Private Secretary to Junior Social Security Ministers
Declared Interests: Director of Ian Bruce Associates Ltd; Eurim Ltd (unpaid)
Employment or office: Parliamentary Advisor to Telecommunications Managers Association; Parliamentary Advisor to Trevor Gilbert and Associates, who are a division of the Recruitment Network Ltd
Financial Sponsorships, Gifts, etc.: Gift of satellite and services from British Sky Broadcasting; 13–14 March 1993 visit to Elveden Forest Holiday Village, paid for by Centre Parcs; Gift of two fax machines for party offices from Southern Electricity plc; Gift of mobile telephone equipment from Talkland International UK Ltd
Overseas Visits: 14–15 September 1992, to ASTRA Satellite Control Station in Luxembourg as a member of the All Party Satellite and Cable Group. Paid for by Société Européene des Satellites; 3–4 June 1993, to the Elf Petroleum Research Centre in Paris, France as a member of the All Party Science Committee, paid for by ELF.

BRUCE, Malcolm

Constituency: Liberal Democrat, Gordon
Parliamentary Activities:
Select Committee Membership: Trade and Industry
Declared Interests: None listed.

BUDGEN, Nicholas

Constituency: Conservative, Wolverhampton South West
Parliamentary Activities:
Select Committee Membership: Treasury and Civil Service
Declared Interests:
Employment or Office: Consultant to Barnett International
Trades or professions: Barrister-at-Law, practising in the Midlands and in London; Farmer in Staffordshire; Occasional journalism and broadcasting
Land and property: Farmland in Staffordshire.

BURDEN, Richard

Constituency: Labour, Birmingham, Northfield
Parliamentary Activities:
Select Committee Membership: None
Declared Interests:
Financial Sponsorships, Gifts, etc.: Sponsored as a Parliamentary Candidate and as Member of Parliament by Transport and General Workers' Union (payments to Birmingham Northfield Labour Party. None to Burden); Assistance with research expenses from NALGO; Gift of fire-proof race suit from Rover Group Ltd, in connection with the Commons v. Lords motor race.

BURNS, Simon

Constituency: Conservative, Chelmsford
Parliamentary Activities: Parliamentary Private Secretary to Gillian Shephard, Secretary of State for Agriculture

Declared Interests:
Employment or Office: Advisor to Scope Communications Management Ltd; Clients: McDonalds; Toyota; W. H. Smith; Rank Xerox; Halfords; Allied Lyons; Member of the political opinion panel of Market Access International Ltd (Money paid to him is distributed to charities in Chelmsford)
Financial Sponsorships, Gifts, etc.: Free membership, for Burns and wife, of Stock Brook Manor Golf Club, of which he is Vice-President; Free off-street parking area loaned by Brookglade Properties Ltd (Chelmsford).

BURT, Alistair

Constituency: Conservative, Bury North
Parliamentary Activities: Parliamentary Under Secretary for Social Security
Declared Interest: None listed.

BUTCHER, John

Constituency: Conservative, Coventry South West
Parliamentary Activities:
Select Committee Membership: None
Declared Interests: Non executive Director and Chairman of the Board of Texas Instruments Ltd; Director of Leslie and Co. Ltd; Chairman of Images Soft Ltd (from June 1993)
Employment or Office: Advisor to the Manufacturing Systems Group of Warwick University; Advisor to Olivetti Systems UK; Advisor to Euro RSCG
Trades or professions: Occasional fees from TV, radio and newspaper journalism, Honorarium from the BBC World Service for addressing seminar of World Service journalist trainees in October 1993
Overseas Visits: 9–22 February 1992, to South Africa, at the invitation and expense of the South African Forum

Comments: From declarations made to Companies House in London, Butcher is also a director of Hudson Bay Trading Company Ltd; Smart Card Technologies Ltd.

BUTLER, Peter

Constituency: Conservative, Milton Keynes North East
Parliamentary Activities:
Select Committee Membership: Home Affairs
Declared Interests: Non-executive Director of Thompson MTS Ltd (from 1.12.92); Director of Bayou Press
Employment or Office: Consultant with Linnells Solicitors
Financial Sponsorships, Gifts, etc.: Visit to Elvedon Forest Holiday Village as a guest of Centre Parcs, 12–14 March 1993
Declarable shareholdings: Bayou Press Ltd
Overseas Visits: 3–10 January 1993, to Israel under the auspices of the Conservative Friends of Israel; 16–25 March 1993, to Japan as a guest of the Members of Foreign Affairs in Japan.

BUTTERFILL, John

Constituency: Conservative, Bournemouth West
Parliamentary Activities:
Select Committee Membership: Trade and Industry

Declared Interests: Director of Conservation Investments Ltd and subsidiary companies; Pavilion Services Group Ltd; Foxwell Securities Ltd
Employment or Office: President, European Property Associates; Panellist for Market Access Ltd; Consultant to Curchod & Co. (Chartered Surveyors); Parliamentary Consultant to British Insurance and Investment Brokers Association (BIIBA)
Trades or Professions: Partner, Butterfill Associates (financial, corporate and real estate consultants); Occasional appearance fees for radio and television; Occasional fees for lectures and journalism
Land and Property: Urban property in Surrey
Declarable Shareholdings: Conservation Investments and Subsidiary companies; Pavilion Services Group Ltd

BYERS, Stephen

Constituency: Labour, Wallsend
Parliamentary Activities:
Select Committee Membership: None
Declared Interests:
Financial Sponsorships, Gifts, etc.: Sponsored as a Parliamentary Candidate by National Union of Public Employees: £2,200 towards election expenses; Sponsored as a Member of Parliament by National Union of Public Employees: £600 p.a. to Wallsend Constituency Labour Party

Comments: From declarations made to Companies House in London, Byers is also a director of Local Information Unit Ltd.

CABORN, Richard

Constituency: Labour, Sheffield Central
Parliamentary Activities:
Select Committee Membership: Chair, Trade and Industry
Declared Interests: Director of Freedom Productions Ltd (no fees or emoluments paid) (from 1988); Sheffield City Trust (no fees or emoluments paid) (from 1990); Sheffield Festival (no fees or emoluments paid) (from 1991)
Financial Sponsorships, Gifts, etc.: The Amalgamated Union of Engineering Workers; Sheffield City Council provides him with premises in Sheffield for use as a parliamentary office, for which he pays no rent. Staff, furniture and running costs (excluding rates) are paid for by him

Comments: From declarations made to Companies House in London, Caborn is also a director of Skillshare Africa; Tribune Publications Ltd.

CALLAGHAN, Jim

Constituency: Labour, Heywood and Middleton
Parliamentary Activities:
Select Committee Membership: National Heritage
Declared Interests: None listed.

CAMPBELL, Anne

Constituency: Labour, Cambridge
Parliamentary Activities:
Select Committee Membership: Science and Technology
Declared Interests:

Financial Sponsorships, Gifts, etc.: Manufacturing Science and Finance Union donated £2,000 to the Cambridge Constituency Labour Party Election fund
Land and Property: Part of his residence in Cambridge is let
Overseas Visits: 18–20 October 1993, to Vienna, to participate in workshop to discuss Parliamentary Technology Assessment as a guest of the Austrian Government who met all costs of the visit.

CAMPBELL, Menzies

Constituency: Liberal Democrat, North East Fife
Parliamentary Activities
Select Committee Membership: Defence
Declared Interests: Director of Westminster Communications Group; Clients: British Railways Board; British Gas
Trades or Professions: Queens Council; Ocasional income from journalism and broadcasting
Financial Sponsorships, Gifts etc.: Gift of a wristwatch from Emir of Bahrein.
Overseas Visits: 1–5 February 1992, to Saudi Arabia, Bahrein and Abu Dhabi, travel paid by Liberal Democrat Middle East Council, accommodation provided by governments of countries visited; July 1992, to New York to attend the Democratic Party Convention. Travel costs paid by Virgin Atlantic Airways Ltd. Accommodation costs borne by him.

CAMPBELL, Ronnie

Constituency: Labour, Blyth Valley
Parliamentary Activities: Parliamentary Commissioner for Administration (Ombudsman)
Declared Interests:
Financial Sponsorships, Gifts, etc: Sponsored as a parliamentary candidate by the National Union of Mineworkers
Overseas Visits: August–September 1992, to China: travel paid for by Campbell, accommodation and hospitality provided by the Chinese Government.

CAMPBELL-SAVOURS, D. N.

Constituency: Labour, Workington
Parliamentary Activities: An Opposition Spokesperson on Food, Agriculture and Rural Affairs
Declared Interests:
Financial Sponsorships, Gifts, etc.: By UNISON. No personal remuneration
Land and Property: Interest in constituency and London homes with my spouse
Overseas Visits: 4–12 January 1992, to India, travel at his expense, some hospitality provided by Indian government; March 1992, to Russia, sponsored by Future of Europe trust (All visits abroad arise out of responsibilities for overseas development brief.)

Comments: From declarations made to Companies House in London, Campbell-Savours is also a director of Shareholder Action Ltd.

CANAVAN, Dennis

Constituency: Labour, Falkirk West
Parliamentary Activities:
Select Committee Membership: Foreign Affairs
Declared Interests: Occasional fees for

broadcasting and writing
Financial Sponsorships, Gifts, etc: Sponsorship by Confederation of Health Service Employees under the Hastings Agreement with the Labour Party.

CANN, Jamie

Constituency: Labour, Ipswich
Parliamentary Activities:
Select Committee Membership: None
Declared Interests: Member of Ipswich Port Authority
Overseas Visits: April 1993, 6-day visit to Turkish Republic of National Cyprus, as a guest of the government of Northern Cyprus. Met the President, Prime Minister and Foreign Minister. 30 May–6 June 1993, 6–day visit to Israel as a guest of Labour Friends of Israel. Met the Prime Minister and Israeli Government officials.

CARLILE, Alex

Constituency: Liberal Democrat, Montgomery
Parliamentary Activities:
Select Committee Membership: Welsh Affairs
Declared Interests:
Employment or Office: Parliamentary Advisor to the Overseas Doctors' Association (no fee)
Trades or Professions: Queens Council, Recorder; Lay Member of the General Medical Council
Financial Sponsorships, Gifts, etc.: Loan of word processor and software from Tandon Computers
Declarable Shareholdings: Chairman of the Special Share Trust of Wynnstay and Clwyd Farmers plc

Comments: From declarations made to Companies House in London, Carlile is also a director of the British Association for Central and Eastern Europe.

CARLISLE, John

Constituency: Conservative, Luton North
Parliamentary Activities:
Select Committee Membership: None
Declared Interests: Non-executive director of Bletchley Motors Group plc (from 8.12.88); Consultant to Barry Simmons PR Ltd.

CARLISLE, Kenneth

Constituency: Conservative, Lincoln
Parliamentary Activities:
Select Committee Membership: None
Declared Interests: Member of Lloyd's
Land and Property: A farm at Wyken Hall Farm, Stanton, Bury St Edmunds.

CARRINGTON, Matthew

Constituency: Conservative, Fulham
Parliamentary Activities: Parliamentary Private Secretary to John Patten, Education Secretary
Declared Interests:
Employment or Office: An advisory position with the Saudi International Bank; Parliamentary Advisor to Henry Butcher & Co. chartered surveyors

Land and Property: Basement flat, 34 Ladbroke Square, London W11
Declarable Shareholdings: Constructive Teaching Centre

Comments: From declarations made to Companies House in London, Carrington is also a director of the University of Westminster (International).

CARTTISS, Michael

Constituency: Conservative, Great Yarmouth
Parliamentary Activities:
Select Committee Membership: None
Declared Interests: Party Consultant to Trett Contract Services Ltd, Great Yarmouth.

CASH, William

Constituency: Conservative, Stafford
Parliamentary Activities:
Select Committee Membership: European Legislation
Declared Interests: Director of The European Foundation (no remuneration)
Employment or Office: Advisor to Institute of Legal Executives; Advisor to Institute of Company Accounts; Advisor to Council for Complementary and Alternative Medicine; Consultant to Radcliffe's and Co.; Advisor to the National Market Traders' Federation; Advisor to Politics International
Trades or Professions: Solicitor – William Cash & Co.; Occasional fees for journalism and radio and television broadcasts
Financial Sponsorships, Gifts, etc.: Research and organisational assistance from the Maastricht Referendum Campaign (nil remuneration)
Land and Property: Land and property at Upton Cressett, Shropshire
Overseas Visits: April 1993, to Antigua for 7 days with the Lords and Commons Cricket Club. Accommodation provided by the St James Club, Antigua

Comments: From declarations made to Companies House in London, Cash is also a director of Stafford Enterprise Ltd.

CHANNON, Rt.Hon. Paul

Constituency: Conservative, Southend West
Parliamentary Activities:
Select Committee Membership: Chairman Transport, Member Finance and Services
Declared Interests:
Land and Property: One tenanted farm in Essex
Declarable Shareholdings: The Iveagh Trustees Ltd; MPG Investment Corporation Ltd; Guinness plc

Comments: Channon was Secretary of State for Trade and Industry 1986–87 and Transport Secretary 1987–89.

CHAPMAN, Sydney

Constituency: Conservative, Chipping Barnet
Parliamentary Activities: Government Whip
Declared Interests: None listed.

CHISHOLM, Malcolm

Constituency: Labour, Edinburgh Leith
Parliamentary Activities:
Select Committee Membership: None
Declared Interests: None listed.

CHURCHILL, Winston

Constituency: Conservative, Davyhulme
Parliamentary Activities:
Select Committee Membership: Defence
Declared Interests:
Land and Property: Rented flat in Central London
Trades and Professions: Author, journalist; Broadcaster, lecturer; Member of Lloyd's
Overseas Visits: June 1992, to Haifa, Israel, to meet ex-President Gorbachev, as the guest of the British Society for Technion (of which Churchill is Vice-President) which was responsible for his air fare and two nights' accommodation in Haifa

Comments: From declarations made to Companies House in London, Churchill is also a director of C. and T. Publications Ltd.

CLAPHAM, Michael

Constituency: Labour, Barnsley West and Penistone
Parliamentary Activities:
Select Committee Membership: Trade and Industry
Declared Interests:
Financial Sponsorships, Gifts, etc.: Sponsored as a parliamentary candidate by the National Union of Mineworkers.

CLAPPISON, James

Constituency: Conservative, Hertsmere
Parliamentary Activities:
Select Committee Membership: Health
Declared Interests: Director of L. Clappison Ltd
Trades and Professions: Barrister; Farmer; Member of Lloyd's
Land and Property: Rental income from L. Clappison Ltd; Rental income from other properties
Declarable Shareholdings: L. Clappison Ltd.

CLARK, Dr David

Constituency: Labour, South Shields
Parliamentary Activities: Shadow Defence Secretary
Declared Interests: Director of Homeowners Friendly Society
Financial Sponsorships, Gifts, etc.: Sponsored by the National Union of Public Employees. No direct financial benefit to him.

CLARK, Dr Michael

Constituency: Conservative, Rochford
Parliamentary Activities:
Select Committee Membership: Trade and Industry
Declared Interests: Director of MAT Group Ltd
Employment or Office: Parliamentary Advisor to Royal Society of Chemistry; Parliamentary Advisor to British Chemical Engineering; Contractors Association; Parliamentary Advisor to British Gas plc
Overseas Visits: 10–12 February 1992, to Moscow, as a guest of the Russian

Government; 13–15 February 1992, to Kiev as a guest of the Ukraine Government.

CLARKE, Eric

Constituency: Labour, Midlothian
Parliamentary Activities:
Select Committee Membership: Scottish Affairs
Declared Interests: Advisor to Mining Scotland Ltd
Financial Sponsorships, Gifts, etc.: Sponsored as a Member of Parliament by the National Union of Mineworkers, under the Hastings Agreement. Yearly administration costs of £750 paid direct to Constituency Labour Party from NUM.

CLARKE, Rt.Hon. Kenneth

Constituency: Conservative, Rushcliffe
Parliamentary Activities: Chancellor of the Exchequer
Declared Interests: None listed.

CLARKE, Tom

Constituency: Labour, Monklands West
Parliamentary Activities: Shadow Overseas Development Minister
Declared Interests:
Financial Sponsorships, Gifts, etc.: Sponsored by General Municipal, Boilermakers and Allied Trades Union.

CLELLAND, David

Constituency: Labour, Tyne Bridge
Parliamentary Activities:
Select Committee Membership: None
Declared Interests:
Financial Sponsorships, Gifts, etc.: Amalgamated Union of Engineering Workers as per Hastings Agreement.

CLIFTON-BROWN, Geoffrey

Constituency: Conservative, Cirencester and Tewkesbury
Parliamentary Activities:
Select Committee Membership: Environment
Declared Interests: Director of GRCB Farming Company, a private unlimited farming company
Trades and Professions: Farming in the UK
Land and Property: Agricultural holdings in Norfolk and Gloucestershire; Small amount of forestry in Scotland
Declarable Shareholdings: Shareholding in Alder Investment Ltd.

CLWYD, Ann

Constituency: Labour, Cynon Valley
Parliamentary Activities: Opposition Spokesperson on Employment
Declared Interests: Sponsored by the Society of Telecom Executives
Financial Sponsorships, Gifts, etc.: Sponsored member of the Transport and General Workers' Union (payment to Constituency Party only)
Overseas Visits: January 1992, to India (part of frontbench responsibilities), where hospitality was provided by the Government of India; February 1992, to

Moscow (part of frontbench responsibilities), paid for by Future of Europe Trust; March 1992, to Turkey for International Women's Day (part of frontbench responsibilities), paid for by Turkish Women's Organisations; June 1992, to Vienna, to first Iraqi Opposition Conference (part of frontbench responsibilities), paid for by Iraqi Opposition groups; May 1993, to Peru, on behalf of parliamentary Human Rights Committee. Expenses paid by Peru Support Group on Human Rights; August 1993, Turkey, at her own expense. Hospitality provided by Turkish Socialist Party.

COE, Sebastion

Constituency: Conservative, Falmouth and Camborne
Parliamentary Activities:
Select Committee Membership: Employment
Declared Interests: Chairman of Diaco Ltd (a company he founded in 1987); director of Comodale Ltd (co-founded in 1990)
Employment or Office: Member of Editorial Board of *Runners' World* magazine
Trades and Professions: He is a regular speaker on a remunerated basis on corporate fitness and sporting/public affairs
Financial Sponsorships, Gifts, etc.: Preferential lease on car from Hertz Europe
Declarable Shareholdings: Diaco Ltd, Comodale Ltd

COFFEY, Ann

Constituency: Labour, Stockport
Parliamentary Activities:
Select Committee Membership: Trades and industry
Declared Interests: Member of the Parliamentary Panel of USDAW (Union of Shop, Distributive and Allied Workers)
Overseas Visits: 17–25 March 1993, to Japan. Sponsored by the Japanese Government.

COHEN, Harry

Constituency: Labour, Leyton
Parliamentary Activities:
Select Committee membership: None
Declared Interests:
Financial Sponsorships Gifts, etc: Sponsored as an MP by Unison (the public service union).

COLVIN, Michael

Constituency: Conservative, Romsey and Waterside
Parliamentary Activities:
Select Committee Membership: Defence
Declared Interests: Director of Accrep Ltd; Ludgate Laud Ltd
Employment or Office: Parliamentary Advisor to the Federation of Retail Licensed Trade (Northern Ireland), for which he receives financial assistance for the employment of a part-time research assistant; Parliamentary Advisor to: Caledonia Investments plc, C.U.K. Ltd, Meridian Broadcasting Ltd, Thames Heliport plc; Chairman, Council of Country Sports; Executive Council

Member of Country Landowners Association; Vice Chairman, British Field Sports Society; Governor, Enham Village Centre
Trades or Professions: Self-employed landowner and farmer; Member of Lloyd's; Forestry interests; Occasional articles and broadcasts
Land and Property: Tangley House, Hampshire; The Cricketers Arms, Tangley, Hampshire; Cramond & Harthill Estates c/o 42 Moray Place, Edinburgh; Colvin Farms Partnerships, Tangley; Langley Woodlands.
Overseas Visits: September 1992, to Malta, as guest of the Malta Government; March 1993, to Hong Kong, as guest of the Hong Kong Government; September 1993, to Taiwan, as guest of the Taipei Republic; September 1993, to Seattle, as guest of Boeing Co.

Comments: From declarations made to Companies House in London, Colvin is also a director of Test Valley Arts Foundation Ltd; The Enham Trust;

CONGDON, David

Constituency: Conservative, Croydon North East
Parliamentary Activities:
Select Committee Membership: Health
Declared Interests: None listed.

CONNARTY, Michael

Constituency: Labour, Falkirk East
Parliamentary Activities:
Select Committee Membership: None
Declared Interests:
Financial Sponsorships, Gifts, etc.: Sponsored by the Union of Communication Workers; Falkirk East Conservative Party receives financial support of £4,000 p.a. towards administration. No personal remuneration received.

CONWAY, Derek

Constituency: Conservative, Shrewsbury and Atcham
Parliamentary Activities: Assistant Government Whip
Declared Interests: Parliamentary Advisor to the British Shops & Stores Association
Land and Property: Lea Farm Holiday Cottages and Apartments
Overseas Visits: October 1992, to Taiwan and Hong Kong with the British–Taiwanese Parliamentary Group, as a guest of respective governments.

COOK, Frank

Constituency: Labour, Stockton North
Parliamentary Activities:
Select Committee Membership: Defence, Chairman's Panel
Declared Interests: Occasional fees from television appearances, radio broadcasts and newspaper articles
Financial Sponsorships, Gifts, etc.: MSF (Manufacturing, Science and Finance) sponsored in accordance with the Hastings Agreements

COOK, Robin

Constituency: Labour, Livingston
Parliamentary Activities: Shadow Trade and Industry Secretary
Declared interests:
Financial Sponsorships, Gifts, etc.: By the National Union of Railwaymen, on the terms of the Hastings Agreement; He receives support towards the cost of his research staff from NALGO, National Communication Union and UCW. In March 1993 the AEEU provided a word processor for his office.

COOMBS, Anthony

Constituency: Conservative, Wyre Forest
Parliamentary Activities:
Select Committee Membership: None
Declared Interests: Director of Grevayne Properties Ltd
Employment or Office: Parliamentary Advisor to the National Bed Federation; Sand U plc
Declarable Shareholdings: Grevayne Properties Ltd; S & U Stores plc; Metalrax Holdings plc
Overseas Visits: 2–5 February 1992, to Washington DC, financed by the Friends of Cyprus; 8–12 February 1992, to Romania to lead delegation on human rights, financed by Jubilee Campaign and Relief Fund for Romania; 16–20 August 1992, to St Paul de Vence, France. Hotel accommodation and return flight his family paid by Unisys for a speaking engagement at their conference

Comments: From declarations made to Companies House in London, Coombs is also a director of Nexbond Ltd; Stanlor Finance and Loans (Hanley) Ltd; Asquith Developments Ltd; Annette Wolverhampton Ltd; Tweedies Sports Centres Ltd; Sartorial Shops Ltd; Boswells Ltd; Airworld Ltd.

COOMBS, Simon

Constituency: Conservative, Swindon
Parliamentary Activities: Parliamentary Private Secretary to Ian Lang, Secretary of State for Scotland
Declared Interests:
Employment or Office: Parliamentary Consultant to Blick International; Parliamentary Consultant to British Telecom; Parliamentary Advisor to the British Standards Institution
Overseas Visits: 14–15 September 1992, to Luxembourg, sponsored by the Society of European Satellites; 27 September–2 October 1992, to United Arab Emirates, sponsored by Emirates Air Line; April 1993, to Kenya, sponsored by Kenya National Tourist Office, Kenya Airways and Lonrho Hotels; 21–22 June 1993, to France, sponsored by Eurotunnel plc

Comments: From declarations made to Companies House in London, Coombs is also a director of Westchester Investments Ltd.

COPE, Rt.Hon. Sir John

Constituency: Conservative, Northavon
Parliamentary Activities: Paymaster General
Declared Interests: None listed.

CORBETT, Robin

Constituency: Labour, Birmingham, Erdington
Parliamentary Activities: Opposition Spokesperson on Broadcasting
Declared Interests:
Employment or Office: Council member, Royal College of Veterinary Surgeons (unremunerated)
Trades or Professions: Occasional broadcasting and lecturing fees
Financial Sponsorships, Gifts, etc.: Sponsored by Union of Shop, Distributive and Allied Workers (no payment to Member).

CORBYN, Jeremy

Constituency: Labour, Islington North
Parliamentary Activities:
Select Committee Membership: Social Security
Declared Interests: Director of Campaign Group News Ltd
Financial Sponsorships, Gifts, etc.: Sponsored as a Member of Parliament by the National Union of Public Employees who paid £2,500 towards election expenses and who pay £100 per year which is used to assist office costs
Declarable Shareholdings: Trustee of North Islington Red Rose Labour and Socialist Club; Hornsey and Wood Green Labour Party Premises Society Ltd (no dividend received).

CORMACK, Patrick

Constituency: Conservative, South Staffordshire
Parliamentary Activities:
Select Committee Membership: Commons Services (Accommodation & Works)
Declared Interests:
Trades or Professions, etc.: Journalism (member of the Institute of Journalists) and other writing and broadcasting; Consultant (Patrick Cormack & Partners); Programme advisor to the Catholic University of America.
Clients: Clients of Patrick Cormack and Partners include: Federation of Recruitment and Employment Services; Machinery Users' Association; Parliamentary Communications Ltd; N.N.E.B.; Linford/ Bridgeman Ltd.

CORSTON, Jean

Constituency: Labour, Bristol East
Parliamentary Activities:
Select Committee Membership: Agriculture
Declared Interests: Barrister-at-Law.

COUCHMAN, James

Constituency: Conservative, Gillingham
Parliamentary Activities:
Select Committee Membership: Public Accounts
Declared Interests: Chairman and Director, Chiswick Caterers Ltd
Employment or Office: Advisor to the Gin and Vodka Association (nominal benefits); Advisor to Pfizer Ltd; Advisor to Denplan Ltd
Declarable Shareholdings: Chiswick Caterers Ltd.

Comments: In 1992 Couchman became embroiled in controversy when he helped to block the Medicines Information Bill while he was a consultant to Pfizer Ltd, the giant pharmaceutical corporation. The Bill was unpopular with pharmaceutical companies because it would have meant revealing vital information about the testing of drugs. Couchman confirmed talking to Pfizer about the Bill but said they offered no briefings or amendments. 'I believe it is not in conflict for me to represent employees in Kent and the pharmaceutical industry as well as representing my constituents on a wider spectrum,' he told Channel 4's 'Checkout' programme.

COUSINS, Jim

Constituency: Labour, Newcastle-upon-Tyne Central
Parliamentary Activities: Opposition Spokesperson on Trade and Industry
Declared Interests:
Financial Sponsorships, Gifts, etc.: The Manufacturing, Science and Finance (MSF) Trade Union sponsors his Constituency Party on his behalf. No payments are made to him. In the 1992 General Election MSF also made a contribution to his election expenses.

COX, Tom

Constituency: Labour, Tooting
Parliamentary Activities:
Select Committee Membership: None
Declared Interests:
Financial Sponsorships, Gifts., etc.: by the Electrical, Electronic, Telecommunication and Plumbing Union.

CRAN, James

Constituency: Conservative, Beverley
Parliamentary Activities:
Select Committee Membership: None
Declared Interests: Member of the Pension Trustee Forum Advisory Council (expenses only received); Various fees from television, surveys and lectures
Overseas Visits: February 1992, to Norway, financed by the Parliamentary Armed Forces Scheme. September 1992, to Malta, financed by the Maltese Government. September/October 1992, to Hong Kong and Taiwan, accompanied by his wife, financed by the Hong Kong and Taiwanese Governments.

CRITCHLEY, Julian

Constituency: Conservative, Aldershot
Parliamentary Activities:
Select Committee Membership: None
Declared Interests: Retainer paid by *Observer*. Author, novelist, freelance journalist
Comments: From declarations made to Companies House in London, Critchley is also a director of British Boxing Board of Control Ltd.

CRYER, Bob

Constituency: Labour, Bradford South
Parliamentary Activities:
Select Committee Membership: Members' Interests
Declared Interest:
Land and Property: Joint owner with Mrs Ann Cryer of 22 Edmund Street, Bradford. Part used as parliamentary constituency office, part let

Declarable Shareholdings: 5 £10 shares in Keighley and Worth Valley Light Railway Ltd, no dividend ever received.

CUMMINGS, John

Constituency: Labour, Easington
Parliamentary Activities:
Select Committee Membership: None
Declared Interests:
Financial Sponsorships, Gifts, etc.: National Union of Mineworkers
Overseas Visits: February 1988, 3-day visit to Iraq, travel and accommodation provided by the Gulf Centre for Strategic Studies; 28 August–12 September 1992, to China at the invitation of the Chinese Association for Friendship and Understanding, who paid travel and accommodation costs. The air fare was paid for by him.

CUNLIFFE, Lawrence

Constituency: Labour, Leigh
Parliamentary Activities:
Select Committee Membership: None
Declared Interests: Advisor, Club Institute Union
Financial Sponsorships, Gifts, etc.: National Union of Mineworkers.

CUNNINGHAM, Jim

Constituency: Labour, Coventry South East
Parliamentary Activities:
Select Committee Membership: None
Declared Interests: Local Councillor.

CUNNINGHAM, Rt. Hon. Dr Jack

Constituency: Labour, Copeland
Parliamentary Activities: Shadow Foreign Secretary
Declared Interests:
Employment or Office: Policy Advisor to Albright and Wilson (UK) Ltd); Advisor to Hays Chemicals; Advisor to Centurion Press Limited
Financial Sponsorships, Gifts, etc.: by General and Municipal Workers' Union as per Hastings Agreement, as a candidate and as a Member, including direct benefit to him
Overseas Visits: February 1993, to South Africa for a conference organised by the African National Congress. He received financial support from the Party of European Socialists, and hospitality

Comments: While Cunningham was Shadow Environment Secretary (1983–89) he was, and remains, a paid advisor to Albright and Wilson UK and Leather Chemicals. Albright and Wilson have a poor pollution record and been fined by the regulatory authorities. 'If people break the law I'm not there to defend them,' Cunningham told *World In Action*. 'I advise people on what I believe they should do. At the forefront of my advice is that at the top of their agenda their organisations must have concern for the environment.'

CURRIE, Edwina

Constituency: Conservative, South Derbyshire
Parliamentary Activities:
Select Committee Membership: None
Declared Interest: Director of Tower House (Findern) Ltd (a family company)

Trades or Professions: I receive an income from broadcasting, journalism, writing and related activities.

CURRY, David

Constituency: Conservative, Skipton and Ripon
Parliamentary Activities: Minister of State for Local Government
Declared Interests: None listed.

DAFIS, Cynog

Constituency: Plaid Cymru, Ceredigion and Pembroke North
Parliamentary Activities:
Select Committee Membership: None
Declared Interests: Party Advisor to the National Union of Teachers
Land and Property: 32 acres of agricultural land.

DALYELL, Tam

Constituency: Labour, Linlithgow
Parliamentary Activities:
Select Committee Membership: None
Declared Interests: Weekly columnist, *New Scientist*
Financial Sponsorships, Gifts, etc.: Sponsored by the National Union of Railwaymen, from whom the constituency party gets about £750 p.a. No personal gain.

DARLING, Alistair

Constituency: Labour, Edinburgh Central
Parliamentary Activities: Opposition Spokesperson on City Affairs
Declared Interests:
Trades or Professions: Advocate; Occasional writing and broadcasting.

DAVIDSON, Ian

Constituency: Labour, Glasgow Govan
Parliamentary Activities:
Select Committee Membership: None
Declared Interests:
Financial Sponsorships, Gifts, etc.: Sponsored as a Parliamentary Candidate by the Co-operative Party.

DAVIES, Bryan

Constituency: Labour, Oldham Central and Royton
Parliamentary Activities:
Select Committee Membership: National Heritage
Declared Interests: None listed.

DAVIES, Rt.Hon. Denzil

Constituency: Labour, Llanelli
Parliamentary Activities:
Select Committee Membership: Public Accounts
Declared Interests: Barrister
Comments: From declarations made to Companies House in London, Davies is also a director of S. Austin (motor body specialists) Ltd.

DAVIES, Quentin

Constituency: Conservative, Stamford and Spalding
Parliamentary Activities:
Select Committee Membership: Treasury and Civil Service
Declared Interests: Director of Dewe Rogerson Consultants Ltd
Employment or Office: Member of Market Access Panel; Advisor to Nat West Securities Ltd; Advisor to Institute of Taxation
Trades or Professions, etc.: Occasional lecturing and broadcasting
Land and Property: A small flock of ewes
Overseas Visits: September 1992, to Italy, conference organised by Konrad Adenauer Foundation; October 1992, to Italy, conference organised by Konrad Adenauer Foundation; November 1992, to Bonn, conference organised by Konrad Adenauer foundation; November 1992, to Spain, organised by Spanish–British Territories; December 1992, to Versailles, organised by Franco–British Collaque.

DAVIES, Ron

Constituency: Labour, Caerphilly
Parliamentary Activities: Shadow Welsh Secretary
Declared Interests:
Financial Sponsorships, Gifts, etc.: Sponsored as a parliamentary candidate by National Union of Public Employees; Assistance with Research, The League Against Cruel Sports.

DAVIS, David

Constituency: Conservative, Boothferry
Parliamentary Activities: Parliamentary Under-Secretary of Office of Public Service and Science
Declared Interests: None listed
Overseas Visits: 23–25 October 1992, to Cadenabbia, Lake Como, Italy, to the third European Round Table Discussion, as a guest of the Konrad Adenauer Stiftung.

DAVIS, Terry

Constituency: Labour, Birmingham, Hodge Hill
Parliamentary Activities:
Select Committee Membership: Public Accounts
Declared Interests:
Employment or Office: Parliamentary Advisor to Inland Revenue Staff Federation who contribute to secretarial and office expenses
Financial Sponsorships, Gifts, etc.: By the MSF (Manufacturing, Science and Finance) Trade Union who contribute to constituency party and election expenses. No payments are received by him; Assistance with the housing and urban renewal problems of people living in Hodge Hill Constituency – received from the full-time employee of a charitable organisation known as the Hodge Hill Housing Advice Project

Comments: From declarations made to Companies House in London, Davis is also director of Job Ownership Ltd.

DAY, Stephen

Constituency: Conservative, Cheadle
Parliamentary Activities:
Select Committee Membership: Social Security
Declared Interests: Parliamentary Consultant to the National Association of Local Government Officers (NALGO).

DENHAM, John

Constituency: Labour, Southampton, Itchen
Parliamentary Activities:
Select Committee Membership: None
Declared Interests: Elected member of Southampton City Council.

DEVA, Nirj

Constituency: Conservative, Brentford and Isleworth
Parliamentary Activities:
Select Committee Membership: Parliamentary Commissioner for Administration (Ombudsman) 1993
Declared Interests: Director of Parliamentary and Public Affairs International Ltd (PPAI); Fitzroy Aviation Ltd (Director Designate); Ceylon and Foreign Trades Ltd (Sri Lanka); First European Communications Corporation Ltd
Employment or Office: Parliamentary Advisor to Turkish Cypriot Association of the UK (April 1992); Parliamentary Advisor to Thomas Howell Group UK Ltd
Land and Property: Family interests in tea, rubber and coconut plantations in Sri Lanka; Distillery and residential property in Sri Lanka
Clients: Principal clients of PPAI with whom he is directly involved: Rothman's International; EDS (Electronic Data Systems Corp.); Laing International Ltd; KHD (Great Britain) Ltd; TECHPRO Ltd
Declarable Shareholdings: Waulegalle Distilleries Ltd (Sri Lanka); Erabodagama Estates Ltd (Sri Lanka)
Overseas Visits: July 1992, 3–day visit to Copenhagen, as Joint Secretary of Aviation Committee, paid for by Thomson CRM; August 1992, 10–day visit to Uganda, entertained as state guest of the President of Uganda; August–September, 14–day visit to Sri Lanka, entertained as state guest of the President of Sri Lanka; October 1992, 5–day visit to Washington DC, as Joint Secretary of Aviation Committee, paid for by British Airways.

DEVLIN, Tim

Constituency: Conservative, Stockton South
Parliamentary Activities:
Select Committee Membership: None
Declared Interests: Director of Fanedge Ltd
Trades or Professions: Barrister (non-practising).

DEWAR, Donald

Constituency: Labour, Glasgow, Garscadden
Parliamentary Activities: Shadow Social Security Secretary
Declared Interests:
Trades or Professions: Partner of Ross Harper & Murphy (Solicitors); Occasional journalism
Financial Sponsorships, Gifts, etc.: by the National Union of Rail, Maritime &

Transport Workers in accordance with the Hastings Agreement.

DICKENS, Geoffrey

Constituency: Conservative, Littleborough and Saddleworth
Parliamentary Activities:
Select Committee Membership: None
Declared Interests: Director of Cunnington and Cooper Ltd (non-executive); Nuclear and General Engineering Ltd (non-executive); F.E.L. Ltd (non-executive)
Employment or Office: Parliamentary consultant to Childwatch (Child Protection) (unpaid); Newhall Publications Ltd.

DICKS, Terry

Constituency: Conservative, Hayes and Harlington
Parliamentary Activities:
Select Committee Membership: None
Declared Interests: Director of Dorcan Investments plc (non-executive)
Employment or Office: Consultant to Associated Nursing Services
Financial Sponsorships, Gifts, etc.: He has been given the use of a car by Hertz (UK) Ltd
Overseas Visits: 5–12 January 1992, to the USA in his capacity as a member of the Conservative Backbench Aviation Committee, sponsored by United Airlines, British Aerospace plc, Rolls Royce plc, Boeing Aircraft Company; 22–23 July 1992, to Copenhagen, courtesy of Thompson CSF Ltd; 14–23 September 1992, to Northern Cyprus, courtesy of Republic of Northern Cyprus; 2–4 October 1992, to Toronto, courtesy of World Sikh Organisation. Air fare paid by World Sikh Organisation but he paid his own hotel expenses; 12–16 October 1992, to Washington, courtesy of British Airways; 5–11 December 1992, to Singapore as a guest of Singapore Airlines; January 1993, to Bahrain, flight courtesy of British Airways. He paid his own travel expenses; June 1993, to Qatar, as member of all-party delegation courtesy of the Government of Qatar; 29–31 October 1993, to Edmonton, to make keynote speech at World Sikh Organisation dinner. Costs met by World Sikh Organisation.

DIXON, Don

Constituency: Labour, Jarrow
Parliamentary Activities:
Select Committee Memberships: Selection, Finance and Services
Declared Interests:
Financial Sponsorships, Gifts, etc.: General Municipal, Boilermakers and Allied Trades Union as per Hastings Agreement.

DOBSON, Frank

Constituency: Labour, Holborn and St Pancras
Parliamentary Activities: Shadow Transport Secretary
Declared Interests:
Financial Sponsorships, Gifts, etc.: Sponsored by Rail, Maritime and Transport Union who pay 80 per cent of election expenses and contribute to salary of agent

Land and Property: House in Dunnington, near York. It is occupied but no income derived.

DONOHOE, Brian

Constituency: Labour, Cunninghame South
Parliamentary Activities:
Select Committee Membership: Transport
Declared Interests:
Financial Sponsorships, Gifts, etc.: Small contribution towards constituency expenses in 1993 by UNISON
Overseas Visits: 21–26 June 1992, to Indonesia, on an inaugural flight sponsored by British Airways; 6–10 December 1992, to Singapore, courtesy of Singapore Airlines.

DORRELL, Stephen

Constituency: Conservative, Loughborough
Parliamentary Activities: Financial Secretary to the Treasury
Declared Interests: None listed
Declarable Shareholdings: Faithful Group Ltd.

DOUGLAS-HAMILTON, Lord James

Constituency: Conservative, Edinburgh West
Parliamentary Activities: Parliamentary Under-Secretary at Scottish Office
Declared Interests:
Trades or Professions: Scots advocate; Author and occasional journalism; Lloyd's underwriter (ceased underwriting in 1985).

DOVER Den

Constituency: Conservative, Chorley
Parliamentary Activities:
Select Committee Membership: None
Declared Interests: Director of Cosalt plc (from 24.3.88); Ancaster Investments Ltd (from 1.1.91); M P Holdings Ltd (from 1.3.91)

Comments: Mr Dover was most reluctant to discuss his business interests. He refused to tell the authors the nature of the companies that pay him. 'I have made my declaration according to the rules and that's it,' he sniffed. From declarations made to Companies House in London, Dover is also a director of Medalworth Ltd; Central Riverside (North Shields) Management Company.

DOWD Jim

Constituency: Labour, Lewisham West
Parliamentary Activities:
Select Committee Membership: None
Declared Interests:
Employment or Office: Councillor, London Borough of Lewisham (small expense allowance only).

DUNCAN Alan

Constituency: Conservative, Rutland and Melton
Parliamentary Activities:
Select Committee Membership: Social Security
Declared Interests:
Employment or Office: Owner of Harcourt Consultants, trading as oil broker and advisor on energy matters

Financial Sponsorships, Gifts, etc.: He receives complimentary membership of the Living Well Health Club, Millbank
Overseas Visits: 14–17 September 1992, to Germany and Hungary, sponsored by the Konrad Adenauer Stiftung.

Select Committee Membership: None
Declared Interests:
Financial Sponsorships, Gifts, etc.: Sponsored by the Amalgamated Engineering Union as per the Hastings Agreement.

DUNCAN-SMITH, Iain

Constituency: Conservative, Chingford
Parliamentary Activities:
Select Committee Membership: None
Declared Interests: Consultant to Jane's Information Group (Publisher)
Overseas Visits: 29 May–2 June 1993, to Azerbaijan, for discussions with the President and other members of the Government and to visit the front line of war in Nagorup-Carabach. Travel and accommodation paid for by BP.

DUNN, Bob

Constituency: Conservative, Dartford
Parliamentary Activities:
Select Committee Memberships: Selection, Members' Interests
Declared Interests: None listed

Comments: From declarations made to Companies House in London, Dunn lists additional interests as a director of Leigh City Technology College.

DUNNACHIE, James

Constituency: Labour, Glasgow, Pollok
Parliamentary Activities:

DUNWOODY, Hon. Mrs Gwyneth

Constituency: Labour, Crewe and Nantwich
Parliamentary Activities:
Select Committee Membership: Transport
Declared Interests: Chairman of the Labour Friends of Israel (unpaid); Consultant to St David's Care in the Community
Financial Sponsorships, Gifts, etc.: Sponsored as a Parliamentary Candidate by the Rail, Maritime and Transport Union who fund 80 per cent of election expenses. Donations received from Messrs Sainsburys and Manweb Electricity plc go towards the running of a Care in the Community helpline from her constituency office.

DURANT, Sir Anthony

Constituency: Conservative, Reading West
Parliamentary Activities:
Select Committee Memberships: Parliamentary Commissioner for Administration (Ombudsman), Members' Interests
Declared Interests: Director of Oriental Press Charitable Fund Association, Hong Kong
Employment or Office: Political Advisor to the National Federation of Demolition Contractors; Advisor to Shire Hall

Communications (a PR company); Advisor to the Police Superintendents' Association of England and Wales.

DYKES, Hugh

Constituency: Conservative, Harrow East
Parliamentary Activities:
Select Committee Membership: European Legislation
Declared Interests: Chairman, ADA Video Systems Ltd; Director of European Movement (British Council) Ltd
Employment or Office: Parliamentary Advisor to British Wine Producers Committee; Chairman, the European Movement in Britain; Advisor to Rogers and Wells; Advisor to the Single Market Services GIE
Land and Property: Land and property in East Anglia, France and Germany (all are held via company investments)
Declarable Shareholdings: Majority shareholder in ADA Video Systems Ltd; Shareholder in Dewe Rogerson Ltd; Shareholder in Single Market Services GIE.

EAGLE, Angela

Constituency: Labour, Wallasey
Parliamentary Activities:
Select Committee Membership: Member's Interests; Welfare
Declared Interests:
Financial Sponsorships, Gifts, etc.: Sponsored as a parliamentary candidate and as a Member of Parliament by COHSE in accordance with the Hastings Agreement (no personal benefit).

EASTHAM, Ken

Constituency: Labour, Manchester, Blackley
Parliamentary Activities:
Select Committee Memberships: Employment, Selection
Declared Interests:
Financial Sponsorship, Gifts, etc.: as a candidate by the Amalgamated Engineering Union (no direct payment to him).

EGGAR, Tim

Constituency: Conservative, Enfield North
Parliamentary Activities: Minister for Coal
Declared Interests: None listed
Overseas Visits: 11–13 September 1992, to a conference in Italy. Expenses were paid by the Konrad Adenauer Foundation.

ELLETSON, Harold

Constituency: Conservative, Blackpool North
Parliamentary Activities:
Select Committee Memberships: Commons Services (Information), Environment
Declared Interests: Director of Harold Elletson Ltd
Employment or Office: Consultant to Quay Consultants Ltd; Consultant to BP Exploration, (Former Soviet Union)
Trades or Professions: Business consultant specialising in assisting companies to develop business in the CIS and Eastern Europe
Financial Sponsorships, Gifts, etc.: Visit to Elvedon Forest Holiday Village as a guest of Centre Parcs, 12–15 March 1993

Declarable Shareholdings: Nationwide Lotteries Ltd; Eco Enterprises Ltd
Comments: From declarations made to Companies House in London, Elletson is also a director of: Harold Elletson Ltd; VZT Ltd (Business Consultant).

EMERY, Rt.Hon. Sir Peter

Constituency: Conservative, Honiton
Parliamentary Activities:
Select Committee Memberships: Chairman Procedure, Member Liaison.
Declared Interests: Director of Winglaw Group Ltd; High Holborn Estates Ltd; East Holborn Estates Ltd; Glenwing Properties Ltd (unremunerated)
Employment or Office: Shenley Trust Services Ltd
Trades or Professions: Occasional fees for writing, television or broadcasting
Declarable Shareholdings: Purchasing Management Services Ltd; Axion Ltd
Comments: From declarations made to Companies House in London, Emery is also a director of National Asthma Campaign; Winglaw Developments Ltd.

ENRIGHT, Derek

Constituency: Labour, Hemsworth
Parliamentary Activities:
Select Committee Membership: European Legislation
Declared Interests:
Trades or Professions: Lecturing, journalism, broadcasting. Rarely remunerated apart from expenses
Financial Sponsorships, Gifts, etc.: Return trip to Paris in return for lecture for European Movement.

ETHERINGTON, Bill

Constituency: Labour, Sunderland North
Parliamentary Activities:
Select Committee Membership: None
Declared interests:
Financial Sponsorship, Gifts, etc.: Sponsored as a parliamentary candidate by the National Union of Mineworkers as per the Hasting Agreement.

EVANS, David

Constituency: Conservative, Welwyn Hatfield
Parliamentary Activities: Parliamentary Private Secretary to John Redwood, Welsh Secretary
Declared Interests: Director of Leapsquare Ltd; Broadreach Group Ltd; Sedgewick Group Development Ltd
Employment or Office: Consultant to the Retail Motor Industry Federation, as a client of Leapsquare Ltd; Roche Products Ltd. (from 1.10.92); Cyril Leonard and Co.
Clients: see above – Retail Motor Industry Federation
Declarable Shareholdings: Leapsquare Ltd; Bradnam Enterprises Ltd; Broadreach Ltd.

EVANS, John

Constituency: Labour, St Helens North
Parliamentary Activities:
Select Committee Membership: None
Declared Interests:
Financial Sponsorship, Gifts, etc.: by the Amalgamated Engineering Union, who pay an agreed proportion of election expenses. Evans receives no payment from them.

EVANS, Jonathan

Constituency: Conservative, Brecon and Radnor
Parliamentary Activities: Parliamentary Private Secretary to David Hunt, Employment Secretary
Select Committee Membership: Welsh Affairs
Declared Interests:
Employment or Office: Consultant on Law and Policy to the National Society for the Prevention of Cruelty to Children
Trades and Professions: Solicitor, with Leo Abse and Cohen, Cardiff
Land and Property: an interest in a block of freehold land in Central Cardiff; a residential property in Lowestoft, Suffolk
Overseas Visits: 1–11 January 1993, to Israel, under the auspices of the Conservative friends of Israel.

EVANS, Nigel

Constituency: Conservative, Ribble Valley
Parliamentary Activities:
Select Committee Membership: None
Declared Interests:
Trades or Professions: Owner of a retail convenience store in Swansea
Financial Sponsorship, Gifts, etc.: 13–15 March 1993, visit to Elvedon Forest Holiday Village, as a guest of Centre Parcs
Overseas Visits: 22 September–2 October 1992, to United Arab Emirates, sponsored by Emirate Airline; 30 May–6 June 1993, to Israel, sponsored by Conservative Friends of Israel.

EVANS, Roger

Constituency: Conservative, Monmouth
Parliamentary Activities:
Select Committee Membership: Welsh Affairs
Declared Interests: Barrister
Declarable Shareholdings: Harcourt Chambers Ltd

Comments: From declarations made to Companies House in London, Evans is also a director of Harcourt Chambers Ltd; Harcourt Associates Ltd; Harcourt Buildings Ltd.

EVENNETT, David

Constituency: Conservative, Erith and Crayford
Parliamentary Activities:
Select Committee Membership: None
Declared Interests: Underwriting Member of Lloyd's.

EWING, Margaret

Constituency: Scottish National Party, Moray
Parliamentary Activities:
Select Committee Membership: European Legislation
Declared Interests:
Trades and Professions: Occasional earnings from media appearances.
Financial Sponsorship, Gifts, etc.: Receipt of £500 to Constituency Association at the General Election from the National Association of Schoolmasters/Union of Women Teachers
Overseas Visits: 3–10 April 1993, to North

Cyprus as a guest of the Turkish Republic of National Cyprus.

FABER, David

Constituency: Conservative, Westbury
Parliamentary Activities:
Select Committee Membership: Social Security
Declared Interests: Director of Sterling Marketing Ltd
Trades or Professions: Underwriting Member of Lloyd's
Declarable Shareholdings: Sterling Markets Ltd (marketing consultants); Cedarsbrook Ltd (property and development).

FABRICANT, Michael

Constituency: Conservative, Mid Staffordshire
Parliamentary Activities:
Select Committee Membership: National Heritage
Declared Interests:
Employment or Office: Technical and Marketing Consultant to BBC Communications
Trades and Professions: Occasional contributions to press and broadcasting.

FAIRBAIRN, Sir Nicholas

Constituency: Conservative, Perth and Kinross
Parliamentary Activities:
Select Committee Membership: Defence, Scottish Affairs
Declared Interests: Director of Penspen Ltd
Trades or Professions: Queens Council; Advocate, writer, journalist, broadcaster, painter, lecturer.

FATCHETT, Derek

Constituency: Labour, Leeds Central
Parliamentary Activities:
Select Committee Membership: None
Declared Interests:
Financial Sponsorship, Gifts, etc.: Annual contribution of £600 to Central Leeds Constituency Labour Party by the Manufacturing Science and Finance Union (MSF); Use of one room as a constituency office, provided, at present, on a rent-free basis by Leeds City Council (he pays full rates).

FAULDS, Andrew

Constituency: Labour, Warley East
Parliamentary Activities:
Select Committee Membership: None
Declared Interests:
Trades or Professions: Actor with a valuable voice; occasional documentary or 'voice-over' work for TV

Comments: From declarations made to Companies House in London, Faulds is also a director of Anglo-Turkish Society.

FENNER, Dame Peggy

Constituency: Conservative, Medway
Parliamentary Activities:
Select Committee Memberships: Members' Interests, Commons Services (Accommodation and Works)

Declared Interests:
Employment or Office: Parliamentary and Legislative Consultant to British Frozen Foods Federation
Clients: British Frozen Foods Federation (a lunch in the House).

FIELD, Barry

Constituency: Conservative, Isle of Wight
Parliamentary Activities:
Select Committee Membership: Environment
Declared Interests: Director of J.D. Field & Sons Ltd; Great Southern Group plc
Employment or Office: Parliamentary Consultant to the National Association of Holiday Centres
Financial Sponsorship, Gifts, etc.: Red Funnel have provided him with a car-parking pass for use at their terminal at Southampton which he uses from time to time, together with a pass (which he uses infrequently) for the Hydrofoil/Red Jet and which expires in 1996.
Declarable Shareholdings: J.D. Field & Sons Ltd, a controlling shareholder in Great Southern Group plc

Comments: From declarations made to Companies House in London, Field is also a director of Crystalgrove Ltd.

FIELD, Frank

Constituency: Labour, Birkenhead
Parliamentary Activities:
Select Committee Memberships: Chairman, Social Security
Declared Interests:
Employment or Office: Parliamentary Consultant to the Civil and Public Services Association (unpaid)
Trades or Professions: Writing and journalism.

FISHBURN, Dudley

Constituency: Conservative, Kensington
Parliamentary Activities:
Select Committee Membership: Members' Interests
Declared Interests: Chairman, University College London Accomodation plc; Chairman, Loughborough University of Technology Accommodation plc; Member of the Board of Overseers, Harvard University (non-remunerated) (from 8.6. 90); Trustee, The Open University Foundation (non-remunerated); Director of English National Ballet (non-remunerated) (from November 1988) Director of HFC plc (from 1.1.90); Member of the Executive Committee, The National Trust (unpaid); Chairman, (non-executive) Principal Portfolios plc; Director of Business Post plc (non-executive) (from 1.4.93)
Employment or Office: Consultant to J.P. Morgan; Consultant to Fishburn, Hedges, Boys, Williams Ltd; Consultant to Shearman and Sterling (US Law Firm)
Trades or Professions: Freelance journalist: *The Economist*; *The Times*; *New York Times*.

Comments: In 1990 Fishburn wrote in the *New York Times* that when he arrived at the Commons after being elected he was told by his fellow MPs to 'get a job'. They suggested 'it would help with the bank account'.

FISHER, Mark

Constituency: Labour, Stoke-on-Trent
Parliamentary Activities: Opposition Spokesperson on National Heritage
Declared Interests:
Employment or Office: Parliamentary Consultant to NUT
Trades or Professions: Occasional fees from articles and broadcasting
Financial Sponsorship, Gifts, etc.: Finance for secretarial and research staff from the Hamlyn Fund until July 1993.

FLYNN, Mark

Constituency: Labour, Newport West
Parliamentary Activities:
Select Committee Membership: Transport
Declared Interests: Occasional fees from journalism and lecturing.

FOOKES, Dame Janet

Constituency: Conservative, Plymouth, Drake
Parliamentary Activities:
Select Committee Membership: None
Declared Interests:
Trades or Professions: Casual fees from the media

Comments: From declarations made to Companies House in London, Dame Janet is also a director of College of St Mark and St John Foundation.

FORMAN, Nigel

Constituency: Conservative, Carshalton and Wallington
Parliamentary Activities:
Select Committee Membership: Treasury and Civil Service
Declared Interests:
Trades or Professions: Modest royalties from previous publications; Occasional fees from lecturing and broadcasting
Employment or Office: Parliamentary Advisor to the Institute of Chartered Accountants; Political Consultant to De Montfort University; Consultant to Gavin Anderson and Company; Council Member (honorary) of the Tavistock Institute

Comments: From declarations made to Companies House in London, Forman is also a director of Job Ownership Ltd; British Association for Central and European Studies; Tavistock Institute of Human Relations.

FORSYTH, Michael

Constituency: Conservative, Stirling
Parliamentary Activities: Minister of State for Employment
Declared Interests: None listed

Comments: Before becoming a Minister Forsyth ran a public relations firm, Michael Forsyth Associates, which represented companies lobbying for privatised contracts in the National Health Service and local government.

FORSYTHE, Clifford

Constituency: Ulster Unionist, South Antrim
Parliamentary Activities:
Select Committee Membership: Social Security
Declared Interests: None listed.

FORTH, Eric

Constituency: Conservative, Mid Worcestershire
Parliamentary Activities: Parliamentary Under-Secretary for Education
Declared Interests: None listed.

FOSTER, Rt. Hon. Derek

Constituency: Labour, Bishop Auckland
Parliamentary Activities: Opposition Chief Whip
Declared Interests:
Financial Sponsorship, Gifts, etc.: Sponsored by Union of Shop, Distributive and Allied Workers (all payment made to Constituency Labour Party under the Hastings Agreements).

FOSTER, Don

Constituency: Liberal Democrat, Bath
Parliamentary Activities:
Select Committee Membership: None
Declared Interests:
Employment or Office: Advisor to Association of Teachers and Lecturers (ATL); Advisor to National Union of Teachers (NUT)
Financial Sponsorships, Gifts, etc.: Temporary access to former company car from previous employers, Pannell Kerr Foster, of Nottingham.

FOULKES, George

Constituency: Labour, Carrick, Cumnock, and Doon Valley
Parliamentary Activities:
Select Committee Membership: None
Declared Interests: Director of Co-operative Press Ltd
Trades or Professions: Occasional income from TV, radio and newspapers
Financial Sponsorships, Gifts, etc.: Sponsorship by Co-operative Party under national agreement. No payment to him personally
Overseas Visits: 11–16 January 1992, to Tokyo, Japan, as a guest of World Parliamentarians' Conference for support of the United Nations

Comments: From declarations made to Companies House in London, Foulkes lists additional interests as a director of John Wheatley Centre; Great Britain China Centre.

FOWLER, Rt. Hon. Sir Norman

Constituency: Conservative, Sutton Coldfield
Parliamentary Activities:
Select Committee Membership: None
Declared Interests: Director of Midland Independent Newspapers Ltd (non-

executive Chairman) (from November 1991); National House Building Council (non-executive chairman) (from June 1992); NFC plc (non-executive) (from 1.6.90); Evered Bardon plc (non-executive) (from 15.3.90)

Employment or Office: Chairman of the Conservative Party Organisation (unremunerated)

Trades or professions, etc.: Member of Lloyd's

Financial Sponsorships, Gifts, etc.: Use of a car provided by the Rover Group plc (in my capacity as chairman of the Conservative Party Organisation)

FOX, Dr Liam

Constituency: Conservative, Woodspring
Parliamentary Activities:
Select Committee Membership: Scottish Affairs
Declared Interests:
Trades or Professions: Lecturer in Emergency Medicine
Overseas Visits: 14–17 September 1992, to Hungary as a guest of the Konrad Adenauer Foundation; 9–11 January 1993, to Macedonia as part of an All Party visit, as a guest of the Macedonia Government.

FOX, Sir Marcus

Constituency: Conservative, Shipley
Parliamentary Activities:
Select Committee Membership: None
Declared Interests: Director of Westminster Communications Ltd; Care Services Group Ltd; McCarthy and Stone plc; Hartley Investment Trust Ltd; Bristol Port Company; Illingworth Morris Ltd; Yorkshire Food Group plc (from March 1993)

Employment or Office: Consultant to 3M (UK) Ltd, Shepherd (Construction) Ltd, Gratte Brothers Ltd; Clients of Westminster Communications: British Gas; Builders Merchant Federation; Standard Life

Comments: From declarations made to Companies House in London, Fox is also a director of First Corporate Shipping Ltd; John McCarthy Foundation.

FRASER, John

Constituency: Labour, Norwood
Parliamentary activities: An Opposition Spokesperson on Legal Affairs
Declared Interests:
Trades or Professions: Solicitor – Lewis Silkin.

FREEMAN, Rt.Hon. Roger

Constituency: Conservative, Kettering
Parliamentary Activities: Minister of State for Public Transport
Declared Interests: None listed.

FRENCH, Douglas

Constituency: Conservative, Gloucester
Parliamentary Activities: Parliamentary Private Secretary to David Curry, Minister of State for Environment
Declared Interests: Director of Westminster

and City Programmes Ltd, P.W. Merkle Ltd, Chairman (non-executive) Pension Trustee Forum Ltd

Employment or Office: Consultant to Alexander Clay and Partners

Trades or Professions: Barrister (non-practising)

Land and Property: Freehold, commercial and residential property

Declarable Shareholdings: P.W. Merkle Ltd, Westminster and City Programmes Ltd

Payments, etc. from abroad: Occasional hospitality provided by Ebor S.A., Geneva.

FRY, Peter Sir

Constituency: Conservative, Wellingborough

Parliamentary Activities:

Select Committee Membership: None

Declared Interests:

Employment or Office: Consultant to Bingo Association of Great Britain; Consultant to PMS Ltd; Consultant to Westminster Advisers Ltd

Clients of PMS Ltd: British Leather Confederation; Clients of Westminster Adviser Ltd: Sally Line Coach Industry Action Group

Overseas Visits: 31 January–12 Febuary 1992, to Brazil, sponsored by Parliamentary Road Passenger Transport Group; June 1992, to Indonesia, courtesy of British Airways; August 1992, to USA, courtesy of Delta Airlines Inc; September 1992, to Turkish Northern Cyprus as a guest of the Government of Northern Cyprus; October 1992, to Washington as a guest of British Airways; May 1993, to Oslo, with Parliamentary Road Study Group, funded by the Roads Campaign Council; October 1993, flight to and from Nice, courtesy of British Midland Airways

Declarable Shareholdings: Parliamentary Monitoring Services Ltd.

FYFE, Maria

Constituency: Labour, Glasgow Maryhill

Parliamentary Activities: An Opposition Spokesperson on Scottish Affairs

Declared Interests:

Financial Sponsorship, Gifts, etc.: Sponsored both as a Parliamentary Candidate and as a member of Parliament by the Transport and General Workers' Union; no payment, direct or indirect, to me personally

Comments: From declarations made to Companies House in London, Fyfe is also a director of Queens Cross Workspace Ltd.

GALBRAITH, Sam

Constituency: Labour, Strathkelvin and Bearsden

Parliamentary Activities: An Opposition Spokesperson on Employment

Declared Interests:

Trades or Professions: Neurosurgeon

Comments: From declarations made to Companies House in London, Galbraith is also a director of Wildcat Stage Productions Ltd.

GALE, Roger

Constituency: Conservative, Thanet North

Parliamentary Activities:

Select Committee Membership: None

Declared Interests:

Employment or Office: Parliamentary Consultant for Scottish and Newcastle Breweries plc; Consultant, Rhone Poulenc Rorer Ltd; Consultant, Organon UK Ltd; Consultant to TMA Ltd.

GALLIE, Philip

Constituency: Conservative, Ayr
Parliamentary Activities:
Select Committee Membership: Scottish Affairs
Declared Interests:
Employment or Office: Parliamentary Liaison Officer to Scottish Power
Financial Sponsorships, Gifts, etc.: Use of a company car provided by Scottish Power (no business miles); Private health care provided by Scottish Power
Overseas Visits: 3–11 January 1993, on fact-finding visit to Israel as a guest of the Conservative Friends of Israel.

GALLOWAY, George

Constituency: Labour, Glasgow Hillhead
Parliamentary Activities:
Select Committee Membership: None
Declared Interests:
Trades or Professions: Occasional freelance journalism; Co-author of *Downfall: The Ceausescus and the Romanian Revolution*; Political consultant (unpaid) to Hawk Communication International Ltd, a company recently established to assist democratic development in the new Palestinian entity.
Financial Sponsorships, Gifts, etc.: Transport and General Workers' Union

Comments: Galloway told the authors that he was considering using the proceeds of his libel damages from the *Daily Mirror* to invest some of the money in a bar in Havana, Cuba, to be run by some relatives.

GAPES, Michael

Constituency: Labour, Ilford South
Parliamentary Activities:
Select Committee Membership: Foreign Affairs
Declared Interests:
Financial Sponsorships, Gifts, etc.: Sponsored as a Parliamentary Candidate by the Co-operative Party who pay 80 per cent of election expenses to the Constituency Party.

GARDINER, Sir George

Constituency: Conservative, Reigate
Parliamentary Activities:
Select Committee Membership: None
Declared Interests:
Trades or Professions: Occasional journalism; Public Affairs Consultant
Clients: Councillors in Public Policy; National Association for Retired Police Officers

Comments: From declarations made to Companies House in London, Gardiner is also a director of Conservative Way Forward Ltd.

GAREL-JONES, Rt. Hon. Tristan

Constituency: Conservative, Watford
Parliamentary Activities:
Select Committee Membership: None
Declared Interests:
Employment or Office: UK Advisor to Union Bank of Switzerland; UK Advisor to Biwater International; Advisor to British Gas plc
Land and Property: Property and investments in Spain

Comments: Garel-Jones was a Minister of State at the Foreign Office from 1990 to 1993.

GARNIER, Edward

Constituency: Conservative, Harborough
Parliamentary Activities:
Select Committee Membership: Home Affairs
Declared Interests:
Trades or Professions: Barrister
Declarable Shareholdings: Tockmore Ltd
Overseas Visits: 5–7 June 1992, attended the International Colloquium of the Hungarian Democratic Forum organised by the Hans Seidel Foundation and the Konrad Adenauer Foundation, funded by Conservative Central Office; 26–28 July 1992, attended the International Conference on Media in Budapest organised and funded by the Hans Seidel Foundation; 16–23 September 1992, attended the British South African Conference in Durban, funded by the British South African Conference; 29 May–2 June 1993, to Azerbaijan, paid for by BP.

GARRETT, John

Constituency: Labour, Norwich South
Parliamentary Activities:
Select Committee Membership: Treasury and Civil Service
Declared Interests:
Trades or Professions: Occasional lecturer; Author.

GEORGE, Bruce

Constituency: Labour, Walsall South
Parliamentary Activities:
Select Committee Membership: Defence (Senior Opposition Member)
Declared Interests:
Trades or Professions: Writer, lecturer on defence-related matters
Financial Sponsorships, Gifts, etc.: Sponsored as a Parliamentary Candidate by APEX, who contributed £600 to 1992 election expenses.

GERRARD, Neil

Constituency: Labour, Walthamstow
Parliamentary Activities:
Select Committee Membership: None
Declared Interests: None listed

Comments: From declarations made to Companies House in London, Gerrard is also a director of Pioneer Theatres Ltd.

GILBERT, Rt. Hon. Dr John

Constituency: Labour, Dudley East
Parliamentary Activities:
Select Committee Membership: None
Declared Interests: Directorships: Edmund Nuttall Ltd (non-executive); Kyle Stewart Ltd (from September 1989) (non-executive); American Heritage Fund Inc.
Employment or Office: International Advisor to Jardine Insurance Brokers International Ltd
Declarable Shareholdings: John Gilbert and Associates
Payments, etc. from Abroad: Occasional lectures
Overseas Visits: February 1992, to Wehrkunde Conference in Munich. Hotel costs only reimbursed.

GILL, Christopher

Constituency: Conservative, Ludlow
Parliamentary Activities:
Select Committee Membership: Agriculture
Declared Interests: None listed
Declarable Shareholdings: F. A. Gill Ltd.

GILLAN, Cheryl

Constituency: Conservative, Chesham and Amersham
Parliamentary Activities:
Select Committee membership: Science and Technology
Declared Interests: Director of Bankers Insurance Company Ltd, Leeming Consultants (Joint Owner)
Employment or Office: Advisor to Chartered Institute of Marketing, Kidsons Impey.
Clients of Leeming Consultants: Kidsons Impey.

GODMAN, Dr Norman

Constituency: Labour, Greenock and Port Glasgow
Parliamentary Activities:
Select Committee Membership: None
Declared Interests: None listed.

GODSIFF, Roger

Constituency: Labour, Birmingham Small Heath
Parliamentary Activities:
Select Committee Membership: None
Declared Interests:
Financial Sponsorships, Gifts, etc.: Sponsored as a Parliamentary Candidate by the GMB Trade Union who pay up to 80 per cent of election expenses.

GOLDING, Llin

Constituency: Labour, Newcastle-under-Lyme
Parliamentary Activities:
Select Committee Membership: None
Declared Interests:
Employment or Office: Parliamentary Advisor to the National Market Traders Association
Financial Sponsorships, Gifts, etc.: by the Ceramic and Allied Trades Union under the Hastings Agreement

GOODLAD, Rt. Hon. Alastair

Constituency: Conservative, Eddisbury
Parliamentary Activities: Minister of State at Foreign Office
Declared Interests:
Trades or Professions: Underwriting Member of Lloyd's.

GOODSON-WICKES, Dr Charles

Constituency: Conservative, Wimbledon
Parliamentary Activities:
Select Committee Membership: Members' Interests, also Parliamentary Private Secretary to Sir George Young, Minister for Housing
Declared Interests: Director of Thomas Greg and Sons Ltd, Nestor BNA plc (from 1.2. 93), Property Reversions plc (from 1.5. 93), Medarc Ltd (from 1.5. 93), Paracelsus (UK) Ltd (from 1.4. 93)
Employment or Office: Self-employed Occupational Physician; Chairman of the Appeals Board, Asbestos Licensing Regulations; Parliamentary Advisor to Upjohn Ltd; Parliamentary Consultant to Chelgate Ltd; Parliamentary Consultant to Eve Group plc; Parliamentary Representative for Retired Officers Association (unpaid); Member of Council of the Dyslexia Institute (unpaid); Clients of Chelgate Ltd: Arnold Project Services; UK Nirex; Wind Energy Association
Trades or Professions: Barrister-at-Law; Regular Army Reserve office (Life Guards)

GORDON, Mildred

Constituency: Labour, Bow and Poplar
Parliamentary Activities:
Select Committee Membership: Education
Declared Interests: Fee for television interview.

GORMAN, Teresa

Constituency: Conservative, Billericay
Parliamentary Activities:
Select Committee Membership: None
Declared Interests: Director of BANTA Ltd
Financial Sponsorships, Gifts, etc.: Financial support received from Wyeth Laboratories towards the cost of employing a research assistant to help me with my work as an MP and particularly in raising the profile of health care for mature women

Comments: From declarations made to Companies House in London, Gorman is also a director of Reamfield Ltd; Amarant Services Ltd; Alliance of Small Firms and Self-Employed People League.

GORST, John

Constituency: Conservative, Hendon North
Parliamentary Activities:
Select Committee Membership: National Heritage
Declared Interests: Director of John Gorst and Associates Ltd
Clients: British Amusement Caterers' Association
Financial Sponsorships, Gifts, etc.: Gift of wine at Christmas from First Team Advisors Ltd
Overseas Visits: 21–23 January 1992, to Taiwan for World Freedom Day at the

invitation of World League for Freedom and Democracy (Republic of China Chapter); 14–15 September 1992, to Luxembourg with the All Party Cable and Satellite Group, sponsored by ASTRA.

GOULD, Bryan

Constituency: Labour, Dagenham
Parliamentary Activities:
Select Committee Membership: None
Declared Interests: None Listed

GRAHAM, Thomas

Constituency: Labour, Renfrew West and Inverclyde
Parliamentary Activities:
Select Committee Membership: None
Declared Interests:
Financial Sponsorships, Gifts, etc.: Sponsored by the Union of Shop, Distributive and Allied Workers.

GRANT, Sir Anthony

Constituency: Conservative, Cambridgeshire South West
Parliamentary Activities:
Select Committee Memberships: Trade and Industry, Commons Services (Broadcasting)
Declared Interests: Director of Guildfare Ltd (unpaid) Cambridge Symphony Orchestra Ltd (unpaid)
Employment or Office: President to the Guild of Experienced Motorists; Advisor to Bowring UK Ltd, Barclays Bank plc, The Guild of Business Travel Agents
Trades or Professions: Occasional fees for lectures and broadcasts
Overseas Visits: 30 May–7 June 1992, to France, to chair annual conference of Guild of Business Travel Agents. Flown by British Midland, accommodated by Inter-Continental Hotels; 2–7 October 1992, to New York for meeting of executive committee of Guild of Business Travel Agents and subsequent meetings with March McLennan (owners of Bowring UK Ltd). Travel for his wife and him financed by British Airways; accommodation financed partly by BA and partly by him; 21–24 October 1993, visit to Prague made by his wife on his behalf to attend meeting of Guild of Business Travel Agents. Travel and accommodation provided by British Airways

Comments: From declarations made to Companies House in London, Grant is also a director of Guild of Freemen of City of London.

GRANT, Bernie

Constituency: Labour, Tottenham
Parliamentary Activities:
Select Committee Membership: None
Declared Interests:
Trades or Professions: Occasional lecturer
Financial Sponsorships, Gifts, etc.: Office equipment provided by GMBATU; Small grant received from the Barrow Cadbury Trust
Payments, etc., from abroad: Febuary 1992, lecturing fees from USA universities
Overseas Visits: January 1992, to Libya sponsored by the Libyan Government; May 1992, to Berlin, to attend Immigrants

Political Forum, who paid travel and accommodation costs; June 1992, to Senegal to attend OAU Summit. Air fare met in part by donations from family and friends in the black community; July 1992, to Martinique, to attend conference on Ethnic Minorities in Europe, sponsored by SERMAC and Conseil General de Martinique; September 1992, to Libya, for fact-finding visit with MPs, lawyers, trades unionists, sponsored by the Libyan Government

Comments: From declarations made to Companies House in London, Grant is also a director of Racial Equality in Europe Trust.

GREENWAY, Harry

Constituency: Conservative, Ealing North
Parliamentary Activities:
Select Committee Membership: Employment
Declared Interests:
Employment or Office: Part-time lecturer; Part-time Consultant to Taylor Woodrow (unremunerated since 31.12.92)
Financial Sponsorships, Gifts, etc.: Use of a company car provided by Taylor Woodrow; Donation made in 1992 to Constituency Conservative Association by supporters' club, members of which were/are private, business and professional people from Ealing North and elsewhere. No personal benefit.

GREENWAY, John

Constituency: Conservative, Ryedale
Parliamentary Activities
Select Committee Membership: Home Affairs
Declared Interests: Director of Greenway Middleton and Co. Ltd (registered insurance brokers)
Employment or Office: Parliamentary Advisor to the Institute of Insurance Brokers; Parliamentary Advisor to Yorkshire Television plc
Trades or Professions: Consultant to Practice Financial Management (independant financial advisors)
Declarable Shareholdings: Green Middleton and Co. Ltd.
Client: Enaged by Langford Exhibitions Ltd, the Institute of Sales Promotion and the British Promotional Merchandising Association for which he will receive some personal payment; He also advises the British Health Care Association (no payment involved); He also receives some small fees for the publication of articles in the insurance press.

GRIFFITHS, Nigel

Constituency: Labour, Edinburgh South
Parliamentary Activities: Opposition Spokesperson on Consumer Affairs
Declared Interests:
Financial Sponsorships, Gifts, etc.: USDAW as per Hastings Agreement. This does not involve any payment to him. USDAW donated £1,500 to Edinburgh South Constituency Labour Party in 1992.

GRIFFITHS, Peter

Constituency: Conservative, Portsmouth North
Parliamentary Activities:

Select Committee Membership: Members' Interests
Declared Interests: None listed.

GRIFFITH, Wyn

Constituency: Labour, Bridgend
Parliamentary Activities: Opposition Spokesperson on Education
Declared Interests:
Employment or Office: Party Consultant to the National Union of Teachers
Trades or Professions: Occasional fees for broadcasting appearances.

GROCOTT, Bruce

Constituency: Labour, The Wrekin
Parliamentary Activities:
Select Committee Membership: None
Declared Interests:
Trades or Professions: Member of the National Union of Journalists, occasional payments from writing and broadcasting

Comments: From declarations made to Companies House in London, Grocott is also a director of Parliamentary Broadcasting Unit Ltd.

GRYLLS, Sir Michael

Constituency: Conservative, Surrey North West
Parliamentary Activities:
Select Committee Membership: None
Declared Interests: Director of Le Carbone Lorraine (GB) Ltd, Armstrong Consulting Services Ltd, Columbus Holdings Ltd, Electrophoretics plc
Employment or Office: Consultant to Association of Authorised Public Accountants; Advisor to the Unitary Tax Campaign; Consultant to Sanofi Winthrop Ltd; Consultant to Digital Equipment Co. Ltd; Consultant to Charter Consolidated plc; Consultant to National Federation of Post Office and BT Pensioners
Clients: Ian Greer Associates

Comments: In 1990 a Select Committee inquiry found that Sir Michael received three 'thank-you' payments for introducing new clients to Ian Greer Associates, a political lobbying company. These were not properly declared at the time and his true commercial relationship with Ian Greer Associates was only registered in October 1989, several years after receiving payments.

GUMMER, Rt.Hon. John Selwyn

Constituency: Conservative, Suffolk Coastal
Parliamentary Activities: Secretary of State for Environment
Declared Interests: Director of Woodward Schools (Southern Division) (unpaid) Walsingham College (Affiliated Schools) Ltd (unpaid)
Employment or Office: Guardian of the Shrine of our Lady of Walsingham, who operate the Walsingham College Trust Association Ltd, the Walsingham College (Yorkshire Properties) Ltd, and the Walsingham College Affiliated Schools Ltd (unpaid)
Trades or Professions: Occasional writings; Visit to his home in Suffolk of the European Community Agriculture Ministers meeting in September 1992

Comments: In 1993 Gummer was rebuked by a Select Committee inquiry for not declaring that Hillsdown Holdings, one of Britain's largest food companies, spent £2,600 to restore a pond at his Suffolk manor house. Gummer was Secretary of State for Agriculture and Food at the time. The work was done just before Gummer was to be host to other European farm ministers at a mini-agricultural show built on the grounds of his home.

GUNNELL, John

Constituency: Labour, Leeds South and Morley
Parliamentary Activities:
Select Committee Membership: Broadcasting
Declared Interests: Chairman, Yorkshire Fund Managers Ltd; In addition the following which are all unremunerated: Yorkshire Enterprise Ltd and its subsidiary companies, White Rose Investments Ltd, White Rose Ventures Ltd, West Yorkshire Enterprise Services Ltd, West Yorkshire Small Firms Fund Ltd, West Yorkshire Small Firms Finance Ltd, White Rose Nominee Investments Ltd, Leeds Theatre Trust Ltd
Trades or Profession: Former university teacher (in receipt of pension)
Financial Sponsorships, Gifts, etc.: Sponsored as a candidate on the parliamentary list of the General, Municipal and Boilermakers Union.

HAGUE William

Constituency: Conservative, Richmond
Parliamentary Activities: Parliamentary Secretary for Social Security
Declared Interests: None listed
Overseas Visits: 14–20 September 1992, to Japan as a guest of the Foreign Ministry of Japan

Comments: From declarations made to Companies House in London, Hague is also a director of Brough Hall Management Co. Ltd, Brough Park Management Co. Ltd.

HAIN Peter

Constituency: Labour, Neath
Parliamentary Activities:
Select Committee Membership: None
Declared Interests: Director of Tribune Newspaper (non-remunerated)
Trades or Professions: Occasional writing, broadcasting and lecturing
Financial Sponsorships, Gifts, etc.: Part-payment of salary of constituency office assistant and expenses, and of election expenses, by the Union of Communication Workers

Comments: From declarations made to Companies House in London, Hain is also a director of Trade Union Research Unit Ltd.

HALL, Mike

Constituency: Labour, Warrington South
Parliamentary Activities:
Select Committee Membership: Public Accounts
Declared Interests: None listed

HAMILTON, Rt.Hon. Sir Archie

Constituency: Conservative, Epsom and Ewell
Parliamentary Activities:
Select Committee Membership: None
Declared Interests: Director of Saladin Holdings Ltd, Woodgate Dairy Farms, Siam Selective Growth Trust plc; James R. Glass Ltd, First Philippine Investment Trust plc, Crownridge Industries Ltd
Employment or Office: Consultant to W.S. Atkins Ltd (Epsom, Surrey); Consultant to Merrill Lynch Europe Ltd, Litton Industries Inc.
Trades or Professions: Farmer; Member of Lloyd's; Fees received for media appearances and contributions to newspapers
Land and Property: Bramley Park Farm

Comments: Hamilton was Parliamentary Private Secretary to Mrs Thatcher 1982–84, Parliamentary Under-Secretary for Defence Procurement 1986–87 and Minister of State for the Armed Forces at the Ministry of Defence 1988–93.

HAMILTON, Neil

Constituency: Conservative, Tatton
Parliamentary Activities: Parliamentary Under-Secretary for Corporate Affairs
Declared Interests: Barrister-at-Law (non-practising).

HAMPSON, Dr Keith

Constituency: Conservative, Leeds North West
Parliamentary Activities:
Select Committee Membership: Trade and Industry
Declared Interests:
Employment or Office: Consultant to the Association of University Teachers; Educational Advisor to Elydon Ltd, Export Projects Consultants; Consultant to Alexander and Alexander UK Ltd; Advisor to NCM Credit Insurance; Advisor to Yorkshire and Humberside Building Employers Confederation.

HANLEY, Jeremy

Constituency: Conservative, Richmond and Barnes
Parliamentary Activities: Ministry of State for Armed Forces
Declared Interests: None listed

Comments: From declarations made to Companies House in London, Hanley is also a director of Sheridan-Hanley Enterprises Ltd, Chartered Accountants.

HANNAM, Sir John

Constituency: Conservative, Exeter
Parliamentary Activities:
Select Committee Membership: Procedure
Declared Interest:
Employment or Office: Parliamentary Advisor, Royal Pharmaceutical Society of Great Britain; Political Advisor to Major Energy Users Council.

HANSON, David

Constituency: Labour, Delyn
Parliamentary Activities:
Select Committee Membership: Welsh Affairs
Declared Interests: None listed.

HARDY, Peter

Constituency: Labour, Wentworth
Parliamentary Activities:
Select Committee Membership: None
Declared Interests:
Financial Sponsorships, Gifts, etc.: by National Association of Colliery Overmen, Deputies and Shotfirers (no personal remuneration provided)

Comments: From declarations made to Companies House in London, Hardy is also a director of Rotherham Chamber of Commerce and Industry Ltd.

HARGREAVES, Andrew

Constituency: Conservative, Birmingham Hall Green
Parliamentary Activities:
Select Committee Membership: Commons Services (Information)
Declared Interests: Director of Foundation Holdings Ltd (expenses only)
Employment or Office: Consultant, Midlands Electricity plc; Honorary Permanent Secretary, European Foundation for Quality and the Environment (expenses only paid)

HARMAN, Harriet

Constituency: Labour, Peckham
Parliamentary Activities: Shadow Chief Secretary to the Treasury
Declared Interests:
Financial Sponsorships, Gifts, etc.: by the Transport and General Workers' Union; Financial contribution from NALGO towards research – no direct financial benefit

Comments: From declarations made to Companies House in London, Harman is also a director of Cambridge House and Talbot.

HARRIS, David

Constituency: Conservative, St Ives
Parliamentary Activities:
Select Committee Memberships: European Legislation, Foreign Affairs, Commons Services (Broadcasting)
Declared Interests: Freelance journalist
Land and Property: Owns his own home and some 28 acres in Cornwall, also his London flat. Commercial property in Devon.

HARVEY, Nick

Constituency: Liberal Democrat, North Devon
Parliamentary Activities:
Select Committee Membership: None
Declared Interests:
Financial Sponsorships, Gifts, etc.: Corporate Communications Strategy Ltd contributes £2,400 per annum to constituency party for secretarial support

Overseas Visits: 6–11 December 1992, to Singapore with members of all parties transport authorities as a guest of Singapore Airlines.

HASELHURST, Alan

Constituency: Conservative, Saffron Walden
Parliamentary Activities:
Select Committee Memberships: Transport, European Legislation,
Declared Interests:
Employment or Office: Consultant to Albright and Wilson Ltd; Consultant to Barrington Jay and Co.; Consultant to Federation of Electronic Industries; Consultant to Johnson Matthey plc; Consultant to National Power plc
Clients of Barrington Jay and Co.: British Aerospace plc, Rolls Royce plc, Racal plc, Bull Computers
Overseas Visits: 6–15 January 1992, to USA, sponsored by United Airlines, BA, Rolls Royce and Boeing in his capacity as Vice-Chairman of the Conservative Backbench Aviation Committee; 22–23 January 1992, to the USA in his capacity as Vice-Chairman of the Conservative Backbench Aviation Committee as a guest of British Aerospace plc; 25–31 May 1992, to USA in his capacity as a member of the Conservative Backbench Aviation Committee, sponsored by Virgin Atlantic Airways, United Airlines, Smiths Industry, Martin Marietta Corperation and IBM; 12–16 October 1992, to the USA as a guest of British Airways in his capacity as a member of the Conservative Backbench Aviation Committee

Comments: From declarations made to Companies House in London, Haselhurst is also a director of CPF Trust.

HATTERSLEY, Rt.Hon. Roy

Constituency: Labour, Birmingham Sparkbrook
Parliamentary Activities:
Select Committee Membership: None
Declared Interests:
Trades or Professions: Writing, broadcasting and occasional lecturing

HAWKINS, Nicholas

Constituency: Conservative, Blackpool South
Parliamentary Activities:
Select Committee Membership: Transport
Declared Interests: Chairman, North West Radio Ltd (unpaid); Director of Revelfree Ltd (corporate advisors) (unpaid)
Employment or Office: Parliamentary Consultant to North West Water (unpaid)
Trade or Professions: Barrister (non-practising); Occasional broadcasting and journalism
Financial Sponsorships, Gifts, etc.: Visit to Elvedon Forest Holiday Village as a guest of Centre Parcs.
Declarable Shareholdings: Quarry Dougall plc; Revelfree Ltd
Overseas Visits: 13–26 September, to USA with British/US Parliamentary Group, partly funded by the Group and partly by the US Information Agency; 4–11 January 1993, to Israel with the Conservative Friends of Israel, paid for by CFI and Isrotel Hotel Management Ltd; 21–22 June 1993, to France, as member of all-party Channel Tunnel Group to view the preparations for international rail services, organised and hosted by European Passenger Services Ltd, P&O Ferries Ltd and Eurotunnel plc.

HAWKSLEY, Warren

Constituency: Conservative, Halesowen and Stourbridge
Parliamentary Activities:
Select Committee Membership: None
Declared Interests:
Trades or Professions: Owner, with wife, of country house hotel near Welshpool, Powys, Wales
Overseas Visits: 14–23 September 1992, to Northern Cyprus as a guest of the Turkish Cypriot Government; 7–8 January 1993, to Lyon and Grenoble as a guest of Control.

HAYES, Jerry

Constituency: Conservative, Harlow
Parliamentary Activities: Parliamentary Private Secretary to Robert Atkins, Minister of State for Northern Ireland
Declared Interests:
Employment or Office: Consultant to Hornagold and Hills; Consultant to Western Provident Association
Trades or Professions: Barrister-at-Law; TV and Radio Presenter, Capital Radio, BBC, Mike Mansfield TV, LBC, GMTV
Overseas Visits: April 1992, to Boston, sponsored by John Hancock Insurance; November 1992, to New York, sponsored by John Hancock Insurance

Comments: From declarations made to Companies House in London, Hayes is also a director of Bassett Business Units Ltd.

HEALD, Oliver

Constituency: Conservative, North Hertfordshire
Parliamentary Activities:
Select Committee Membership: Employment
Declared Interests:
Trades or Professions: Barrister, practising in Cambridge and London.

HEATH, Rt.Hon. Sir Edward

Constituency: Conservative, Old Bexley and Sidcup
Parliamentary Activities:
Select Committee Membership: None
Declared Interests: Director of Dumpton Gap Company
Employment or Office: Member of the Public Review Board of Arthur Anderson and Co; Member of the Board of Governors of the Centre for Global Energy Studies; Development Advisor to the China Investment and Development Fund Ltd and to Kleinwort Benson China Management Ltd; Advisor to the China Ocean Shipping Company
Trades or Professions: Writing books and press articles, lecturing, making television and radio broadcasts on behalf of Dumpton Gap Company; Member of Lloyd's
Declarable Share holdings: Dumpton Gap Company

Comments: From declarations made to Companies House in London, Sir Edward is also a director of New Queens Hall Orchestra.

HEATHCOAT-AMORY, David

Constituency: Conservative, Wells
Parliamentary Activities: Minister of State at the Foreign Office
Declared Interests:
Land or Property: farm in Scotland
Declarable Shareholdings: Lowman Manufacturing Co. Ltd; LDT Ltd.

HENDERSON, Doug

Constituency: Labour, Newcastle-upon-Tyne, North
Parliamentary Activities: Opposition Spokesperson on the Environment
Declared Interests:
Employment or Office: Elected Official of the GMB, no salary; Consultant to the Machine Tool Technologies Association
Financial Sponsorships, Gifts, etc.: Sponsored by the GMB, minor material benefit.

HENDRON, Dr Joseph

Constituency: Social Democrat and Labour Party, Belfast West
Parliamentary Activities:
Select Committee Membership: None
Declared Interests: Medical Practitioner (GP).

HENDRY, Charles

Constituency: Conservative, High Peak
Parliamentary Activities:
Select Committee Membership: Procedure
Declared Interests:
Employment or Office: Consultant to Oracle Corporation; Consultant to Andersen Consulting; Consultant to Fleishman-Hillard
Clients of Fleishman-Hillard: Energis; Anhauser-Busch
Overseas Visits: 14–17 September 1992, to Stuttgart and Budapest, courtesy of the Konrad Adenauer Foundation.

HEPPELL, John

Constituency: Labour, Nottingham East
Parliamentary Activities:
Select Committee Membership: None
Declared Interest:
Financial Sponsorships, Gifts, etc.: Sponsored both as a Parliamentary Candidate and as Member of Parliament by the Rail, Maritime and Transport Union. No payment to the Member either directly or indirectly

Comments: From declarations made to Companies House in London, Heppell is also a director of Greater Nottingham Rapid Transit Ltd.

HESELTINE, Rt.Hon. Michael

Constituency: Conservative, Henley
Parliamentary Activities: President of the Board of Trade
Declared Interests:
Land and Property: Owner-Occupier of houses in London and Northamptonshire
Declarable Shareholdings: Haymarket Group, consisting of five companies: Haymarket Publishing Group Ltd, Haymarket Publishing Group Services Ltd (including Haymarket Exhibitions Ltd and

BBC Haymarket Exhibitions Ltd), Haymarket Medical Publications Ltd, Haymarket Marketing Publications Ltd, Haymarket Magazines Ltd and their subsidiaries. The Group has significant interests in local radio stations operating in the South of England. In addition the Group owns significant property, including its own offices, principally in: Lancaster Gate Properties Ltd, Teddington Properties Ltd, Ansdell Street Properties Ltd, Thenhurst Agricultural Ltd. In addition: J. Pridmore (Swansea) Ltd, Yoka Developments Ltd, Kensington Freeholds Ltd.

HICKS, Robert

Constituency: Conservative, Cornwall South East
Parliamentary Activities:
Select Committee Membership: European Legislation
Declared Interests:
Employment or Office: Parliamentary Liaison Officer, British Hospitality Association; Parliamentary Advisor to the Milk Marketing Board
Trades or Professions, etc.: Occasional television, radio and journalism.

HIGGINS, Rt.Hon. Terence

Constituency: Conservative, Worthing
Parliamentary Activities:
Select Committee Membership: None
Declared Interests: Director of Langley Sports Ltd (Chairman) Owners Abroad Group (from May 1991)
Employment or Office: Economic Consultant to Lex Service Group plc; Advisor to KPMG Peat Marwick
Trades or Professions: Economist; Occasional Lecturer
Declarable Shareholdings: Langley Sport Ltd

Comments: From declarations made to Companies House in London, Higgins is also a director of Institute of Advanced Motorists Ltd; Policy Studies Institute; Lex Service plc.

HILL, James

Constituency: Conservative, Southampton Test
Parliamentary Activities:
Select Committee Membership: Chairmen's Panel, Procedure
Declared Interests: Director of Clanfield Properties Ltd; Two family owned businesses mainly concerned with long-term investments
Employment or Office: Consultant to the Glass and Glazing Federation
Financial Sponsorships, Gifts, etc.: Research assistance allowance from Associated British Ports; Partner in Gunsfield Farm.

HILL, Keith

Constituency: Labour, Streatham
Parliamentary Activities:
Select Committee Membership: Transport
Declared Interests:
Financial Sponsorships, Gifts, etc.: Sponsored as a Parliamentary Candidate by the National Union of Rail, Maritime

and Transport Workers. £600 donated by RMT towards expenses of constituency party (no personal financial benefit).

HINCHLIFFE, David

Constituency: Labour, Wakefield
Parliamentary Activities: Shadow Minister for Personal Social Services
Declared Interests:
Trades or Professions: Occasional articles for *Social Work Today* magazine and other social work publications
Financial Sponsorships, Gifts, etc.: Sponsored by the National Union of Public Employees under the terms of the Hastings Agreement. No personal financial benefit. UNISON give a grant of £5,000 per year for the employment of a part-time researcher assisting with frontbench duties.
Declarable Shareholdings: 500 shares in Wakefield Trinity Rugby League Football Club Ltd.

HOEY, Kate

Constituency: Labour, Vauxhall
Parliamentary Activities:
Select Committee Membership: Commons Services (Broadcasting)
Declared Interests:
Employment or Office: Member of the Advisory Board of London Weekend Television
Trades or Professions: Occasional fees from TV, radio and newspapers
Financial Sponsorships, Gifts, etc.: Part payment of office expenses from the Union of Communication Workers.

HOGG, Rt. Hon. Douglas

Constituency: Conservative, Grantham
Parliamentary Activities: Minister of State at the Foreign Office
Declared interests: Barrister (non-practising).

HOGG, Norman

Constituency: Labour, Cumbernauld and Kilsyth
Parliamentary Activities:
Select Committee Membership: None
Declared Interests: Director of Kelvin Central Buses Ltd (from 28.3.91) (non-executive)
Employment or Office: Parliamentary Consultant to the National and Local Government Officers Association; Parliamentary Advisor to the Bus and Coach Council
Overseas Visits: 31 January–11 February 1992, to Brazil under the auspices of the All Party Road Passenger Transport Group.

HOME ROBERTSON, John

Constituency: Labour, East Lothian
Parliamentary Activities:
Select Committee Membership: Defence
Declared Interests: Farmer
Financial Sponsorships, Gifts, etc.: Sponsored by the Transport Salaried Staffs Association; payments made directly to East Lothian Constituency Labour Party
Land and property: Paxton South Mains and Overhowden farms, Berwickshire
Overseas Visits: 28–29 June 1992, to USA, to visit a nuclear installation in Colorado as a guest of Scottish Nuclear.

HOOD, Jimmy

Constituency: Labour, Clydesdale
Parliamentary Activities:
Select Committee Membership: Chairman European Legislation
Declared Interests:
Financial Sponsorships, Gifts, etc.: Sponsored by the National Union of Mineworkers.

HOON, Geoffrey

Constituency: Labour, Ashfield
Parliamentary Activities:
Select Committee Membership: None
Declared Interests: Member of the European Parliament until July 1994
Overseas Visits: 3–4 December 1992, to Paris, to attend a seminar organised by the Franco-British Colloque. Return flight to Paris and overnight accommodation paid for by the Franco-British Colloque.

HORAM, John

Constituency: Conservative, Orpington
Parliamentary Activities:
Select Committee Membership: Public Accounts
Declared Interests: Managing Director of CRU International Ltd; Director of CRU International Holdings Ltd; CRU Publishing Ltd; CRU Publishing (Holdings) Ltd

Comments: From declarations made to Companies House in London, Horam is also a director of Forex Research Ltd; Resources Development Group Ltd; CRU Share Scheme Trustees Ltd; Purley Press (Holdings) Ltd; Mount Pleasant Trustee Ltd; CRU Associated Trustee Ltd; Diamond Research and Publishing Ltd; British Sulphur Corporation Ltd; Jewellery Research and Publishing Ltd; Circle 33 Commercial Properties Ltd; Purley Press Ltd.

HORDERN, Rt. Hon. Sir Peter

Constituency: Conservative, Horsham
Parliamentary Activities:
Select Committee Membership: None
Declared Interests: Director of F. and C. Smaller Companies Investment plc, Fina plc, T.R. Technology Investment Trust
Employment or Office: Consultant to Pannell, Kerr, Forster
Trades or Professions: Occasional broadcasting and articles in newspapers

Comments: From declarations made to Companies House in London, Hordern is also a director of Pountney Hill Holdings Ltd; Tragen Finance Company Ltd; Earl of March's Trust Company Ltd.

HOWARD, Rt. Hon. Michael

Constituency: Conservative, Folkestone and Hythe
Parliamentary Activities: Home Secretary
Declared Interests: Queen's Counsel (ceased practising on 2 September 1985).

HOWARTH, Alan

Constituency: Conservative, Stratford-on-Avon
Parliamentary Activities:
Select Committee Membership: National Heritage
Declared Interests:
Employment or Office: Advisor to Richard Branson, whose business interests include Virgin Atlantic Airways Ltd, package holidays and retailing
Trades or Professions: Member of Lloyd's
Land and Property: Owner-occupied house in London.

HOWARTH, George

Constituency: Labour, Knowsley North
Parliamentary Activities:
Select Committee Membership: None
Declared Interests: Chairman of Pendleton's Ice Cream Ltd (unpaid)
Financial Sponsorships, Gifts, etc.: Sponsored by AEU.

HOWELL, Rt.Hon. David

Constituency: Conservative, Guildford
Parliamentary Activities:
Select Committee Membership: Chairman, Foreign Affairs
Declared Interests: Director of Trafalgar House plc (non-executive, from 5.12.90), Jardine Insurance Brokers plc, (non-executive) (from 1.10.91), Monks Investment Trust plc (non-executive) (from 27.5.93)
Employment or Office: Economic Advisor to Coopers, Lybrand, Deloittes; Member of the International Advisory Council, the Swiss Bank Corporation; Economic Advisor to Swiss Bank Corporation (UK)
Trades or Professions: Journalist; Columnist for the *Japan Times* and *Wall Street Journal*; Economic Consultant
Payments, etc., from abroad: Fees from overseas articles and lectures

Comments: Howell was Secretary of State for Energy 1979–81 and Transport Secretary 1981–83. According to records at Companies House in London, Howell is also a director of UK–Japan 2000 Group; Trafalger House Trustees (1990) Ltd.

HOWELL, Sir Ralph

Constituency: Conservative, Norfolk North
Parliamentary Activities:
Select Committee Membership: None
Declared Interests:
Trades or Professions: Farmer; Underwriting Member of Lloyd's
Land and Property: Owner-Occupier of farms in Norfolk

Comments: From declarations made to Companies House in London, Sir Ralph is also a director of Anglo-Austrian Society; Savers Union Ltd.

HOWELLS, Dr Kim

Constituency: Labour, Pontypridd
Parliamentary Activities:
Select Committee Membership: Public Accounts
Declared Interests: None listed

Overseas Visits: 27 June–1 July 1992, to Colorado, USA, to visit nuclear dry storage facility, funded by Scottish Nuclear Ltd.

HOYLE, Doug

Constituency: Labour, Warrington North
Parliamentary Activities:
Select Committee Membership: None
Declared Interests:
Employment or Office: Past President of the Manufacturing, Science and Finance Union (unpaid)
Financial Sponsorships, Gifts, etc.: by the Manufacturing, Science and Finance Union. No money is paid to me in respect of this sponsorship

Comments: From declarations made to Companies House in London, Hoyle is also a director of ASTMS Insurance Selection Ltd; MPU Insurance Selection Ltd.

HUGHES, Kevin

Constituency: Labour, Doncaster North
Parliamentary Activities:
Select Committee Membership: None
Declared Interests:
Financial Sponsorships, Gifts, etc.: Sponsored as a parliamentary candidate by the National Union of Mineworkers who pay £400 towards administration expenses

Comments: From declarations made to Companies House in London, Hughes is also a director of Doncaster Leisure Management Ltd.

HUGHES, Robert

Constituency: Labour, Aberdeen North
Parliamentary Activities:
Select Committee Membership: Scottish Affairs (ex-Chairman)
Declared Interests:
Financial Sponsorships, Gifts, etc.: Amalgamated Union of Engineering Workers (no monies paid directly to me).

HUGHES, Robert G.

Constituency: Conservative, Harrow West
Parliamentary Activities:
Select Committee Membership: Commons Services (Broadcasting)
Declared Interests: None
Overseas Visits: 23–25 October 1992, to Cadenabbia, Lake Como, Italy, to the third Round Table Discussion, as a guest of the Konrad Adenauer Stiftung

Comments: From declarations made to Companies House in London, Hughes is also a director of Arden Housing Ltd.

HUGHES, Roy

Constituency: Labour, Newport East
Parliamentary Activities:
Select Committee Membership: Chairman Welsh Grand Committee
Declared Interests:
Financial Sponsorships, Gifts, etc.: Sponsored by Transport and General Workers' Union who pay £2,000 in election expenses
Overseas Visits: 5–13 April 1993, to Turkish Republic of Cyprus, as a guest of the Government of the Turkish Republic of

Cyprus. He was accompanied by his wife whose air travel he paid for.

HUGHES, Simon

Constituency: Liberal Democrat, Southwark and Bermondsey
Parliamentary Activities:
Select Committee Membership: Commons Services (Accommodation and Works)
Declared Interests: Director of Cambridge University Mission Ltd (£1 share otherwise unremunerated); Rose Theatre Trust Ltd (£1 share otherwise unremunerated); Thames Heritage Parade Ltd (£1 share otherwise unremunerated)
Trades or Professions: Barrister; Occasional broadcasting, lectures and writing.

HUME, John

Constituency: Social Democratic and Labour Party, Foyle
Parliamentary Activities:
Select Committee Membership: None
Declared Interests: None listed.

HUNT, Rt.Hon. David

Constituency: Conservative, Wirral West
Parliamentary Activities: Secretary of State for Employment
Declared Interests:
Trades or Professions: Partner, Beachcroft Stanleys (Solicitors); Underwriting Member of Lloyd's (External).

HUNT, Sir John

Constituency: Conservative, Ravensbourne
Parliamentary Activities:
Select Committee Membership: None
Declared Interests:
Employment or Office: Parliamentary Advisor to the National Hairdressers' Federation.

HUNTER, Andrew

Constituency: Conservative, Basingstoke
Parliamentary Activities:
Select Committee Membership: Agriculture
Declared Interests: Director of Maestro Trading Ltd (from 1.6.89) (not trading) (unpaid); Maestro Trading (Botswana) Ltd (from 1.1.90) (not trading) (unpaid); Maestro Properties (Botswana) Ltd (from 1.8.90) (not trading) (unpaid); The Training and Business Group plc (from 1.1.93)
Declarable Shareholdings: Maestro Trading Ltd (which wholly owns Maestro Trading Botswana Ltd) (not trading); Maestro Properties (Botswana) Ltd (not trading)
Overseas Visits: January 1992, to Mozambique as a guest of the Mozambique Institute, London; May 1992, to Bophuthatswana and KwaZulu as a guest of the Bophuthatswana and KwaZulu Governments

HURD, Rt.Hon. Douglas

Constituency: Conservative, Witney
Parliamentary Activities: Foreign Secretary
Declared Interests:
Trades or Professions: Novelist.

HUTTON, John

Constituency: Labour, Barrow and Furness
Parliamentary Activities:
Select Committee Membership: None
Declared interests: None listed
Overseas Visits: 12–24 September 1992, to USA with the British-American Parliamentary Group, partly funded by the Group and partly by the US Information Service.

ILLSLEY, Eric

Constituency: Labour, Barnsley Central
Parliamentary Activities:
Select Committee Membership: Procedure
Declared Interests:
Employment or Office: Occasional fees for market research from Access Opinions
Financial Sponsorships, Gifts, etc.: Sponsored by the National Union of Mineworkers
Overseas Visits: 1–8 December 1992, to the US, accompanied by his wife, to attend an Annual Parliament-Congressional Conference, as a member of a British-American Parliamentary Group Delegation. Travel within the US paid for by the US Government

Comments: From declarations made to Companies House in London, Illsley is also a director of Barnsley College Educational Trust.

INGRAM, Adam

Constituency: Labour, East Kilbride
Parliamentary Activities:
Select Committee Membership: Trade and Industry
Declared Interests:
Financial Sponsorships, Gifts, etc.: Sponsored by the Transport and General Workers' Union; Payment of £500 from UNISON (the public service union) for parliamentary work done on their behalf
Overseas Visits: 27–30 June 1992, to Fort St Vrain, Colorado, USA, as a guest of Scottish Nuclear plc, to view a dry storage facility for spent nuclear fuel; June 1993, to Paris Air Show under auspices of the Parliamentary Space Committee, part funded by the UK International Space Committee.

JACK, Michael

Constituency: Conservative, Fylde
Parliamentary Activities: Minister of State for Agriculture
Declared Interests: None listed.

JACKSON, Glenda

Constituency: Labour, Hampstead and Highgate
Parliamentary Activities:
Select Committee Membership: None
Declared Interests: Director of RGD Productions Ltd
Financial Sponsorships, Gifts, etc.: Sponsored as a Parliamentary Candidate by ASLEF.

JACKSON, Helen

Constituency: Labour, Hillsborough
Parliamentary Activities:

Select Committee Membership: Environment
Declared Interests: Occasional fees from media work
Comments: From declarations made to Companies House in London, Jackson is also a director of Soutcerule Ltd.

JACKSON, Robert

Constituency: Conservative, Wantage
Parliamentary Activities:
Select Committee Membership: Public Accounts
Declared Interests: None listed

Comments: From declarations made to Companies House in London, Jackson is also a director of Round Table Ltd; Hattori Trust Company Ltd.

JAMIESON, David

Constituency: Labour, Plymouth Devonport
Parliamentary Activities:
Select Committee Membership: Education
Declared Interests: None listed.

JANNER, Hon. Greville

Constituency: Labour, Leicester West
Parliamentary Activities:
Select Committee Membership: Chair, Employment
Declared Interests: Director of Ladbroke plc (non-executive); JSB Group (from July 1989)
Trades or Professions: Queen's Counsel, barrister; Writer, lecturer and trainer, working mainly through JSB Group; Broadcaster
Declarable Shareholdings: JSB Group Ltd
Overseas Visits: 13–19 October 1992, to Sweden, Latvia and Lithuania, sponsored by Holocaust Educational Trust and the Inter-Parliamentary Council Against Anti-semitism. Some hospitality and transport received within their countries from the three parliaments concerned

Comments: From declarations made to Companies House in London, Janner is also a director of Effective Presentational Skills Ltd; Jewish Museum London; Institute of Jewish Affairs; Jewish Chronicle Trust Ltd.

JENKIN, Bernard

Constituency: Conservative, Colchester North
Parliamentary Activities:
Select Committee Membership: None
Declared Interests:
Employment or Office: Advisor to Legal and General Group plc
Trades and Professions: Occasional journalism
Overseas Visits: 30 May-4 June 1993, to Israel with the Conservative Friends of Israel, accompanied by his wife. He paid for his wife's air ticket but his own and all hospitality was provided by the Israeli Government.

JESSEL, Toby

Constituency: Conservative, Twickenham
Parliamentary Activities:
Select Committee Membership: National Heritage
Declared Interests: Director of Huzback Securities (unpaid)
Declarable Shareholdings: Shell Transport
Comments: From declarations made to Companies House in London, Jessel is also a director of Faraday Yard Company Ltd.

JOHNSON-SMITH, Sir Geoffrey

Constituency: Conservative, Wealden
Parliamentary Activities:
Select Committee Membership: Chairman, Member's Interests
Declared Interests: Director of (Non-executive) Taylor Alden Ltd (Industrial Public Relations and Marketing); (Non-executive) Glengate Holdings plc (Commercial and Industrial Property); (Non-executive) MDA (Blenelux) S.A. Construction consultants and Quantity Surveyors; (Non-executive) Brands Hatch Leisure plc
Employment or Office: Consultant to Eagle Star Group; Consultant to Philips Communications Systems, Cambridge

Comments: Despite being a long-serving chairman of the Commons Select Committee on Members' Interests, Sir Geoffrey has himself sailed close to the wind on his own business interests. One of his former consultancies was with MEL, a major defence contractor owned by Philips Electronics. During the 1988 Defence Estimates debate, Sir Geoffrey strongly opposed reductions in defence spending without declaring his own interest.

JOHNSTON, Sir Russell

Constituency: Liberal Democrat, Inverness, Nairn and Lochaber
Parliamentary Activities:
Select Committee Membership: None
Declared Interests:
Trades or Professions: Occasional journalism, TV and radio
Overseas Visits: May 1992, to Kosovo for unofficial elections, paid for by the Kosovan LDK Party; August 1992, to Serbian controlled area of Bosnia, paid for by the Yugoslav Government; September 1992, to Cyprus as guest of the President of the Cypriot Assembly

Comments: From declarations made to Companies House in London, Johnston is also a director of Scottish Telethon Trust Ltd.

JONES, Barry

Constituency: Labour, Alyn and Deeside
Parliamentary Activities:
Select Committee Membership: None
Declared Interests:
Financial Sponsorships, Gifts, etc.: Sponsored by the Transport and General Workers' Union.

JONES, Gwilym

Constituency: Conservative, Cardiff North
Parliamentary Activities: Parliamentary Under-Secretary for Wales
Declared Interests:
Land and Property: Family home in Cardiff and small flat in London

Comments: From declarations made to Companies House in London, Jones is also a director of Bowring Wales Ltd, Insurance Brokers.

JONES, Ieuan Wyn

Constituency: Plaid Cymru, Ynys Mon
Parliamentary Activities:
Select Committee Membership: Agriculture
Declared Interests: Solicitor.

JONES, Jon Owen

Constituency: Labour, Cardiff Central
Parliamentary Activities:
Select Committee Membership: None
Declared Interests:
Employment or Office: Member of Cardiff City Council

Financial Sponsorships, Gifts, etc.: Sponsored as a Parliamentary Candidate and as a Member of Parliament by the Co-operative Party.

JONES, Lynne

Constituency: Labour, Birmingham Selly Oak
Parliamentary Activities:
Select Committee Membership: Science and Technology
Declared Interests: Councillor, Birmingham City Council

Comments: From declarations made to Companies House in London, Jones is also a director of Birmingham Tribunal Unit.

JONES, Martyn

Constituency: Labour, South West Clwyd
Parliamentary Activities:
Select Committee Membership: Agriculture
Declared Interests:
Employment or Office: Parliamentary Advisor to the Brewers Society (the fee, after tax and deductions, is paid to the Labour Party at local, regional and national level)
Financial Sponsorships, Gifts, etc.: Sponsored by the Transport and General Workers' Union (paid directly to the Clwyd South West Labour Party).

JONES, Nigel

Constituency: Liberal Democrat, Cheltenham
Parliamentary Activities:
Select Committee Membership: None
Declared Interests:
Employment or Office: Consultant to International Computers Ltd, Government and Major Companies Division.

JONES, Robert

Constituency: Conservative, Hertfordshire West
Parliamentary Activities:
Select Committee Membership: Chairman, Environment
Declared Interests: Vice-Chairman of SGS Yarsley Quality Assured Firms Ltd
Trades or Professions: Income from sundry writing and broadcasting
Overseas Visits: September 1992, to the Turkish Republic of North Cyprus, to learn

at first hand the prospect of a political settlement there, at the expense of the local administration

Comments: From declarations made to Companies House in London, Jones is also a director of SGS Yarsley International Certification Services Ltd.

JOPLING, Rt.Hon. Michael

Constituency: Conservative, Westmorland and Lonsdale
Parliamentary Activities:
Select Committee Membership: Foreign Affairs
Declared Interests: Director of Blagden Industries plc (from March 1989)
Employment or Office: Consultant to Hill and Knowlton (UK) Ltd; President of the Auto-Cycle Union (no remuneration except for occasional expenses paid for events run under an ACU licence)
Trades or Professions: Farmer; Member of Lloyd's; Occasional fees from writing, broadcasting or lecturing
Land and Property: Has an interests in land and property
Declarable Shareholdings: Ryeland Properties Ltd
Clients: Police Superintendents Association; Royal Armouries; Chiquita Brands International; Vernons Organisation; Nuclear Electric; Vaux plc; Railtrack; American Express; European Recovery and Recycling Association; Union Bank of Switzerland, Games for Good Causes plc

Comments: Jopling was Government Chief Whip from 1979 to 1983 and Secretary of State for Agriculture 1983–87. From declarations made to Companies House in London, Jopling lists additional interests as a director of Art Study Tours Ltd.

JOWELL, Tessa

Constituency: Labour, Dulwich
Parliamentary Activities:
Select Committee Membership: Health
Declared Interests:
Employment or Office: Part-time advisor on community care to Joseph Rowntree Foundation and Islington Council (completing contracts undertaken before election, to be finished by March 1993); Member of the Royal College of Nursing's Party Panel (the College pay my accommodation charges at the annual Party Conference)
Trades or Professions: Periodic consultancy on community care
Financial Sponsorships, Gifts, etc.: Sponsored as a Parliamentary Candidate by the Transport and General Workers' Union
Overseas Visits: 25–27 January 1993, to Bonn under the auspices of the Friedrich Ebert Stiftung, who met all travel and accommodation costs.

KAUFMAN, Rt.Hon. Gerald

Constituency: Labour, Manchester Gorton
Parliamentary Activities:
Select Committee Membership: National Heritage Chairman
Declared Interests:
Financial Sponsorships, Gifts, etc.: Sponsored as a Candidate by the General, Municipal, Boilermakers and Allied Trades Union

Comments: From declarations made to Companies House in London, Kaufman is also a director of Greater Manchester Arts Centre Ltd.

KEEN, Alan

Constituency: Labour, Feltham and Heston
Parliamentary Activities:
Select Committee Membership: None
Declared interests:
Financial Sponsorships, Gifts, etc.: Sponsored as a Parliamentary Candidate by the Co-operative Party
Declarable Shareholdings: Safe and Sound Fire Technology Ltd.

KELLETT-BOWMAN, Dame Elaine

Constituency: Conservative, Lancaster
Parliamentary Activities:
Select Committee Membership: None
Declared interests:
Trades or Professions: Member of Lloyd's; Barrister, no longer practising
Land and Property: Owner-Occupier, 149 acres.

KENNEDY, Charles

Constituency: Liberal Democrat, Ross, Cromarty and Skye
Parliamentary Activities:
Select Committee Membership: None
Declared Interests:
Trades or Professions: Occasional journalism (articles and/or broadcasting) and lecturing
Overseas Visits: 30 May–6 June 1993, to Israel, financed by Labour Friends of Israel

Comments: From declarations made to Companies House in London, Kennedy is also a director of Block 10 Ashley Gardens Ltd; Parliamentary Broadcasting Unit Ltd.

KENNEDY, Jane

Constituency: Labour, Liverpool Broadgreen
Parliamentary Activities:
Select Committee Membership: Social Security
Declared Interests:
Financial Sponsorship Gifts, etc.: Sponsored as a Member of Parliament by UNISON.

KEY, Robert

Constituency: Conservative, Salisbury
Parliamentary Activities: Parliamentary Under-Secretary for Transport
Declared Interests: None listed.

KHABRA, Piara

Constituency: Labour, Ealing Southall
Parliamentary Activities:
Select Committee Membership: None
Declared Interests: None listed

Comments: From declarations made to Companies House in London, Khabra is also a director of Southall Day Centre Ltd; Southall Community Projects Committee; Ealing Borough Law Centre.

KILFEDDER, Sir James

Constituency: Ulster Popular Unionist Party, Down North
Parliamentary Activities:
Select Committee Membership: None
Declared Interests: None listed.

Comments: From declarations made to Companies House in London, Kilfedder is a director of Optionright Ltd.

KILFOYLE, Peter

Constituency: Labour, Liverpool Walton
Parliamentary Activities:
Select Committee Membership: None
Declared Interests: None listed.

KING, Rt. Hon. Tom

Constituency: Conservative, Bridgwater
Parliamentary Activities:
Select Committee Membership: None
Declared Interests: Director of Electra Investment Trust plc; Consultant to British Water
Trades or Professions: Occasional broadcasting, writing and lecturing
Land and Property: Small farm and woodlands
Declarable Shareholdings: Fosters Rooms Ltd; Excel Mouldings Ltd

Comments: King was a Cabinet Minister between 1983 and 1992 in the following successive Departments of State: Environment, Transport, Employment, Northern Ireland and Defence. From declarations made to Companies House in London, King lists additional interests as a director of: Electra Kingsway General Partner Ltd; St Michael's School Tawstock Ltd; Electra Kingsway Managers Holdings Ltd.

KINNOCK, Rt. Hon. Neil

Constituency: Labour, Islwyn
Parliamentary Activities:
Select Committee Membership: None
Declared Interests: Director of Residents Opposed to Ci'Lonydd Quarry Ltd (unpaid)
Financial Sponsorships, Gifts, etc.: Sponsored by Transport and General Workers' Union according to provision of Hastings Agreement. All payments go directly to constituency party funds.
Employment or office: Advisor to Caparo Group plc

Comments: From declarations made to Companies House in London, Kinnock is also a director of Coleg Harlech.

KIRKHOPE, Timothy

Constituency: Conservative, Leeds North East
Parliamentary Activities: a Government Whip
Declared Interests:
Employment or Office: Consultant with R. V. Clerey and Co.
Trades and Professions: Solicitor
Land and Property: The owner of several family properties from which rental income is received, as well as homes in London, Northumberland and Yorkshire.

KIRKWOOD, Archy

Constituency: Liberal Democrat, Roxburgh and Berwickshire
Parliamentary Activities:
Select Committee Memberships: Selection, Liaison, Finance and Services
Declared Interests: None listed

Comments: From declarations made to Companies House in London, Kirkwood is also a director of Family Budget Unit.

KNAPMAN, Roger

Constituency: Conservative, Stroud
Parliamentary Activities:
Select Committee Membership: None
Declared Interests:
Trades or Professions: Partner, R.J. and R.M. Knapman, Builders; Member of Lloyd's underwriting syndicates; Associate partner, Carters, Chartered Surveyors.

KNIGHT, Angela

Constituency: Conservative, Erewash
Parliamentary Activities: Parliamentary Private Secretary to Tim Sainsbury, Minister for Industry
Declared Interests:
Employment or Office: Consultant to William Cook plc
Financial Sponsorships, Gifts, etc.: August 1993 – Gift of one adult and two children return tickets to Guernsey from British Midland
Declarable Shareholdings: William Cook plc.

KNIGHT, Greg

Constituency: Conservative, Derby North
Parliamentary Activities:
Select Committee Memberships: Commons Services (Broadcasting), Finance and Services
Declared Interests:
Employment or Office: Owns a recording studio in Leicestershire. Occasional session work and journalism.

KNIGHT, Dame Jill

Constituency: Conservative, Birmingham Edgbaston
Parliamentary Activities:
Select Committee Membership: Home Affairs
Declared Interests: Director of Computeach International (from 25.4.90); Teachware Ltd (a subsidiary of Computeach) (from 1.12.90)
Trades or Professions: Occasional broadcasting and journalism.

KNOX, Sir David

Constituency: Conservative, Staffordshire Moorlands
Parliamentary Activities:
Select Committee Memberships: European Legislation, Chairman's Panel, Unopposed Bills
Declared Interests:
Employment or Office: Economic Advisor to Lucas Industries Ltd, Birmingham; Parliamentary Advisor to the Chartered Institute of Management Accountants.

KYNOCH, George

Constituency: Conservative, Kincardine and Deeside
Parliamentary Activities:
Select Committee Membership: Scottish Affairs
Declared Interests: Director of Kynoch Group (non-executive); Aardwark Holdings Ltd (non-executive)
Land and Property: Income received from let of two fields adjacent to constituency home

Comments: From declarations made to Companies House in London, Kynoch is also a director of C. and J. Hirst Fabrics Ltd.

LAIT, Jacqui

Constituency: Conservative, Hastings and Rye
Parliamentary Activities:
Select Committee Membership: Health
Declared Interests:
Trades or Professions: Member of Lloyd's 1986–91 (resigned from 31 December 1991)
Overseas Visits: 17–18 January 1993, to Germany, sponsored by Starcky Industries in my capacity as a Fellow Elect of the Industry Parliamentary Trust; 2–7 August 1993, to USA, sponsored by Staveley Industries plc, as part of fellowship of Industry and Parliamentary Trust.

LAMONT, Rt.Hon. Norman

Constituency: Conservative, Kingston-upon-Thames
Parliamentary Activities:
Select Committee Membership: None
Declared Interests: Director of N.M. Rothschild and Sons Ltd; First Philippine Investment Trust; Taiwan Investment Trust plc
Land and Property: a house in London W11

Comments: Lamont was Minister of State for Industry 1981–85, Minister for Defence Procurement 1985–86, Financial Secretary to the Treasury 1986–89, Chief Secretary to the Treasury 1989–90 and Chancellor of the Exchequer 1990–93. Within months of leaving the Treasury, the former Chancellor joined the board of N.M. Rothschild, the merchant bank which had been the beneficiary of several privatisation commissions in the 1980s. While Chancellor he received £4,700 of public money to reimburse legal expenses incurred to evict a sex therapist from one of his properties. Both the Select Committee for Members' Interests and the Inland Revenue stated he should have declared the payments as well as the £18,400 Lamont received from an anonymous Tory Party donor.

LANG, Rt.Hon. Ian

Constituency: Conservative, Galloway and Upper Nithsdale
Parliamentary Activities: Secretary of State for Scotland
Declared Interests:
Trades or Professions: Member of Lloyd's (ceased underwriting December 1990)
Declarable Shareholdings: Lang and Fulton Ltd.

LAWRENCE, Sir Ivan

Constituency: Conservative, Burton
Parliamentary Activities:
Select Committee Membership: Chairman, Home Affairs.
Declared Interests:
Employment or Office: Chairman of the Burton-on-Trent Artisan Dwelling Co. Ltd
Trades or Professions: Barrister-at-Law (Queen's Counsel); Recorder of the Crown Courts; Broadcasting; Occasional lecturing and journalism
Overseas Visits: 3–12 April 1993, to Cyprus, as a guest of the Turkish Republic of Northern Cyprus.

LEGG, Barry

Constituency: Conservative, Milton Keynes South West
Parliamentary Activities: Treasury and Civil Service

Comments: From declarations made to Companies House in London, Legg is also a director of Conservative Way Forward Ltd.

LEIGH, Edward

Constituency: Conservative, Gainsborough and Horncastle
Parliamentary Activities:
Select Committee Membership: None
Declared Interests:
Trades or Professions: Barrister (non-practising)

Comments: From declarations made to Companies House in London, Leigh is also a director of Formatstar Ltd.

LENNOX-BOYD, Mark

Constituency: Conservative, Morecambe and Lunesdale
Parliamentary Activities: Parliamentary Under-Secretary at the Foreign Office
Declared Interests: None Listed
Declarable Shareholdings: The Iveagh Trustees Ltd; Duke Seabridge Ltd; Guinness plc; Mintel International Group Ltd.

LESTER, Jim

Constituency: Conservative, Broxtowe
Parliamentary Activities:
Select Committee Membership: Foreign Affairs
Declared Interests:
Employment or Office: Parliamentary Consultant to: Direct Selling Association, Association of First Division Civil Servants, BAT Industries, CMA (Communication Managers Association), Phonographic Performance Ltd, Priory Hospital Group Ltd

Comments: From declarations made to Companies House in London, Lester is also a director of Third World Educational Clearing House; Family Budget Unit.

LESTOR, Joan

Constituency: Labour, Eccles
Parliamentary Activities:
Select Committee Membership: None
Declared Interests:
Financial Sponsorships, Gifts, etc.: As an MP sponsored by the General Municipal Boilermakers and Allied Trades Union. No payment to Member personally.

LEWIS, Terry

Constituency: Labour, Worsley
Parliamentary Activities:
Select Committee Membership: Members' Interest
Declared Interests:
Financial Sponsorships, Gifts, etc.: Sponsored by the Transport and General Workers' Union; Constituency Party receives £750 per annum; financial support at a General Election reflects an agreement between the TGWU and the Labour Party. No payments are paid to Lewis.

LIDINGTON, David

Constituency: Conservative, Aylesbury
Parliamentary Activities:
Select Committee Membership: Education
Declared Interests:
Land and Property: Freehold house in Enfield, Middlesex, yielding a nominal ground rent
Overseas Visits: 1–8 August 1992, to Hong Kong with my wife as guests of the Hong Kong Government; 14–17 September 1992, to Stuttgart and Budapest as guest of the Konrad Adenauer Stiftung; 23–25 October 1992, to Caddenabia, Italy, for Anglo-German Conference as guest of the Konrad Adenauer Stiftung; 9–11 January 1993, member of an All Party visit to the Republic of Macedonia, as a guest of the Macedonian Parliament.

LIGHTBROWN, David

Constituency: Conservative, Staffordshire South East
Parliamentary Activities:
Select Committee Memberships: Commons Services (Accommodation and Works), Government Whip
Declared Interests: None listed

Comments: From declarations made to Companies House in London, Lightbrown is a director of Brunel Lodge Management Company.

LILLEY, Rt. Hon. Peter

Constituency: Conservative, St Albans
Parliamentary Activities: Secretary of State for Social Security
Declared Interests: None listed.

LITHERLAND, Robert

Constituency: Labour, Manchester Central
Parliamentary Activities:
Select Committee Membership: None
Declared Interests:
Financial Sponsorships, Gifts, etc.: Graphical, Paper and Media Union.

LIVINGSTONE, Ken

Constituency: Labour, Brent East
Parliamentary Activities:
Select Committee Membership: None
Declared Interests: Director of Localaction Ltd (company formed to cover the publication of my books, *Socialist Economic Bulletin* and other writing and media work).
Financial Sponsorships, Gifts, etc.: Sponsored as an MP by TGWU – annual payment of £600 to constituency Labour party

LLOYD, Peter

Constituency: Conservative, Fareham
Parliamentary Activities: Minister of State at Home Office
Declared Interests: Member of Lloyd's.

LLOYD, Tony

Constituency: Labour, Stretford
Parliamentary Activities: An Opposition Spokesperson on Employment
Declared Interests:
Financial Sponsorships, Gifts, etc.: Sponsored by the Graphical, Paper and Media Union.

LLWYD, Elfyn

Constituency: Plaid Cymru, Meirionnydd Nant Cowy
Parliamentary Activities:
Select Committee Membership: Welsh Affairs
Declared Interests:
Employment or Office: Consultant to Messrs Guthrie Jones and Jones, Solicitors, Dolgellau, Gwynedd.

LOFTHOUSE, Geoffrey

Constituency: Labour, Pontefract and Castleford
Parliamentary Activities:
Select Committee Membership: None.
Declared Interests:
Financial Sponsorships, Gifts, etc.: Sponsored as a Parliamentary Candidate by GMB Apex Union, who contributed £1,125 to my election expenses.

LORD, Michael

Constituency: Conservative, Suffolk Central
Parliamentary Activities: Parliamentary Commissioner for Administration (Ombudsman)
Declared Interests: Director of the Palmer Family Trust (from October 1988)
Employment or Office: Parliamentary Consultant to the British Printing Industries Federation; Parliamentary Consultant to the Country Houses Association Ltd
Trades or Professions, etc.: Arboricultural consultant.

LOYDEN, Eddie

Constituency: Labour, Liverpool Garston
Parliamentary Activities:
Select Committee Membership: None
Declared Interests:
Financial Sponsorships, Gifts, etc.: Sponsored by Transport and General Workers' Union, financial assistance is direct to constituency.

LUFF, Peter

Constituency: Conservative, Worcester
Parliamentary Activities:
Select Committee Membership: Welsh Affairs, Transport
Declared Interests:
Employment or Office: Consultant in

corporate and public affairs to Lowe Bell Consultants Ltd – Principal Clients of Lowe Bell Consultants Ltd: Bibby Line Ltd; Securicor Security Services; the Chamber of Shipping; Saloman Brothers International Ltd; Consultant to Visa International
Declarable Shareholdings: Luff and Sons Ltd, a small family stationery company
Overseas Visits: September 1992, 4–day visit to Germany and Hungary, as a guest of the Konrad Adenauer Foundation; June 1993, to Calais, Lille and Lyon to view the Channel Tunnel infrastructure work and related French railway investment, as guest of Eurotunnel plc and BR European Passenger Services.

LYELL, Rt. Hon. Sir Nicholas

Constituency: Conservative, Mid Bedfordshire
Parliamentary Activities:
Select Committee Membership: None
Declared Interests:
Trades or Professions: Barrister, Queen's Counsel; Recorder; Member of Lloyd's
Land and Property: Small Holding (house let) and share in holiday house (some rentals)

Comments: From declarations made to Companies House in London, Lyell is also a director of Stowe School Ltd; Council of Law Reporting.

LYNNE, Liz

Constituency: Liberal Democrat, Rochdale
Parliamentary Activities:
Select Committee Membership: None
Declared Interests:
Occassional fees for TV and Radio appearances

McALLION, John

Constituency: Labour, Dundee East
Parliamentary Activities:
Select Committee Membership: None
Declared Interests:
Employment or Office: Parliamentary Consultant to the Union of Civil and Public Servants (fee paid to local constituency Labour Party)
Financial Sponsorships, Gifts, etc.: He also has premises provided by Dundee District Council free of charge for his surgeries once every two weeks. This provision is extended to all locally elected representatives.

Comments: From declarations made to Companies House, McAllion is also a director of the Dundee Enterprise Trust Ltd.

McAVOY, Thomas

Constituency: Labour, Glasgow Rutherglen
Parliamentary Activities:
Select Committee Membership: None
Declared Interests:
Financial Sponsorships, Gifts, etc.: Sponsored as a Parliamentary Candidate by the Co-operative Party who pay an annual contribution to his constituency party. No fees are paid to McAvoy personally
Land and Property: Owns a property in London SE11 which is occasionally let.

McCARTNEY, Ian

Constituency: Labour, Makerfield
Parliamentary Activities: Opposition Spokesperson on Health
Declared Interests:
Employment or Office: Council member of the Child Accident Prevention Trust
Financial Sponsorships, Gifts, etc.: Sponsored by the Transport and General Workers' Union. Fees paid to the Makerfield Constituency Labour Party as per the Hastings Agreement.

McCREA, Rev. William

Constituency: Democratic Unionist, Mid Ulster
Parliamentary Activities:
Select Committee Membership: None
Declared Interests:
Trades or Professions: Minister of Calvary Free Presbyterian Church in Magherafelt; Member of Magherafelt District Council; Gospel recording artist
Land and Property: Owns 64 acres of land in County Tyrone, one residential property in Coleraine and another residential property in Castledawson.

MACDONALD, Calum

Constituency: Labour, Western Isles
Parliamentary Activities:
Select Committee Membership: None
Declared Interests: Joint Chairman and Director of Future of Europe Trust Ltd. This is a company limited by guarantee. Macdonald only receives travel costs.
Land and Property: One residential rented property in London

McFALL, John

Constituency: Labour, Dumbarton
Parliamentary Activities: an Opposition Spokesperson on Scottish Affairs. Also member of Select Committee on Services and Information
Declared Interests:
Financial Sponsorships, Gifts, etc.: Sponsored as a candidate by the Co-operative Party
Overseas Visits: February 1992, to Israel, through Labour Friends of Israel, at the invitation of the Israeli Government; September 1992, to Japan, through the British–Japanese Party Group, at the invitation of the Japanese Government; October 1992, to Hong Kong, through the British–Hong Kong Party Group, at the invitation of the Hong Kong Commission.

McGRADY, Eddie

Constituency: Social and Democratic Labour Party, South Down
Parliamentary Activities:
Select Committee Membership: None
Declared Interests:
Trades or Professions: Chartered Accountant

MacGREGOR, John

Constituency: Conservative, South Norfolk
Parliamentary Activities: Secretary of State for Transport
Declared Interests: None listed

MacKAY, Andrew

Constituency: Conservative, East Berkshire
Parliamentary Activities: Government Whip
Select Committee Membership: Procedure
Declared Interests: None listed

Comments: From declarations made to Companies House, he resigned 29 directorships after the 1992 General Election on becoming a Government Whip. MacKay also used to be a consultant to Morgan Grenfell, the merchant bankers. In 1988 an internal company memorandum stated: 'He [Mackay] advises us on our political strategy and it is no small credit to him that we have recovered our political acceptability in Whitehall and Westminster. . . . Many companies under-estimate how much their MP can do for them.'

McKELVEY, William

Constituency: Labour, Kilmarnock and Loudoun
Parliamentary Activities:
Select Committee Membership: Chairman, Scottish Affairs
Declared Interests:
Financial Sponsorships, Gifts, etc.: Sponsored by the Amalgamated Engineering Union as per the Hastings Agreement.

MACKINLAY, Andrew

Constituency: Labour, Thurrock
Parliamentary Activities: Opposition Whip
Select Committee Membership: Transport
Declared Interests:
Financial Sponsorships, Gifts, etc.: Sponsored as a candidate at the 1992 General Election by the Transport and General Workers' Union who made a donation to his campaign funds. This fee exceeded 25 per cent of his expenses. He is also sponsored as a member of the TGWU who make an annual grant of £600 to his Constituency Labour Party. Mackinlay personally receives no money from the union
Overseas Visits: 12–16 September 1992, to the United States with the British-American Party Group, partly funded by the Group and partly by the US Information Service. 2–8 August 1993, to Israel, as guest of Labour Friends of Israel, accompanied by spouse. Mackinlay paid the cost of his spouse's travel.

MACLEAN, David

Constituency: Conservative, Penrith and The Border
Parliamentary Activities: Minister of State at the Home Office
Declared Interests: None listed.

McLEISH, Henry

Constituency: Labour, Central Fife
Parliamentary Activities: an Opposition Spokesperson on Scottish Affairs
Declared Interests:
Financial Sponsorships, Gifts, etc.: Sponsored by UNISON, who pay part cost of a research assistant

Comments: From declarations made to Companies House, he is also a director of the John Wheatley Centre.

MACLENNAN, Robert

Constituency: Liberal Democrat, Caithness and Sutherland
Parliamentary Activities: Member of Commons Public Accounts Committee and Spokesperson on Home Affairs and Heritage
Declared Interests: Director of Atlantic Tele-Network Inc. since 1 February 1992
Employment or Office: Consultant to *Encyclopaedia Britannica*
Trades or Professions: Barrister

Comments: From declarations made to Companies House, he is also a director of the North Lands Festival, Cancer Research Campaign, Fotofeis Ltd, Foundation for Management Education and the Tower Shakespeare Company.

McLOUGHLIN, Patrick

Constituency: Conservative, West Derbyshire
Parliamentary Activities: Parliamentary Under-Secretary at Department of Trade and Industry
Declared Interests: None listed.

McMASTER, Gordon

Constituency: Labour, Paisley South
Parliamentary Activities:
Select Committee Membership: Procedure
Declared Interests:
Trades or Professions: Occasional income for writing, broadcasting and lecturing
Financial Sponsorships, Gifts, etc.: He is sponsored by the Co-operative Party under the national agreement. No payment made to McMaster personally.

McNAIR-WILSON, Sir Patrick

Constituency: Conservative, New Forest
Parliamentary Activities:
Select Committee Membership: None
Declared Interests:
Employment or Office: Consultant to: Praxair Ltd; Rhone Poulenc plc

Comments: Sir Patrick's consultancy with Re-Chem International Ltd for the Fawley Plant brought him criticism from local environmentalists, for the company has breached its emission regulations on 14 tests carried out by the local river authority for making chemical discharges higher than granted under licence.

McNAMARA, Kevin

Constituency: Labour, Kingston-upon-Hull North
Parliamentary Activities: Chief Spokesperson on Northern Ireland
Declared Interests:
Trades or Professions: Lecturing (at home and abroad) and occasional TV appearances
Financial Sponsorships, Gifts, etc.: Sponsored by the Transport and General Workers' Union in accordance with the Hastings Agreement
Overseas Visits: 7 February 1992, to Dublin, paid for by Trinity College Labour Club; 20 February 1992, to Dublin, paid for by Trinity College Law Society.

McWILLIAM, John

Constituency: Labour, Blaydon
Parliamentary Activities:

Select Committee Memberhsip: Defence
Declared Interests: Director of Eurim Ltd (unpaid)
Financial Sponsorships, Gifts, etc.: Sponsored by the National Communications Union (Engineering Section) who pay 80 per cent of his election expenses and make an annual grant to his constituency in accordance with the Labour Party agreement
Overseas Visits: June 1993, to the Paris Air Show on behalf of the Parliamentary Space Committee, part paid for by the UK Industrial Space Committee.

MADDEN, Max

Constituency: Labour, Bradford West
Parliamentary Activities:
Select Committee Membership: None
Declared Interests:
Trades or Professions: Modest fees from journalism and broadcasting
Financial Sponsorships, Gifts, etc.: Sponsored by the Transport and General Workers' Union. His constituency party receives £600 per year. All financial support at General Elections is based on an agreement between the TGWU and the Labour Party.

MADDOCK, Diana

Constituency: Liberal Democrat, Christchurch
Parliamentary Activities:
Select Committee Membership: None
Declared Interests: Occasional broadcasting and lecturing

MADEL, David

Constituency: Conservative, South West Bedfordshire
Parliamentary Activities:
Select Committee Membership: European Legislation and Commons Services (Administration)
Declared Interests:
Trades or Professions: Fees from some broadcasting
Employment or Office: Consultant to National Council of Building Material Producers

MAGINNIS, Ken

Constituency: Official Ulster Unionist, Fermanagh and South Tyrone
Parliamentary Activities:
Select Committee Membership: None
Declared Interests:
Employment or Office: Advisor to the Royal Ulster Constabulary Federation. Since 1 June 1990, half the cost of a researcher (£4,000 gross) has been met by the Royal Ulster Constabulary Federation.

MAHON, Alice

Constituency: Labour, Halifax
Parliamentary Activities:
Select Committee Membership: Health
Declared Interests:
Financial Sponsorships, Gifts, etc.: Sponsored as a Parliamentary Candidate by the National Union of Public Employees. £600 paid to Halifax Constituency Labour Party each year. Also some financial help with General Election expenses.

MAITLAND, Lady Olga

Constituency: Conservative, Sutton and Cheam
Parliamentary Activities:
Select Committee Memberships: Education, Procedure
Declared Interests:
Overseas Benefits: Christmas 1993 – gifts from Sheikh Salem Al-Sabah, of earrings and brooch for her and Cartier pen for husband
Trades or Professions: Freelance Journalist
Overseas Visits: 13–19 September 1992, to Israel, sponsored by the British Israel Public Affairs Centre; 16–19 August 1993, to Kuwait, at the invitation of Sheikh Salem Al-Sabah as a guest of the Kuwaiti National Committee for the Missing Prisoners of War; 2–26 September 1993, to South Africa on fact-finding tour arranged by South African Ambassador H.E. Mr Kent Durr and South Africa Forum.

MAJOR, Rt.Hon. John

Constituency: Conservative, Huntingdon
Parliamentary Activities: Prime Minister
Declared Interests: None listed.

MALLON, Seamus

Constituency: Social and Democratic Labour Party, Newry and Armagh
Parliamentary Activities:
Select Committee Membership: None
Declared Interests: None listed.

MALONE, Gerald

Constituency: Conservative, Winchester
Parliamentary Activities:
Select Committee Membership: None
Declared Interests: Director of Cleveden Services Ltd, Country Gentlemen's Association (CGA) Services Ltd, Devanha Group plc, Aberdeen Cable Services Ltd
Employment or Office: Consultant: Contributor's contract with *The Sunday Times*, Texaco Ltd, Norton Rose, McCann Erickson
Trades or Professions: Solicitor; Journalist; Broadcaster
Declarable Shareholdings: Cleveden Services Ltd; CGA Services Ltd
Clients: Peterkins Solicitors, McGrigor Donald Solicitors, Grampian Television plc, Abtrust

Comments: Until the summer of 1993, Malone was a consultant to Morgan and Rogerson Ltd, a public relations company that represented Asil Nadir, the fugitive businessman.

MANDELSON, Peter

Constituency: Labour, Hartlepool
Parliamentary Activities:
Select Committee Membership: None
Declared Interests: None Listed
Overseas Visits: 12–15 July 1992: Joint Party visit to Democratic Party Convention in New York City. Visitors' programme funded by Goldman Sachs

Comments: From declarations made to Companies House, he is also a director of NS Publishing Ltd.

MANS, Keith

Constituency: Conservative, Wyre
Parliamentary Activities:
Select Committee Membership: None
Declared Interests:
Trades or Professions: Pilot in the Royal Air Force Reserve
Overseas Visits: October 1992, to USA, hosted by US Air; December 1992, to Singapore, hosted by Singapore Airlines; January 1993, to Brussels, hosted by British Airways.

MAREK, Dr John

Constituency: Labour, Wrexham
Parliamentary Activities:
Select Committee Membership: None
Declared Interests:
Financial Sponsorships, Gifts, etc.: Sponsored by the National Union of Rail, Maritime and Transport Workers.
Overseas Visits: 10–16 October 1992, to Hong Kong, at the invitation of the Hong Kong Government; 14 June 1993, to the Paris Air Show, courtesy of British Aerospace.

MARLAND, Paul

Constituency: Conservative, West Gloucestershire
Parliamentary Activities:
Select Committee Membership: Agriculture
Declared Interests: Director of Marland's English Table Waters Ltd (also Chairman)
Employment or Office: Consultant: British Scrap Metal Federation, Unigate Dairies Ltd, The Reclamation Association
Trades or Professions: Member of Lloyd's
Land and Property: Farm
Overseas Visits: 7–10 December 1992, to Singapore, at the invitation of Singapore Airlines; 6–7 January 1993, to Brussels, to attend a conference on air liberalisation at the invitation of British Airways;
23–24 April 1993, to Seoul, Republic of Korea, as a guest of the Korean Government

Comments: From declarations made to Companies House, Marland is also a director of Tender Assistance Scheme Ltd.

MARLOW, Tony

Constituency: Conservative, Northampton North
Parliamentary Activities:
Select Committee Membership: European Legislation
Declared Interests:
Employment or Office: Consultant to Gulf Centre for Strategic Studies
Land and Property: Owner of tenanted accommodation
Declarable Shareholdings: Clive E. Green and Co. Ltd; Toddingtons Ltd
Comments: From declarations made to Companies House, Marlow is also a director of Clive E. Green and Co. Ltd.

MARSHALL, David

Constituency: Labour, Glasgow Shettleston
Parliamentary Activities:
Select Committees Membership: None
Declared Interests: Director of East End Partnership Ltd (unpaid). Registered charity set up by Strathclyde Regional Council,

Glasgow District Council and Glasgow Development Agency
Financial Sponsorships, Gifts, etc.: Sponsored by the Transport and General Workers' Union as per the Hastings Agreement. No money is paid to him – only to his Constituency Party for political purposes
Overseas Visits: To Oslo, Norway, sponsored by the Parliamentary Roads Study Group.

MARSHALL, Jim

Constituency: Labour, Leicester South
Parliamentary Activities:
Select Committee Membership: None
Declared Interests:
Employment or Office: Parliamentary Advisor to the National Federation of Market Traders
Financial Sponsorships, Gifts, etc.: Sponsored by the Graphical, Paper and Media Union (no personal financial gain).

MARSHALL, John

Constituency: Conservative, Hendon South
Parliamentary Activities: Parliamentary Private Secretary to Tony Newton, Leader of the House of Commons
Declared Interests: Director of Beta Global Emerging Markets Investment Trust plc
Employment or Office: Parliamentary Consultant to the Bus and Coach Council; Stockbroking with London Wall Equities, a subsidiary of Shaw and Co.
Overseas Visits: May 28–1 June 1992, to Jerusalem to speak at the Jerusalem Day Dinner, organised by the Herut Movement. His travelling and hotel expenses were paid for by the Herut Movement; September 28–1 October 1993, to Republic of Cyprus to study the Cyprus issue. The Greek Cypriot Brotherhood of Great Britain paid the air fares and cost of hotel accommodation.

MARSHALL, Sir Michael

Constituency: Conservative, Arundel
Parliamentary Activities:
Select Committee Membership: Procedure
Declared Interests: Director of Marshall Consultants (also Managing Partner), SHL Systemhouse, General Offshore UK Ltd
Employment or Office: Parliamentary Advisor to: British Aerospace plc, Cable and Wireless plc, Willis Caroon Inspace, Society of West End Theatres, William Holdings
Trades or Professions: Member of Lloyd's; Author and broadcaster
Declarable Shareholdings: Direct Business Satellite Systems Ltd; Integrated Information Technology Ltd
Payment from abroad: As President of the Inter-Parliamentary Union, he receives a number of small gifts from visiting parliamentary delegations and when making overseas visits on behalf of the Union
Overseas Visits: February 1992: as President of the Inter-Parliamentary Union, his accommodation was provided by his hosts – the Speakers of India and Pakistan – during a visit

Comments: As a consultant to British Aerospace plc, Sir Michael played an active role in the Westland affair. He was also Parliamentary Private Secretary to Leon Brittan, then Trade and Industry Secretary.

MARTIN, David

Constituency: Conservative, Portsmouth South
Parliamentary Activities: Parliamentary Private Secretary to Douglas Hurd, Secretary of State for Foreign Affairs
Declared Interests:
Trades or Professions: Partner in ADP and E Farmers. He has a shared interest in up to eight acres of land which has planning permission for industrial and residential development. He also has a shared interest in three hectares of orchard pasture in North Brittany.

MARTIN, Michael

Constituency: Labour, Glasgow Springburn
Parliamentary Activities:
Select Committee Membership: None
Declared Interests:
Financial Sponsorships, Gifts, etc.: He is sponsored by his trade union, Management, Science and Finance (MSF), who provide a donation to the Springburn Constituency Labour Party. No payment is made to Martin and he receives no personal financial benefit.

MARTLEW, Eric

Constituency: Labour, Carlisle
Parliamentary Activities: Opposition Spokesperson on Defence – RAF
Declared Interests:
Financial Sponsorships, Gifts, etc.: Sponsored by the Transport and General Workers' Union. £600 per year is paid to Carlisle Constituency Labour Party and £3,000 towards General Election expenses.

MATES, Michael

Constituency: Conservative, East Hampshire
Parliamentary Activities:
Select Committee Membership: None
Declared Interests: Director of Broadgate Mercantile plc (not currently paid); Consultant to Unex Cherrygren Ltd

Comments: Colonel Mates has a chequered record in his dealings with businessmen. In 1986 he became Chairman of the Commons Select Committee on Defence. That year he also became a Consultant to Link Miles Ltd, a major defence contractor. In 1990 Mates was appointed a Consultant to SGL Ltd, a PR company set up to act for defence contractors. It was an obvious potential conflict of interests. Within a few months a Commons inquiry found that Mates was 'in error' for not declaring these clients properly during Defence Select Committee hearings. In 1993, as Northern Ireland Security Minister, he was embroiled in controversy for his private support for Asil Nadir. Mates sent the fugitive businessman, wanted for theft charges, a watch with the inscription: 'Don't let the buggers get you down.'

MAWHINNEY, Dr Brian

Constituency: Conservative, Peterborough
Parliamentary Activities: Minister for Health
Declared Interests: None listed.

MAXTON, John

Constituency: Labour, Glasgow Cathcart
Parliamentary Activities:
Select Committee Membership: National Heritage
Declared Interests: Director of Glasgow International Jazz Festival Ltd (unpaid, but receives free tickets for concerts).

MAYHEW, Rt.Hon. Sir Patrick

Constituency: Conservative, Tunbridge Wells
Parliamentary Activities: Secretary of State for Northern Ireland
Declared Interests:
Trades or Professions: Queen's Counsel – no private practice during tenure of Government Office.
Land and Property: Rent income from farm land, farm buildings and flat. Also occasional rents from holiday house.

MEACHER, Michael

Constituency: Labour, Oldham West
Parliamentary Activities: Shadow Minister on Citizens' Charter
Declared Interests:
Financial Sponsorships, Gifts, etc.: Sponsored as a Member by the Confederation of Health Service Employees. £650 per year is paid by the Union to his Constituency Party. No payment is made to Meacher.

MEALE, Alan

Constituency: Labour, Mansfield
Parliamentary Activities: Opposition Whip on Home Affairs, Social Security and Transport
Declared Interests: Director of Sherwood TV Ltd (unpaid). This is a small TV company based in North Nottinghamshire specialising in local productions to promote the area; Mansfield 2010 (unpaid). This is an economic development organisation made up jointly of local authorities and companies whose remit is to develop new jobs and businesses into the Mansfield area.
Financial Sponsorships, Gifts, etc.: Sponsored by Management, Science and Finance Trade Union which pays £600 per year, plus a percentage of his election costs is paid to his constituency party. Mansfield District Council provides Meale with premises for use as constituency offices for which he pays a nominal rent. Staff, furniture, services and running costs (excluding rates) are paid by Meale.
Declarable Shareholdings: Mansfield Town AFC (non-recoverable); Co-operative Society.

MELLOR, Rt.Hon. David

Constituency: Conservative, Putney
Parliamentary Activities:
Select Committee Membership: None
Declared Interests: Director of Abela Holdings UK Ltd, Sports Aid Foundation Ltd (unpaid), English National Opera (unpaid), National Youth Orchestra of GB (unpaid), Richmond Theatre Trust Ltd (unpaid)
Employment or Office: Consultant: Middle East Broadcasting Centre, Middle East Economic Digest, GL Holdings (Bermuda)

Ltd, RACAL Tacticom Ltd, Millwall Holdings plc, Crosby Associates UK, Investcorp, Shandwick Consultants, Ernst and Young. In relation to Shandwick he works as a public affairs consultant. On the other consultancies, he works on business development unrelated to his position as an MP.

Clients: He is available to advise certain Shandwick clients from time to time about matters relevant to their business. He says he does not lobby Ministers on their behalf or speak on behalf of their clients in the Commons or table questions related to their interests.

Trades or Professions: Barrister (not practising); Fees from journalism and from appearances on TV and radio either as an interviewee or presenter; Fees from lecturing and public speaking

Comments: Mellor resigned as Secretary of State for National Heritage in October 1992. Since leaving the Cabinet he has acquired an impressive list of clients. Mellor was also in the Cabinet as Chief Secretary to the Treasury and has also been a Home Office (twice), Energy, Health and Foreign Office Minister. Most of Mellor's new business interests are Middle East based. After the retirement of Sir Ian Gilmour and Sir Dennis Walters, he is now seen as the heir apparent to head the Arab lobby. So much so that he is known by his colleagues as 'Daud bin Akers'.

MERCHANT, Piers

Constituency: Conservative, Beckenham
Parliamentary Activities: Parliamentary Private Secretary to Peter Lilley, Secretary of State for Social Security
Declared Interests:

Trades or Professions: Occasional fees from broadcasting and journalism; Occasional small payments (£50 or less) to Beckenham Conservative Association by Access Opinions in return for help by him and others in completing occasional opinion questionaire.

MICHAEL, Alun

Constituency: Labour, Cardiff South and Penarth
Parliamentary Activities: an Opposition Spokesperson on Home Affairs
Declared Interests:

Trades or Professions: Occasional journalism, radio and TV items

Financial Sponsorships, Gifts, etc.: Sponsored by the Co-operative Party under national agreement, involving no payment to Michael personally.

MICHIE, Bill

Constituency: Labour, Sheffield Heeley
Parliamentary Activities:

Select Committee Membership: Members' Interests

Declared Interests:

Financial Sponsorships, Gifts, etc.: Sponsored by the Amalgamated Engineering and Electrical Union. Sheffield City Council provides Michie with premises in Sheffield for use as a parliamentary office for which he pays no rent. Staff, furniture, services and running costs (excluding rates) are paid for by him Labour Party by Access Opinions in return for help by him in completing questionaires.

Declarable Shareholdings: £20 worth of shares held in The People's Press Printing Society Ltd (no dividend paid); £5 worth of shares held in Wortley Hall (no dividend paid.

MICHIE, Ray

Constituency: Liberal Democrat, Argyll and Bute
Parliamentary Activities:
Select Committee Membership: Scottish Affairs
Declared Interests: None listed.

MILBURN, Alan

Constituency: Labour, Darlington
Parliamentary Activities:
Select Committee Membership: None
Declared Interests:
Financial Sponsorships, Gifts, etc.: Gift of a pager. Payment of its running costs met by Hutchison Telecom, a company in his constituency.

MILLER, Andrew

Constituency: Labour, Ellesmere Port and Neston
Parliamentary Activities:
Select Committee Membership: Science and Technology
Declared Interests:
Financial Sponsorships, Gifts, etc.: Contribution of more than 25 per cent of election expenses received from central and local political funds of the Manufacturing, Science and Finance Union.

MILLS, Alain

Constituency: Conservative, Meriden
Parliamentary Activities:
Select Committee Membership: None
Declared Interests: Director of Interbrand Group plc
Employment or Office: Consultant: National Tyre Distributers Association, Grant, Spencer, Caisley and Co., Industrial Anti-Counterfeiting Group, Dial Ltd, Small Independent Brewers Association
Overseas Visits: 14–15 August 1992, to Hungary, sponsored by the Ford Motor Company.

MITCHELL, Andrew

Constituency: Conservative, Gedling
Parliamentary Activities: Assistant Government Whip
Declared Interests: None listed
Declarable Shareholdings: Shareholder in El Vino Company Ltd.

MITCHELL, Dr Austin

Constituency: Labour, Great Grimsby
Parliamentary Activities:
Select Committee Membership: None
Declared Interests:
Trades or Professions: Associate Editor of *House* magazine; Presenter of the 'Target' programme on Sky Television; Occasional journalism for newspapers and publications; Occasional television and radio programmes; Author of occasional books
Financial Sponsorships, Gifts, etc.: Sponsored by the General, Municipal and Boilermakers Union which contributes to

his constituency party only and well under 25 per cent of election expenses

Comments: From declarations made to Companies House, Mitchell is also a director of Triangular Median Ltd.

MITCHELL, Sir David

Constituency: Conservative, North-West Hampshire
Parliamentary Activities:
Select Committee Membership: None
Declared Interests: Director of El Vino Company Ltd (wine merchants)
Declarable Shareholdings: El Vino Company Ltd.

MOATE, Sir Roger

Constituency: Conservative, Faversham
Parliamentary Activities:
Select Committee Membership: None
Declared Interests: Director of Robinco AG
Employment or Office: Consultant to Woollams, Moira, Gaskin, O'Malley, British Paper and Board Industry Federation
Trades or Professions: Member of Lloyd's (ceased in 1990).

MOLYNEAUX, Rt.Hon. James

Constituency: Official Ulster Unionist, Lagan Valley
Parliamentary Activities:
Select Committee Membership: None
Declared Interests: None listed.

MONRO, Sir Hector

Constituency: Conservative, Dumfries
Parliamentary Activities: Parliamentary Under-Secretary at Scottish Office
Declared Interests:
Trades or Professions: Farmer.

MONTGOMERY, Sir Fergus

Constituency: Conservative, Altrincham and Sale
Parliamentary Activities: Chairman of the Selection Committee (this appoints Members to Select Committees)
Declared Interests: Director of Messenger Television Productions Ltd, Clos-O-Mat (GB) Ltd
Employment or Office: Consultant to Welbeck Public Relations Ltd, National Association of Bookmakers, National Breakdown.

MOONIE, Dr Lewis

Constituency: Labour, Kirkcaldy
Parliamentary Activities: an Opposition Spokesperson on Science and Technology
Declared Interests:
Financial Sponsorships, Gifts, etc.: Sponsored as a Parliamentary Candidate by the Co-operative Party.

MORGAN, Rhodri

Constituency: Labour, Cardiff West
Parliamentary Activities: an Opposition Spokesperson on Welsh Affairs

Declared Interests:
Trades or Professions: Occasional fees from broadcasting
Financial Sponsorships, Gifts, etc.: Sponsored as a Parliamentary Candidate in 1992 by the Transport and General Workers' Union (TGWU) as per the Hastings Agreement. An annual contribution is paid by the TGWU to constituency party funds as per the Hastings Agreement of 1989.
Overseas Visits: February 1992, to Moscow, paid for by the Future of Europe Trust; December 1992, to the USA, as part of a delegation from the British–American Parliamentary Group. Travel within the USA was paid for by the US Government.

MORLEY, Elliot

Constituency: Labour, Glanford and Scunthorpe
Parliamentary Activities: an Opposition Spokesperson on Agriculture
Declared Interests:
Financial Sponsorships, Gifts, etc.: Sponsored by the General Municipal and Boilermakers Union. The fee is £300 per year paid direct to his constituency party for their use.

MORRIS, Rt.Hon. Alfred

Constituency: Labour, Manchester Wythenshawe
Parliamentary Activities:
Select Committee Membership: None
Declared Interests:
Financial Sponsorship, Gifts, etc.: Sponsored as a Candidate by the Co-operative Party.

MORRIS, Estelle

Constituency: Labour, Yardley
Parliamentary Activities:
Select Committee Membership: None
Declared Interests:
Employment or Office: Consultant to the National Union of Teachers
Financial Sponsorships, Gifts, etc.: Part of the salary of his constituency office assistant, office expenses and election expenses is paid by the Union of Communication Workers.

MORRIS, Rt.Hon. John, QC

Constituency: Labour, Aberavon
Parliamentary Activities: Shadow Attorney-General
Declared Interests:
Employment or Office: Queen's Counsel; Recorder of the Crown Court
Financial Sponsorship, Gifts, etc.: Sponsored by the General and Municipal Workers on the usual terms.

MORRIS, Michael

Constituency: Conservative, Northampton South
Parliamentary Activities:
Select Committee Membership: None
Declared Interests: Director of Modern Personnel Ltd, Chariots Trust Ltd (honorary – charity), Tunbridge Wells Equitable Friendly Society (honorary)
Land and Property: Caesar's Camp, Sandy, Bedfordshire; 250 acres of woodland in Bedfordshire, Suffolk and Herefordshire
Declarable Shareholdings: Modern Personnel Ltd

MOSS, Malcolm

Constituency: Conservative, Cambridgeshire North East
Parliamentary Activities: Parliamentary Private Secretary to Sir Patrick Mayhew, Secretary of State for Northern Ireland
Declared Interests: Director of Mandrake Associates Ltd; Consultant to Hambro Countrywide plc
Declarable Shareholdings: Hambro Countrywide plc

Comments: From declarations made to Companies House, Moss is also a director of the Fens Business Enterprise Trust Ltd.

MOWLAM, Marjorie

Constituency: Labour, Redcar
Parliamentary Activities: Chief Opposition Spokesperson on National Heritage
Declared Interests:
Employment or Office: Parliamentary Consultant to the Banking, Insurance and Finance Sector Union (BIFU). Mowlam's fee is paid to her constituency office, with no personal benefit to her
Trades or Professions: Small fees for broadcasting and publication of articles
Financial Sponsorships, Gifts, etc.: Sponsored by the Confederation of Health Service Employees. She also has a full-time research assistant paid for by NALGO, reviewed on an annual basis
Clients: She has also worked for the Victor Faux Consultancy, of Orion House, Upper St Martin's Lane, London WC2, for whom she sponsored a single function at the House of Commons in June 1993.

Comments: From declarations made to Companies House, Mowlam is also a director of the UK-Japan 2000 Group.

MUDIE, George

Constituency: Labour, Leeds East
Parliamentary Activities:
Select Committee Membership: None
Declared Interests: None Listed

MULLIN, Chris

Constituency: Labour, Sunderland South
Parliamentary Activities:
Select Committee Membership: Home Affairs
Declared Interests:
Trades or Professions: Occasional income from newspaper articles; Royalties and film rights from four books written between 1982 and 1987
Overseas Visits: 14–25 September 1992, to the United States as part of a parliamentary delegation sponsored jointly by the British–American Parliamentary Group and the United States Information Agency. The costs of the internal flights were funded by the American Government.

MURPHY, Paul

Constituency: Labour, Torfaen
Parliamentary Activities: an Opposition Spokesperson on Welsh Affairs
Declared Interests:
Employment or Office: Parliamentary Consultant to the National Association of Teachers in Further and Higher Education (NATFHE)
Financial Sponsorships, Gifts, etc.: Sponsored by the Transport and General Workers' Union
Overseas Visits: February 1992, to Israel with Labour Friends of Israel, sponsored by the Israeli Government.

NEEDHAM, Richard

Constituency: Conservative, North Wiltshire
Parliamentary Activities: Minister for Trade
Declared Interests:
Trades or Professions: Member of Lloyd's
Declarable Shareholdings: RGM Print Holdings Ltd.

NELSON, Anthony

Constituency: Conservative, Chichester
Parliamentary Activities: Economic Secretary to the Treasury
Declared Interests: None listed.

NEUBERT, Sir Michael

Constituency: Conservative, Romford
Parliamentary Activities: Member of Commons Selection Committee (this appoints members of Select Committees)
Declared Interests:
Employment or Office: Parliamentary Advisor: National Market Traders Federation; Federation of Master Builders
Overseas Visits: 14 September 1992, to Luxembourg as the guest and at the expense of Société Europëene des Satellites (ASTRA). Stayed one night only as a member of the All Party Cable and Satellite Group.

NEWTON, Rt. Hon. Tony

Constituency: Conservative, Braintree
Parliamentary Activities: Leader of the House of Commons and Lord President of the Council
Declared Interests: None listed.

NICHOLLS, Patrick

Constituency: Conservative, Teignbridge
Parliamentary Activities:
Select Committee Membership: None
Declared Interests:
Employment or Office: Consultant to Hill and Smith Holdings plc, Federation of Associations of Specialists and Sub-Contractors, National Sub-Contractors Council, Port Enterprises Ltd, MinOtels Europe Group, Howard de Walden Estates Ltd, Waterfront Partnership, Channel Express Ltd, British Shops and Stores Association
Trades or Professions: Partner in Messrs Dunn and Baker Solicitors
Land and Property: Owns office premises and agricultural land
Overseas Visits: 21–26 June 1992, to Indonesia. Travel and expenses paid by British Airways

Comments: Nicholls acquired his nine consultancies after spells as a Junior Employment Minister and then in the Department of the Environment. In October 1990 he resigned after a drunken-driving charge in Bournemouth during the Conservative Party conference.

NICHOLSON, David

Constituency: Conservative, Taunton
Parliamentary Activities:
Select Committee Membership: Public Accounts
Declared Interests:
Employment or Office: Consultant to Association of British Chambers of Commerce, Economic and Regulatory Analysts, London, National Association of Cider Makers
Overseas Visits: September 1992, to Como, Italy, for 4-day conference with European Parliamentarians as guest of the Konrad Adenauer Foundation; October 1992, to Como, Italy, for 2-day Anglo-German conference as guest of the Konrad Adenauer Foundation.

NICHOLSON, Emma

Constituency: Conservative, Torridge and West Devon
Parliamentary Activities: Parliamentary Private Secretary to Michael Jack, Minister of State for Agriculture
Declared Interests: None listed
Overseas Visits: Regular charitable visits to Iran and Iraq, part sponsored by the Iraq Humanitarian Relief Committee, AMAR appeal and other donors, part paid personally. Occasional visits to other countries for charitable purposes, sometimes part-sponsored by relevant appeal donors and part paid personally
Comments: From declarations made to Companies House, she is also a director of Cities in Schools Ltd.

NORRIS, Steven

Constituency: Conservative, Epping Forest
Parliamentary Activities: Parliamentary Under-Secretary for Transport
Declared Interests: None listed
Declarable Shareholdings: Anthony Ince Ltd.

OAKES, Rt.Hon. Gordon

Constituency: Labour, Halton
Parliamentary Activities:
Select Committee Membership: None
Declared Interests:
Employment or Office: Public Affairs Consultant to 3M United Kingdom Ltd, Royal Pharmaceutical Society of GB, Caravan Club (expenses)
Trades or Professions: Solicitor (not practising)
Financial Sponsorships, Gifts, etc.: Sponsored by the Transport and General Workers' Union, paying £740 per year to Halton Constituency Labour Party

Comments: From declarations made to Companies House, Oakes is a director of Halton Chemical Industry Museum Trust Ltd.

O'BRIEN, Michael

Constituency: Labour, Warwickshire North
Parliamentary Activities:
Select Committee Membership: Home Affairs
Declared Interests:
Trades or Professions: Solicitor in criminal law (non-practising); Advisor to Police Federation of England and Wales – receives

financial assistance to employ a researcher
Financial Sponsorships, Gifts, etc.: Donation to election expenses by GMB Apex.

O'BRIEN, William

Constituency: Labour, Normanton
Parliamentary Activities: an Opposition Spokesperson on Northern Ireland
Declared Interests: None listed
Overseas Visits: January 1992, to Israel, sponsored by Labour Friends of Israel.

O'HARA, Edward

Constituency: Labour, Knowsley South
Parliamentary Activities:
Select Committee Membership: Education
Declared Interests:
Overseas Visits: July 1992, to Cyprus, paid for by the Government of Cyprus; June 1993, to Greece, for sea-borne conference hosted by the Foundation for Hellenic Culture; August 1993, to Cyprus, to commemorate the nineteenth anniversary of the occupation of Famagusta, as a guest of the municipality of Famagusta.

OLNER, William

Constituency: Labour, Nuneaton
Parliamentary Activities:
Select Committee Membership: None
Declared Interests:
Financial Sponsorships, Gifts, etc.: Sponsored as a Parliamentary Candidate by the Amalgamated Engineering Union.

O'NEILL, Martin

Constituency: Labour, Clackmannan
Parliamentary Activities: Opposition Spokesperson on Energy
Declared Interests:
Financial Sponsorships, Gifts, etc.: Sponsored by the Graphical, Media and Paper Union under the Hastings Agreement by which £1,500 is paid per year directly to Clackmannan Constituency Labour Party with a donation at General Elections of 80 per cent of expenses; Clackmannan District Council provide the exclusive use of one room in Alloa to the sitting Member, regardless of political affiliation.

ONSLOW, Rt. Hon. Sir Cranley

Constituency: Conservative, Woking
Parliamentary Activities:
Select Committee Membership: Trade and Industry
Declared Interests: Director of Redifon Holdings Ltd (also Chairman), Elmdale Investments Ltd, Scatsouth E01–36
Employment or Office: Consultant to Argyll Group plc, Bristow Helicopters, LEK Partnership (associate), Generics Holdings Corporation
Overseas Visits: October 1992, to Hong Kong as a guest of the Hong Kong Government

Comments: From declarations made to Companies House, Onslow is also a director of ACA Trustee Company Ltd and Nautical Museum Trust Ltd.

OPPENHEIM, Phillip

Constituency: Conservative, Amber Valley
Parliamentary Activities: Parliamentary Private Secretary to Kenneth Clarke, Chancellor of the Exchequer
Declared Interests:
Financial Sponsorships, Gifts, etc.: Gift of voucher for two flights by British Midland Airways
Land and Property: Owner of a 240-acre farm – no net income
Overseas Visits: June 1993, to Jackson Hole, Wyoming, to participate in the Big Horn Mountain Foundation trade conference. Flights and accommodation paid for by the conference organisers.

ORME, Rt. Hon. Stanley

Constituency: Labour, Salford East
Parliamentary Activities:
Select Committee Membership: None
Declared Interests:
Financial Sponsorships, Gifts, etc.: Sponsored by the Amalgamated Union of Engineering Workers, details as published by the Union.

OTTAWAY, Richard

Constituency: Conservative, Croydon South
Parliamentary Activities: Parliamentary Private Secretary to Michael Heseltine, Secretary of State for Trade and Industry
Declared Interests: Director of Coastal Europe Ltd, Coastal States Holdings UK Ltd
Employment or Office: Political Consultant to the Baltic Exchange

PAGE, Richard

Constituency: Conservative, Hertfordshire South-West
Parliamentary Activities:
Select Committee Membership: Public Accounts
Declared Interests: Director of Page Holdings Ltd and associated companies
Employment or Office: Parliamentary Advisor to Electrical Manufacturers Association Ltd and Association of British Travel Agents
Declarable Shareholdings: Page Holdings Ltd
Overseas Visits: 7–14 September 1992, to Japan, at the invitation of a consortium of British manufacturers; 24–29 April 1993, to Mallorca, courtesy of Association of British Travel Agents; 14–15 June 1993, to Paris, courtesy of Parliamentary Space Committee

Comments: From declarations made to Companies House, he is also a director of the following companies, some of which are clearly associated companies of Page Holdings Ltd: Somber Development Company Ltd, Reg Heynes and Sons Ltd, Derby Finance Ltd, Page (Motors) Leatherhead Ltd, Page Motors Epsom Ltd, Page Chelmsford Ltd, Pagehire Ltd, Page Motors Bournemouth Ltd, Page Motors Ferndown Ltd, Page Motors Ltd, Wedd and White Coachworks Ltd and Rickmansworth Masonic School Ltd.

PAICE, James

Constituency: Conservative, South-East Cambridgeshire
Parliamentary Activities: Parliamentary Private Secretary to John Gummer, Secretary of State for Agriculture

Declared Interests: Director of United Framlingham Farmers Ltd, Governor of Writtle College (expenses only)
Employment or Office: Public Affairs Advisor to Dixons plc; Parliamentary Advisor to National Training Federation and British Fibreboard Association
Overseas Visits: September 1992, to Como, Italy, as guest of the Konrad Adenauer Foundation.

PAISLEY, Rev. Ian

Constituency: Democratic Unionist, North Antrim
Parliamentary Activities: Leader of the Democratic Unionist Party
Declared Interests: Director of Voice Newspapers Ltd (honorary), Protestant Telegraph Ltd (honorary)
Trades or Professions: Member of the European Parliament; Minister of the Martyrs Memorial Free Presbyterian Church, Belfast (expenses only); President of Whitefield College of the Bible (honorary); Occasional television appearances and journalism etc. Any fees are donated to the Church. He also receives royalties from publications.

PARRY, Robert

Constituency: Labour, Liverpool Riverside
Parliamentary Activities: Member of Selection Committee (this appoints Members to Select Committees)
Declared Interests:
Financial Sponsorships, Gifts, etc.: Sponsored by the Transport and General Workers' Union as per the Hastings Agreement. No payment to Parry. The payments are made directly to the Constituency Party.

PATCHETT, Terry

Constituency: Labour, Barnsley East
Parliamentary Activities:
Select Committee Membership: None
Declared Interests:
Financial Sponsorships, Gifts, etc.: Sponsored by the National Union of Mineworkers.

PATNICK, Irvine

Constituency: Conservative, Sheffield Hallam
Parliamentary Activities: Government Whip (Lord Commissioner of the Treasury)
Declared Interests: None listed.

PATTEN, Rt.Hon. John

Constituency: Conservative, Oxford West and Abingdon
Parliamentary Activities: Secretary of State for Education
Declared Interests:
Trades or Professions: Supernumerary Fellow of Hertford College, Oxford (non-stipendiary); Royalties from published books.

PATTIE, Rt.Hon. Sir Geoffrey

Constituency: Conservative, Chertsey and Walton
Declared Interests: Director of GEC Marconi (also Chairman); Leica BV
Employment or Office: Partner of Terrington Management. Its clients are: Knight Piesold and T. I. plc
Overseas Visits: As Vice-Chairman (International) of the Conservative Party, Pattie makes visits abroad at the Party's expense.

Comments: Pattie was Minister of State for Defence Procurement from 1983 to 1984 and then Minister for Industry 1984–87. A measure of the amount of money being paid was in 1991 when, as chairman of Nexus Marketing Ltd, the company provided communication and marketing advice to Leica Group plc for which £69,000 was paid. From declarations made to Companies House, Pattie is also a director of International Co-operation Fund Ltd.

PAWSEY, James

Constituency: Conservative, Rugby and Kenilworth
Parliamentary Activities:
Select Committee Membership: None
Declared Interests: Director of Autobar Group Ltd, St Martin's Hospitals, Ranelagh Ltd
Employment or Office: Parliamentary Consultant to Severn Trent and Association of Teachers and Lecturers
Trades or Professions: Member of Lloyd's; Occasional fees from writing, broadcasting and speaking
Clients of Ranelagh Ltd: Institute of Electrical Engineers; Institute of Chemical Engineers.

PEACOCK, Elizabeth

Constituency: Conservative, Batley and Spen
Parliamentary Activities:
Select Committee Membership: None
Declared Interests: Director of Coal Investments plc, Transpennine Group Ltd
Employment or Office: Consultant: British Furniture Manufacturers Association, Meetings Industry Association, Forest Forever Campaign
Declarable Shareholdings: Shilton Investments Ltd.

PENDRY, Tom

Constituency: Labour, Stalybridge and Hyde
Parliamentary Activities: an Opposition Spokesperson on National Heritage
Declared Interests:
Financial Sponsorships, Gifts, etc.: Pendry is sponsored by UNISON who pay a flat sum towards his election expenses. NUPE also donate an annual grant to cover constituency party and parliamentary expenses arising out of the above arrangements.
Overseas Visits: August 1992, to Barcelona to attend the Olympic Games as a guest of the British Olympic Association (in his capacity as Shadow Minister of Sport)

Comments: From declarations made to Companies House, Pendry is a director of the British Boxing Board of Control Ltd.

PICKLES, Eric

Constituency: Conservative, Brentwood and Ongar
Parliamentary Activities:
Select Committee Membership: None
Declared Interests:
Employment or Office: Parliamentary Advisor to Coopers and Lybrand
Overseas Visits: 3–11 January 1993, to Israel at the invitation of Conservative Friends of Israel.

PICKTHALL, Colin

Constituency: Labour, Lancashire West
Parliamentary Activities:
Select Committee Membership: Agriculture
Declared Interests: Lecturer in Higher Education

PIKE, Peter

Constituency: Labour, Burnley
Parliamentary Activities: Opposition Spokesperson on Housing
Declared Interests:
Financial Sponsorships, Gifts, etc.: His constituency is financially supported by the General Boilermakers and Allied Trades Union – not fully sponsored in accord with the Hastings Agreement.

POPE, Greg

Constituency: Labour, Hyndburn
Parliamentary Activities:
Select Committee Membership: None
Declared Interests:
Trades or Professions: Occasional journalism
Financial Sponsorships, Gifts, etc.: Occasional contribution from UNISON, the public service union.

PORTER, Barry

Constituency: Conservative, Wirral South
Parliamentary Activities:
Select Committee Membership: Trade and Industry
Declared Interests: Director of Congress International Ltd, Porter Cooke Ltd, Impac plc, Planning International Ltd
Employment or Office: Consultant to Wang (UK) Ltd, Air Boss Ltd, Hearing Aids Association, Airline Maintenance Associates Ltd
Trades or Professions: Solicitor with Fanshaw Porter and Hazelhurst.
Clients of Porter Cooke: Wang plc; Ingress Ltd; Whirlpool plc

PORTER, David

Constituency: Conservative, Waveney
Parliamentary Activities:
Select Committee Membership: Education
Declared Interests:
Land and Property: Rental income from small retail outlets in Lowestoft.

PORTILLO, Rt.Hon. Michael

Constituency: Conservative, Enfield Southgate
Parliamentary Activities: Chief Secretary to the Treasury
Declared Interests:
Financial Sponsorships, Gifts, etc.: Gift of a Persian rug from Mr F. Matini who is a member of the Enfield Southgate Conservative Association

Comments: Before becoming a Minister in 1987, Portillo was a paid consultant to British Airways.

POWELL, Ray

Constituency: Labour, Ogmore
Parliamentary Activities:
Select Committee Membership: None
Declared Interests:
Financial Sponsoredships, Gifts. etc.: Sponsored by the Union of Shop, Distributive and Allied Workers (USDAW) as a Candidate and as a Member.

POWELL, William

Constituency: Conservative, Corby
Parliamentary Activities:
Select Committee Membership: Science and Technology
Declared Interests:
Employment or Office: Consultant: The Unquoted Companies Group, McNicholas Construction Company, British Technology Group European Study Tours
Trades or Professions: Barrister (non-practising)
Overseas Visits: 14–19 September 1992, to Malta, as a guest of the Government of Malta; 29 September–12 October 1992, to Hong Kong and Taiwan, as a guest of the Government of Hong Kong and Taiwan

Comments: From declarations made to Companies House, Powell is also a director of Anchorwise Ltd.

PRENTICE, Bridget

Constituency: Labour, Lewisham East
Parliamentary Activities:
Select Committee Membership: None
Declared Interests:
Financial Sponsorships, Gifts, etc: Sponsored as a Parliamentary Candidate and MP by the General Municipal and Boilermakers Union. £500 is donated per year to constituency party.

PRENTICE, Gordon

Constituency: Labour, Pendle
Parliamentary Activities:
Select Committee Membership: None
Declared Interests: None listed
Overseas Visits: October 1993, to Egypt for five-day visit paid for by the Egyptian Government.

PRESCOTT, John

Constituency: Labour, Hull East
Parliamentary Acvities: Shadow Employment Secretary
Declared Interests:
Financial Sponsorships, Gifts, etc.: Sponsored by the Railway and Maritime

Transport Union. No personal payment to Prescott.
Overseas Visits: 9–13 October 1992, to Cyprus. Flight and accommodation paid by Cyprus Morphu District Association (GB).

PRIMAROLO, Dawn

Constituency: Labour, Bristol South
Parliamentary Activities: Opposition Spokesperson on Health
Declared Interests:
Financial Sponsorships, Gift, etc.: Sponsored by the Manufacturing Science and Finance Union (MSF) which contributed £2,500 towards General Election expenses in 1992. MSF also sponsors Primarolo as an MP and pays £600 per year direct to Bristol South Constituency Party. No personal financial gain to Primarolo.

PURCHASE, Ken

Constituency: Labour, Wolverhampton North East
Parliamentary Activities:
Select Committee Membership: None
Declared Interests:
Financial Sponsorships, Gifts, etc.: Sponsored as a Parliamentary Candidate by the Co-operative Party.

QUIN, Joyce

Constituency: Labour, Gateshead East
Parliamentary Activities: an Opposition Spokesperson on European Affairs
Declared Interests:
Financial Sponsorships, Gifts, etc.: Sponsored as a Parliamentary Candidate and MP by the Transport and General Workers' Union. Fees are paid to the constituency party. No personal expenses for Quin

Comments: From declarations made to Companies House, Quin is also a director of Folkworks Ltd.

RADICE, Giles

Constituency: Labour, North Durham
Parliamentary Activities:
Select Committee Memberships: Treasury and Civil Service
Declared Interests:
Financial Sponsorships, Gifts, etc.: Sponsored by the General and Municipal Workers Union
Trades or Professions: Occasional journalism and authorship

Comments: From declarations made to Companies House, Radice is a director of the Anglo-Austrian Society, British Association for Central and East European Studies and UK–Japan 2000 Group.

RANDALL, Stuart

Constituency: Labour, Hull West
Parliamentary Activities:
Select Committee Membership: None
Declared Interests:
Employment or Office: Consultant to Magellan Medical Communications Ltd. One of their clients is Parke-Davis

Financial Sponsorships, Gifts, etc.: Sponsored by the Amalgamated Engineering and Electrical Union.

RATHBONE, Tim

Constituency: Conservative, Lewes
Parliamentary Activities:
Select Committee Membership: None
Declared Interests: Director of VJF Property Ltd, VJF Property Two Ltd, Vulture 1–19 plc, Vulture 27–47 plc, Business Against Drugs (registered charity)
Employment or Office: Consultant: Chanel Ltd, South East Electricity Board plc (SEEBOARD), European Investment and Development plc, Eurotunnel plc
Overseas Visits: 1–8 January 1993, to the Kingdom of Jordan, as guest of the Jordanian Government.

RAYNSFORD, Nick

Constituency: Labour, Greenwich
Parliamentary Activities:
Select Committee Membership: Environment
Declared Interests:
Employment or Office:
Consultant to HACAS
Trades or Professions: Occasional articles for journals

Comments: From declarations made to Companies House, Raynsford is a director of the National Energy Foundation, Notting Hill Care Services and Notting Hill Commercial Properties Ltd.

REDMOND, Martin

Constituency: Labour, Don Valley
Parliamentary Activities:
Select Committee Membership: None
Declared Interests: Director of Doncaster Leisure (Management) Ltd (unremunerated)
Financial Sponsorships, Gifts, etc.: Sponsored by the National Union of Mineworkers

REDWOOD, Rt.Hon. John

Constituency: Conservative, Wokingham
Parliamentary Activities: Secretary of State for Wales
Declared Interests:
Trades or Professions: Book royalties.

REID, Dr John

Constituency: Labour, Motherwell North
Parliamentary Activities: an Opposition Spokesperson on Defence (Army)
Declared Interests:
Financial Sponsorships, Gifts, etc.: Sponsored by the Transport and General Workers' Union

RENTON, Rt.Hon. Timothy

Constituency: Conservative, Mid Sussex
Parliamentary Activities:
Select Committee Membership: None
Declared Interests: Director of Fleming Continental European Investment Trust, City Renaissance plc, Interactive Telephone Services Ltd, ITS Group plc (holding company of Interactive Telephone Services Ltd)

Employment or Office: Parliamentary Consultant to Robert Fleming Holdings Ltd
Trades or Professions: Member of Lloyd's underwriting syndicates; Writer of occasional articles
Declarable Shareholdings: ITS Group plc; City Renaissance plc
Overseas Visits: 3–10 October 1992, to Hong Kong with his wife, as guests of the Hong Kong Government who paid the air fares; 10–11 October 1992, to South China with his wife as guests of the Chinese Government.

RICHARDS, Rod

Constituency: Conservative, Clwyd North West
Parliamentary Activities: Parliamentary Private Secretary to David Heathcoat-Amory, Minister of State at Foreign Office
Declared Interests:
Employment or Office: Member of a panel for market research. Receives a small monthly fee.
Land and Property: Joint owner of a hotel in Powys, Wales.

RIDDICK, Graham

Constituency: Conservative, Colne Valley
Parliamentary Activities: Parliamentary Private Secretary to John MacGregor, Secretary of State for Transport
Declared Interests:
Employment or Office: Parliamentary Advisor to the Brewers Society
Trades or Professions: Member of Lloyd's; Occasional broadcasting fees
Overseas Visits: June 1992, to Indonesia, as a guest of British Airways.

RIFKIND, Rt.Hon. Malcolm, QC

Constituency: Conservative, Edinburgh Pentlands
Parliamentary Activity: Secretary of State for Defence
Declared Interests:
Trades or Professions: Non-practising member of Faculty of Advocates.

ROBATHAN, Andrew

Constituency: Conservative, Blaby
Parliamentary Activities:
Select Committee Membership: Employment
Declared Interests: None listed.

ROBERTS, Rt.Hon. Sir Wyn

Constituency: Conservative, Conwy
Parliamentary Activities: Minister of State at Welsh Office
Declared Interests: None listed.

ROBERTSON, George

Constituency: Labour, Hamilton
Parliamentary Activities: Shadow Scottish Secretary
Declared Interests:
Financial Sponsorships, Gifts, etc.:

Regional organiser of the General Municipal and Boilermakers Union (on leave of absence); Sponsored by the General Municipal and Boilermakers Union
Trades or Professions: Occasional articles, broadcasting and lecturing.

ROBERTSON, Raymond

Constituency: Conservative, Aberdeen South
Parliamentary Activities:
Select Committee Membership: Scottish Affairs
Declared Interests:
Employment or Office: Parliamentary Consultant to Mining (Scotland) Ltd; Member of political opinion panel of Opinion Leader Research. All fees are paid directly to charities in Aberdeen; Consultant to William Hill Organisation and Clay Colliery Company Ltd
Financial Sponsorships, Gifts, etc.: Aberdeen Cable Services are cabling the Parliamentary TV channel into his constituency office free of charge; His research assistant is partly funded by Dr Francis Clarke, and his car is supplied by Mr D. Jackson of Wylies Ltd, Glasgow
Overseas Visits: 14–17 September 1992, to Stuttgart, Germany, and Budapest, Hungary, on a study visit as a guest of the Konrad Adenauer Stiftung; 30 May–6 June 1993, study visit to Israel, paid for by the Conservative Friends of Israel.

ROBINSON, Geoffrey

Constituency: Labour, Coventry North West
Pariamentary Activities:
Select Committee Membership: None
Declared Interests: Director of Transfer Technology Group plc (also Chairman), Agie UK Ltd, Yamato Lock Inspection Systems Ltd and Kleinwort Smaller Companies Investment Trust plc
Declarable Shareholdings: Transfer Technology Group plc

Comments: From declarations made to Companies House, Robinson is also a director of the following companies: Fenworth Ltd, Fenworth (Woodchester) Ltd; Lock International Ltd (also Chairman); Forceleague Ltd; Holcombe Holdings plc; Technology Trustees Ltd; Earby Light Engineers Ltd; Matrix Grinding Technologies Ltd; Laserspeak Developments Ltd; Sarclad International Ltd; Newton Chambers and Co. plc; M.H. Marine plc; Hollis Industries plc (now dissolved); Robert Fraser (Ipswich) Ltd and Robert Fraser Second Development Co Ltd.

ROBINSON, Mark

Constituency: Conservative, Somerton and Frome
Parliamentary Activities: Parliamentary Private Secretary to Baroness Chalker and Mark Lennox-Boyd, Ministers of State at the Foreign Office
Declared Interests: Director of Leopold Joseph and Sons Ltd.

ROBINSON, Peter

Constituency: Democratic Unionist, Belfast East
Parliamentary Activities:
Select Committee Membership: None
Declared Interests: Director of Crown Publications, Voice Newspapers Ltd (honorary)
Employment or Office: Occasional television and radio appearances; Newspaper articles, books, booklets and lectures.

ROCHE, Barbara

Constituency: Labour, Hornsey and Wood Green
Parliamentary Activities:
Select Committee Membership: Home Affairs
Declared Interests:
Financial Sponsorships, Gifts, etc.: She receives an annual sum of £500 from the former NALGO Political Fund Committee as a member of the Parliamentary Group. This is used towards the running of her constituency office.
Overseas Visits: 10–11 October 1992, to Cyprus at the invitation of the Morphou District Association UK who paid for one night's accommodation. Roche paid for her return air ticket.

ROE, Marion

Constituency: Conservative, Broxbourne
Parliamentary Activities:
Select Committee Membership: Health (Chairperson)
Declared Interests:
Employment or Office: Parliamentary Consultant to the Horticultural Trades Association
Overseas Visits: 17–30 July 1992, to the Seychelles, to monitor the Elections as the UK representative on the seven–member Commonwealth Observer Group organised by Secretary–General of the Commonwealth. All her expenses were paid by the Commonwealth Secretariat; 27 September 1992–2 October 1992, to Angola, to monitor the Elections as a member of the UK Parliamentary Observer Group sponsored by UNITA, one of the main parties fighting the elections. This was in accordance with agreements negotiated by all parties in those elections. All her expenses were paid by UNITA.

ROGERS, Allan

Constituency: Labour, Rhondda
Parliamentary Activities: Opposition Spokesperson on Defence
Declared Interests:
Financial Sponsorships, Gifts, etc.: Sponsored as a Parliamentary Candidate by the Confederation of Health Service Employees.

ROOKER, Jeff

Constituency: Labour, Birmingham Perry Barr
Parliamentary Activities:
Select Committee Membership: None
Declared Interests: None listed
Overseas Visits: 5–8 October 1992, study visit to Federal Republic of Germany as the guest of the Friedrich Ebert Foundation.

ROONEY, Terry

Constituency: Labour, Bradford North
Parliamentary Activities:
Select Committee Membership: None
Declared Interests: Sponsored by Graphical, Paper and Media Union who make payments direct to his constituency party.

ROSS, Ernie

Constituency: Labour, Dundee West
Parliamentary Activities:
Select Committee Membership: Employment
Declared Interests:
Financial Sponsorships, Gifts, etc.: Sponsored by the Manufacturing, Science and Finance Union according to the Hastings Agreement; Premises are also provided by Dundee District Council free of charge for Ross's surgeries once every two weeks. This provision is extended to all local elected representatives.

ROSS, William

Constituency: Official Ulster Unionist, Londonderry East
Parliamentary Activities:
Select Committee Membership: None
Declared Interests:
Land and Property: Farmer and owner of farmland.

ROWE, Andrew

Constituency: Conservative, Mid Kent
Parliamentary Activities: Parliamentary Private Secretary to Richard Needham, Minister for Trade
Declared Interests:
Employment or Office: Parliamentary Advisor to Amway plc
Financial Sponsorships, Gifts, etc. Occasional research services provided by Nicholas Kent
Overseas Visits: 22 October 1992, to inspect the French and English ends of the Channel Tunnel, as a guest of Eurotunnel and British Rail

Comments: From declarations made to Companies House, Rowe is a director of Kent County Engineering Society Ltd and the Community Service Trust.

ROWLANDS, Ted

Constituency: Labour, Merthyr Tydfil and Rhymney
Parliamentary Activities:
Select Committee Membership: Foreign Affairs
Declared Interests:
Financial Sponsorships, Gifts, etc.: Rowlands' Constituency Party is sponsored by the Union of Shop, Distributive and Allied Workers

Comments: From declarations made to Companies House, Rowlands is also a director of the Institute of Development Studies Ltd.

RUDDOCK, Joan

Constituency: Labour, Lewisham Deptford
Parliamentary Activities: an Opposition Spokesperson on Home Affairs
Declared Interests:
Financial Sponsorships, Gifts, etc.: Sponsored by the Transport and General Workers Union. £200 is paid by ASLEF, the train drivers union, for help with research on transport and publication of a report. £1,000 was received from Peter Crampton, MEP, for the same project.

RUMBOLD, Rt.Hon. Dame Angela

Constituency: Conservative, Mitcham and Morden
Declared Interests: Director of Decision Makers Ltd; Clients of Decision Makers: Hunting Engineering Ltd, Blue Circle Properties, Dartford Borough Council, Citibank, Sevenoaks District Council, Richard Ellis, Swale District Council, Local Government Consortium, Barclays Mercantile, John Brown, European Food and Packaging Association, McDonalds
Employment or Office: Deputy Chairman of the Conservative Party
Land and Property: Sole owner of a property in St Aignan, Brittany, France
Overseas Visits: August 1992, flight from London to Houston donated by British Airways to enable Rumbold to attend the Republican Convention; Parliamentary visit to Turkish Republic of Northern Cyprus made by her husband on her behalf. Flight and some other expenses paid by himself. Some hospitality was provided.

RYDER, Rt.Hon. Richard

Constituency: Conservative, Mid Norfolk
Parliamentary Activities: Government Chief Whip
Declared Interests:
Land and Property: Land in Suffolk
Declarable Shareholdings: Great Bradley Farms Company, Great Bradley Estates Ltd.

SACKVILLE, Hon. Tom

Constituency: Conservative, Bolton West
Parliamentary Activities: Parliamentary Under-Secretary for Health
Declared Interests: Director of Sackville Investments (PVT) Ltd (unpaid).

SAINSBURY, Rt.Hon. Timothy

Constituency: Conservative, Hove
Parliamentary Activities: Minister for Industry
Declared Interests:
Land and Property: Owner of two farms, including separately tenanted residential properties, and one industrial building
Declarable Shareholdings: J. Sainsbury plc; Tacil Ltd; No. 47 and 49 Palmeira Ave Management Ltd; Branch Securities Ltd; Daunt Books Ltd; Brown Oak Third Assured Tenancies; Brown Oak (Eastern) Assured Tenancies Ltd

Comments: Sainsbury is estimated to be Britain's seventieth-richest individual. As of October 1993, he owned 49.5 million shares in the family supermarket chain. At that time they were worth £207 million. An MP since 1973, he resigned as a director of J.

Sainsbury in 1983. From declarations made to Companies House, Sainsbury is also a director of 47 and 49 Palmeira Avenue Management Ltd.

SALMOND, Alex

Constituency: Scottish Nationalist Party, Banff and Buchan
Parliamentary Activities:
Select Committee Membership: None
Declared Interests: None listed.

SCOTT, Rt.Hon. Nicholas

Constituency: Conservative, Chelsea
Parliamentary Activities: Minister of State for Social Security
Declared Interests: None listed.

SEDGEMORE, Brian

Constituency: Labour, Hackney South and Shoreditch
Parliamentary Activities:
Select Committee Membership: Treasury and Civil Service
Declared Interests: Freelance journalist.

SHAW, David

Constituency: Conservative, Dover
Parliamentary Activities:
Select Committee Membership: Social Security
Declared Interests: Director of Sabrelance Ltd, The Adscene Group plc, Raptor Residential Investment plc
Employment or Office: Member of Advisory Board of Novecon Corporation (unpaid); Parliamentary Consultant to the Enterprise Zone Property Unit Trust Association
Declarable Shareholdings:
Sabrelance Ltd; Corporate and Public Affairs Strategy Ltd (dormant)

SHAW, Sir Giles

Constituency: Conservative, Pudsey
Parliamentary Activities:
Select Committee Membership: Science and Technology (Chairman)
Declared Interests: Director of Yorkshire Water plc, British Steel plc, Broadcasters Audience Research Board Ltd
Employment or Office: Consultant to Philip Harris Group plc

Comments: Sir Giles was Minister of State for Industry, responsible for the steel industry, between September 1986 and June 1987. The following year British Steel was privatised and Sir Giles became a director. He left the board of British Steel plc in 1990 but rejoined two years later.

SHEERMAN, Barry

Constituency: Labour, Huddersfield
Parliamentary Activities:
Select Committee Membership: None
Declared Interests: Director of National Education, Research and Development Trust, unpaid, Parliamentary Advisory Council for Transport Safety, unpaid

Employment or Office: Partner in COPTECH (Co-operative Technology Development). Its clients are: Hanson plc, Malta Development Corporation, West Glamorgan Co-operative Development Agency, Credit Union Educational Trust; Academic advisor to Cornell University and Beaver College, Pennsylvania
Financial Sponsorships, Gifts, etc.: Sponsored by the Co-operative Party.

SHELDON, Rt.Hon. Robert

Constituency: Labour, Ashton-under-Lyne
Parliamentary Activities:
Select Committee Membership: Public Accounts (Chairman)
Declared Interests:
Employment or Office: Business advisor to R.E. Sheldon Ltd and Acronyl Ltd
Declarable Shareholdings: R.E. Sheldon Ltd; Acronyl Ltd.

SHEPHARD, Rt.Hon. Gillian

Constituency: Conservative, Norfolk South West
Parliamentary Activities: Secretary of State for Agriculture
Declared Interests: None listed.

SHEPHERD, Colin

Constituency: Conservative, Hereford
Parliamentary Activities:
Select Committee Membership: None
Declared Interests: Director of the Haigh Group Ltd, Haigh Engineering Co Ltd, Haih Tweeny Co Ltd, Stork Haigh Netherlands
Employment or Office: Parliamentary Advisor to Balfour Beatty Ltd
Financial Sponsorships, Gifts, etc.: Shepherd has the use of an office provided by the Haigh Group Ltd. He also receives occasional part-time assistance of a student through the auspices of Educational Programmes Abroad.
Declarable Shareholdings: The Haigh Group Ltd; H.S.C. Investments Ltd

Comments: From declarations made to Companies House, Shepherd is also a director of C. and H. Waste Processing Ltd.

SHEPHERD, Richard

Constituency: Conservative, Aldridge Brownhills
Parliamentary Activities:
Select Committee Membership: None
Declared Interests: Director of Partridges of Sloane Street Ltd, Shepherd Foods (London) Ltd
Trades or Professions: Member of Lloyd's
Declarable Sharholdinga: Shepherd Foods (London) Ltd; Partridges of Sloane Street Ltd
Comments: From declarations made to Companies House, Shepherd is also a director of Shepherd Foods (Marylebone) Ltd and C. and J. Carpets Ltd.

SHERSBY, Michael

Constituency: Conservative, Uxbridge
Parliamentary Activities:
Select Committee Membership: Public Accounts
Declared Interests: Director of World Sugar Research Organisation Ltd (unpaid)
Employment or Office: Advisor to the Sugar Bureau; Police Federation of England and Wales; Clients of Sugar Bureau: British Sugar plc; Tate and Lyle plc; UK Sugar Merchants Association
Financial Sponsorships, Gifts etc.: Shersby's private secretary also receives a fee from the Police Federation of England and Wales; Accommodation and hospitality for a weekend in Scotland was provided by Tate and Lyle plc, 29–30 May 1993

Comments: From declarations made to Companies House, Shersby is also a director of Abbeyfield Uxbridge Society Ltd.

SHORE, Rt.Hon. Peter

Constituency: Labour, Bethnal Green
Parliamentary Activities:
Select Committee Membership: Foreign Affairs
Declared Interests:
Financial Sponsorships, Gifts, etc.: Sponsored by the Transport and General Workers' Union
Overseas Visits:
August 1992, to Hong Kong, as guest of the Hong Kong Government

Comments: From declarations made to Companies House, Shore is a director of Universities Settlement in East London Ltd.

SHORT, Clare

Constituency: Labour, Birmingham Ladywood
Parliamentary Activities:
Select Committee Membership: None
Declared Interests:
Employment or Office: Fee received to act as a judge for the 1994 NCR book award for non-fiction
Financial Sponsorships, Gifts, etc.: Grant of £15,000 received during the parliamentary session of 1991–92 from the Joseph Rowntree Social Services Trust to employ extra staff for a temporary period; Sponsored by the National Union of Public Employees. £600 is paid to Ladywood Constituency Labour Party and £2,100 towards General Election expenses.
Overseas Visits: 25–29 August 1992, to Zambia to work with all the political parties to help establish a new multi-party democratic system. Funded by Westminster Foundation for Democracy

Comments: From declarations made to Companies House, Short is a director of Tribune Publications Ltd.

SIMPSON, Alan

Constituency: Labour, Nottingham South
Parliamentary Activities:
Select Committee Membership: None
Declared Interests: Director of Waste-Notts Ltd (a waste disposal company set up by Nottinghamshire County Council, of which he is a councillor)
Overseas Visits: 15–18 September 1992, to Libya, as a guest of the Libyan Foreign Ministry.

SIMS, Roger

Constituency: Conservative, Chislehurst
Parliamentary Activities:
Select Committee Membership: Health
Declared Interests:
Employment or Office: Parliamentary Advisor to the Scotch Whisky Association
Financial Sponsorships Gifts etc.: Nominal payment as a lay screener General Medical Council.
Overseas Visits: 3–10 January 1993, to Hong Kong, paid for by the Hong Kong Government

SKEET, Sir Trevor

Constituency: Conservative, Bedford North
Parliamentary Activities:
Select Committee Membership: Science and Technology
Declared Interests: None listed.

SKINNER, Dennis

Constituency: Labour, Bolsover
Parliamentary Activities:
Select Committee Membership: None
Declared Interests:
Financial Sponsorships, Gifts, etc.: Sponsored by the National Union of Mineworkers, in accordance with the Hastings Agreement. No personal remuneration.

SMITH, Andrew

Constituency: Labour, Oxford East
Parliamentary Activities: an Opposition Spokesperson on Treasury and Economic Affairs
Declared Interests:
Trades or Professions: Occasional fees from broadcasting and lectures
Financial Sponsorships, Gifts, etc.: Sponsored as a Candidate and as an MP by the Union of Shop, Distributive and Allied Workers (USDAW) which contributes 80 per cent of election expenses plus some other miscellaneous expenses. The Union also contributes £600 per year to the Constituency Party. In 1991 a donation of £2,000 was paid to the Constituency Party to cover the financial years of 1990–92.

SMITH, Chris

Constituency: Labour, Islington South and Finsbury
Parliamentary Activities: Chief Spokesperson on Environmental Protection
Declared Interests: Director of New Century Magazines Ltd (unpaid)
Employment or Office: Trustee of the John Muir Trust (unpaid)
Trades or Professions: Occasional writing, broadcasting and lecturing
Financial Sponsorships, Gifts, etc.: Sponsored by the Union of Communication Workers which provides financial support to the Constituency Party. The Constituency Party is also assisted by the Broadcasting, Entertainment, Cinematograph and Theatre Union.
Overseas Visits: February 1992, to Bonn, Dresden, Frankfurt, Hamburg and Bielefeld, at the invitation of the Deutsch–Englische Gesellschaft.

SMITH, Sir Dudley

Constituency: Conservative, Warwick and Leamington
Parliamentary Activities:
Select Committee Membership: None
Declared Interests:
Employment or Office: Partner in the Dudley Smith Management Consultancy
Clients (of Dudley Smith Management Consultancy): Celltech plc, London International Group, SmithKline Beecham plc, British Plastics Federation, Whitehall Laboratories Ltd, The Cosmetic Toiletry and Perfumery Association, The Procordia Group of Sweden (including Svenska Tobak), F.H. Faulding (UK) Ltd, Volvo UK Ltd, Pielle Corporate Communications Ltd, Gillette Management Inc, CareAssist Group Ltd, Trident Group of Pennsylvania USA (currently unpaid)
Overseas Visits: January 1993, to Gibraltar, for two days' working visit with all – party group at the invitation of the Gibraltar Government.

SMITH, Rt. Hon. John

Constituency: Labour, Monklands East
Parliamentary Activities: Leader of the Opposition
Declared Interests:
Trades or Professions: Queen's Counsel (Scotland)
Financial Sponsorships, Gifts, etc.: Sponsored by the General Municipal and Boilermakers Union in terms of the Hastings Agreement
Overseas Visits: 2–6 February 1992, to Bonn, Brussels and Paris. Received assistance with expenses from Friedrich Ebert Stiftung and the Rowntree Trust.

SMITH, Llewellyn

Constituency: Labour, Blaenau Gwent
Parliamentary Activities:
Select Committee Membership: None
Declared Interests:
Trades or Professions: Receives occasional fees for broadcasting.

SMITH, Tim

Constituency: Conservative, Beaconsfield
Parliamentary Activities:
Select Committee Membership: None
Declared Interests: None listed

Comments: Smith was very active in the Commons on Price Waterhouse's behalf in the late 1980s. In February 1988, for example, he put down 58 parliamentary questions to government departments for detailed information on management consultancy contracts. It transpired that this data was useful for Price Waterhouse who were preparing a marketing and business plan for their clients.

SMYTH, Rev. Martin

Constituency: Official Ulster Unionist, Belfast South
Parliamentary Activities:
Select Committee Membership: Health
Declared Interests:
Trades or Professions: Minister, without charge, of the Presbyterian Church in Ireland (unpaid).

SNAPE, Peter

Constituency: Labour, West Bromwich East
Parliamentary Activities:
Select Committee Membership: None
Declared Interests: Director of West Midlands Travel plc
Financial Sponsorships, Gifts, etc.: Sponsored by the Rail, Maritime and Transport Union who pay £600 per year to West Bromwich East Labour Party. 80 per cent of his election expenses are paid by the Rail, Maritime and Transport Union; Occasional donations from the Musicians Union.
Overseas Visits: 21–26 June 1992, Inaugural British Airways flight from London to Jakarta, courtesy of British Airways; 12–21 October 1992, as Opposition Transport Spokesperson, to San Diego to attend the American Public Transit Association annual meeting – courtesy of West Midlands Travel plc; 21–22 June 1993, to Lille and Lyon, France, looking at Trans–Europe railway services, courtesy of Eurotunnel.

SOAMES, Hon. Nicholas

Constituency: Conservative, Crawley
Parliamentary Activities: Parliamentary Under-Secretary at Ministry of Agriculture (Minister for Food)
Declared Interests: None listed

Comments: From declarations made to Companies House, Soames is a director of Sedgwick Group Development Ltd.

SOLEY, Clive

Constituency: Labour, Hammersmith
Parliamentary Activities:
Select Committee Membership: None
Declared Interests:
Financial Sponsorships, Gifts, etc.: Sponsored by the General, Municipal, Boilermakers and Allied Trades Union.

SPEARING, Nigel

Constituency: Labour, Newham South
Parliamentary Activities:
Select Committee Membership: None
Declared Interests: None listed
Overseas Visits: 2–6 April 1993, to Sweden, at the invitation of the Nytil EG Kongress. Hospitality provided for three nights. Other expenses and fares paid for by Spearing.

SPEED, Sir Keith

Constituency: Conservative, Ashford
Parliamentary Activities:
Select Committee Membership: None
Declared Interests: Director of Folkestone and Dover Water Services plc, Westminster Communications Ltd.
Employment or Office: Consultant to Professional Association of Teachers and Association for the Instrumentation Control of the Automation Industry in the UK (GAMBICA)
Declarable Shareholdings: Westminster Communications Ltd
Clients (of Westminster Communications Ltd): Inter City Division of British Rail, The Motor Cycle Association, ICL, Independent Distillers Company Ltd, TSB, British Gas plc, Thomas Cook Group plc,

Caribbean Banana Exporters Association
Overseas Visits: 3–10 October 1993, to Qatar, as part of a parliamentary group as a guest of the Qatar Government

Comments: From declarations made to Companies House, Sir Keith is also a director of Independent Distillers Company Ltd.

SPELLAR, John

Constituency: Labour, Warley West
Parliamentary Activities:
Select Committee Membership: None
Declared Interests:
Employment or Office: Political Officer of the Electronic, Telecommunication and Plumbing Union (EETPU); Advisor to PQ Parliamentary Information Services. No payment to Spellar. Fees are paid to Warley West Constituency Party
Financial Sponsorships, Gifts, etc.: He is also sponsored as a parliamentary candidate by the EETPU
Overseas Visits: 8–10 June 1992, to Washington, to attend conference organised by the Centre for Strategic and International Studies, sponsored by the Centre; 16–25 March 1993, to Japan, with a delegation as a guest of the Japanese Ministry of Foreign Affairs; 31 March 1993, to Paris, to attend conference sponsored by the Centre for Strategic and International Studies.

SPENCER, Sir Derek, QC

Constituency: Conservative, Pavilion
Parliamentary Activities: Solicitor-General
Declared Interests: None listed.

SPICER, Sir James

Constituency: Conservative, Dorset West
Parliamentary Activities:
Select Committee Membership: None
Declared Interests: Director of Fitness for Industry Ltd (also Chair), Thames and Kennet Marina Ltd (unpaid)
Declarable Shareholdings: Fitness for Industry Ltd; Thames and Kennet Marina Ltd
Overseas Visits: Occasional trips as International Chairman of the Conservative Party; September 1992, 2–week visit to South Africa, sponsored by the South African government for meeting with political representatives across the spectrum

Comments: From declarations made to Companies House, Sir James is a director of the Westminster Foundation for Democracy Ltd and the Parnham Trust.

SPICER, Michael

Constituency: Conservative, Worcester South
Parliamentary Activities:
Select Committee Membership: None
Declared Interests: Director of Association of Independent Electricity Producers
Trades or Professions: Income from occasional writing, broadcasting, speeches
Overseas Visits: 12–13 December 1992, to Denmark, sponsored by Harris and Sheldon of Meridan Warwick; 2–4 April 1993, to Denmark, sponsored by Harris and Sheldon of Meridan Warwick; 3–6 June 1993, to USA for an overseas International Trade Conference sponsored by the Big Horn Mountain Federation.

SPINK, Dr Robert

Constituency: Conservative, Castle Point
Parliamentary Activities:
Select Committee Membership: Education
Declared Interests:
Employment or Office: Self-employed Management Consultant
Trades or Professions: County Councillor
Land and Property: Owner of two residential properties in Dorset and one residential properties in London SE11
Payments from Abroad: Received payment from OEB (Cyprus Employers Federation) in pursuance of a private consultancy contract which began in 1989 and is part-funded by the International Labour Organisation and United Nations in Geneva
Overseas Visits: 12–23 September 1992, to America, organised by the British–American Parliamentary Group and co-sponsored by the United States Information Agency and BAPG.

SPRING, Richard

Constituency: Conservative, Bury St Edmunds
Parliamentary Activities:
Select Committee Membership: Employment
Declared Interests: Director of Abbey Regent Global Fund
Employment or Office: Consultant to Xerox Furman Selz, Protravel, Malabar Capital Ltd
Trades or Professions: Occasional Lecturing
Overseas Visits: 5–10 April 1993, to Turkish Republic of Northern Cyprus as a member of an all-party group, as a guest of that Government.

SPROAT, Iain

Constituency: Conservative, Harwich
Parliamentary Activities: Parliamentary Under-Secretary for National Heritage
Declared Interests: None listed
Payments from Abroad: American Airlines
Overseas Visits: 22–23 July 1992, return flight from London to Copenhagen as a member of the Conservative backbench Aviation Committee, sponsored by CSF–Thomsen; 27–29 September 1992, return flight from London to Stockholm, sponsored by BA; 15–16 October 1992, to Austin, Texas, USA, to lecture at University of Texas. The University paid for two nights' accommodation and travel was provided by American Airlines; January 1993, to Washington DC. Return flight provided by American Airlines.

SQUIRE, Rachel

Constituency: Labour, Dunfermline West
Parliamentary Activities:
Select Committee Membership: None
Declared Interests:
Financial Sponsorships, Gifts, etc.: Contribution towards General Election expenses paid by National Union of Public Employees (NUPE). A payment once every three months is donated to the constituency by UNISON.

SQUIRE, Robin

Constituency: Conservative, Hornchurch
Parliamentary Activities: Parliamentary Under-Secretary for Education
Declared Interests: None listed.

STANLEY, Sir John

Constituency: Conservative, Tonbridge and Malling
Parliamentary Activities:
Select Committee Membership: Foreign Affairs
Declared Interests: Director of Henderson Highland Trust plc, Latin American Capital Fund Ltd, Latin American Capital Fund (Chile) Ltd
Employment or Office: Consultant to European Capital Company Ltd and Fidelity Investment Management Ltd
Overseas Visits: 22–23 April 1992, to Sweden, for constituency purposes, financed by SCA Aylesford Ltd; 17–20 September 1992, to Durban, South Africa, to attend the Britain–South Africa conference. Fares and hotel accommodation paid for by the Conference; Occasional visits abroad on behalf of Action Aid of which Stanley is an unpaid trustee.

STEEL, Rt.Hon. Sir David

Constituency: Liberal Democrat, Tweedale, Ettrick and Lauderdale
Parliamentary Activities: Liberal Democrat Spokesperson on Foreign Affairs
Declared Interests: Director of Heritage Oil and Gas Ltd, Border Television plc, Central Scotland Radio, Byres of Aikwood Trust (unpaid)
Trades or Professions: Regular broadcasting, writing and lecturing
Overseas Visits: Sir David makes overseas visits as President-elect of Liberal International, paid for by that organisation or its member parties; January to February 1992, tour of Egypt, Saudi Arabia, Bahrein and Abu Dhabi, paid for by the Liberal Middle East Council and Middle East Digest; February 1992, to Tulsa, paid for by the University of Tulsa; May 1992, to Botswana, paid for by the Alliance of Western Parliamentarians Against Apartheid. Also trip to Uganda, paid for by the Global Coalition for Africa.

STEEN, Anthony

Constituency: Conservative, South Hams
Parliamentary Activities: Parliamentary Private Secretary to Peter Brooke, Secretary of State for National Heritage
Declared Interests:
Employment or Office: Advisor to Airlines of Great Britain. This also involves regular travel on a number of airlines in connection with airline work in the UK and Europe. Steen receives occasional free air travel for immediate family in the UK and Europe; Advisor to The Communication Group plc; English Vineyards Association
Trades or Professions: Barrister; Member of Lloyd's
Financial Sponsorships, Gifts, etc.: In May 1992, Steen received a gift of salmon and flat fish from Brixham fishermen – worth approximately £150 – in recognition of services to the local industry
Overseas Visits: 6–15 January 1992, to Phoenix, Arizona, as a member of the Parliamentary Tennis Team v. the US Senate, to raise money for the Hospice Movement. Travel provided by US Air.

STEINBERG, Gerry

Constituency: Labour, City of Durham
Parliamentary Activities:
Select Committee Membership: Education

Declared Interests:
Employment or Office: Consultant to Educational Psychologists Association and National Union of Teachers
Financial Sponsorships, Gifts, etc.: Sponsored by the Transport and General Workers' Union (no personal benefit to Steinberg); Durham City Council provides him with office accommodation at a reduced rent
Overseas Visits: 30 May 1993–6 June 1993, to Israel, sponsored by Labour Friends of Israel.

STEPHEN, Michael

Constituency: Conservative, Shoreham
Parliamentary Activities:
Select Committee Membership: None
Declared Interests:
Employment or Office: Consultant to Parliamentary and Public Affairs International and Cyprus Turkish Association of the UK
Land and Property: Owner of a block of flats in Chelsea
Declarable Shareholdings: Parliamentary and Public Affairs International Ltd (PPAI)
Client (of PPAI Ltd): Electronic Data Systems Scicon Ltd
Overseas Visits: 3–4 June 1993, to Pau, France. Member of delegation from the Parliamentary Scientific Committee which visited the research facilities of Elf Aquitaine, as guests of that company.

STERN, Michael

Constituency: Conservative, Bristol North West
Parliamentary Activities:
Selct Committee Membership: Public Accounts
Declared Interests:
Employment or Office: Consultant to Cory Environmental Ltd and Cohen Arnold and Co. Ltd; Client of Cohen Arnold and Co.: Faircharm Investments Ltd.

STEVENSON, George

Constituency: Labour, Stoke-on-Trent South
Parliamentary Activities:
Select Committee Membership: Agriculture
Declared Interests:
Financial Sponsorships, Gifts, etc.: Sponsored as an MP by the Transport and General Workers' Union, who also make a payment towards election expenses

Comments: From declarations made to Companies House, he is also a director of 55 Chester Way Ltd.

STEWART, Allan

Constituency: Conservative, Eastwood
Parliamentary Activities:
Select Committee Membership: None
Declared Interests: None listed.

STOTT, Roger

Constituency: Labour, Wigan
Parliamentary Activities:
Select Committee Membership: None
Declared Interests:
Financial Sponsorships, Gifts, etc.: Sponsored as a Parliamentary Candidate

by the National Communications Union which also pays the salary of Stott's constituency agent.

STRANG, Dr Gavin

Constituency: Labour, Edinburgh East
Parliamentary Activities: an Opposition Spokesperon on Agriculture
Declared Interests:
Financial Sponsorships, Gifts, etc.: Sponsored by the Transport and General Workers' Union, according to the Hastings Agreement.

STRAW, Jack

Constituency: Labour, Blackburn
Parliamentary Activities: Shadow Environment Secretary
Declared Interests:
Employment or Office: Advisor to the Association of University Teachers
Trades or Professions: Writing, broadcasting and lecturing
Financial Sponsorships, Gifts, etc.: Sponsored by the General, Municipal and Boilermakers Union. No personal payment or personal material benefit is derived; Research assistance is provided by the National Association of Local Government Officers; Gift of a day at the races paid for by British Airways
Overseas Visits: 8–11 December 1992, to Pakistan, as guest of the Pakistan Government of Azad Kashmir. Expenses within Pakistan and Azad Kashmir were met by these governments.

STREETER, Gary

Constituency: Conservative, Plymouth Sutton
Parliamentary Activities: Parliamentary Private Secretary to Sir Derek Spencer, the Solicitor-General
Declared Interests:
Employment or Office: Consultant to Institute of Housing and Cruelty Free Manufacturing Ltd
Trades or Professions: Partner at Foot and Bowden, Solicitors
Overseas Visits: 3–11 January 1993, Streeter and his wife visited Israel as guests of the Conservative Friends of Israel.

SUMBERG, David

Constituency: Conservative, Bury South
Parliamentary Activities:
Select Committee Membership: Foreign Affairs
Declared Interests:
Employment or Office: Consultant to Jacques and Lewis Solicitors, Peninsula Bus Services Ltd, Consensus (Scotland) Ltd
Overseas Visits: 13–19 October 1992, to Sweden, Latvia and Lithuania, on behalf of the Inter–Parliamentary Council Against Anti-Semitism. Hospitality and transport was provided by the three Parliaments of the countries concerned.

SWEENEY, Walter

Constituency: Conservative, Vale of Glamorgan
Parliamentary Activities:
Select Committee Membership: None
Declared Interests:

Trades or Professions: Consultant with Gordon Kemp and Co. Solicitors; Solicitor in private practice in own firm, known as Walter Sweeney.

SYKES, John

Constituency: Conservative, Scarborough
Parliamentary Activities:
Select Committee Membership: National Heritage
Declared Interests: Director of Farnley Estates Ltd, Shaws Petroleum Ltd, EMJ Plastics Ltd
Land and Property: Farnley Estates (owns a third share with brothers); Sykes and Sons (owns a half share with brothers)
Declarable Shareholdings: Farnley Estates Ltd, Shaws Petroleum Ltd, Sykes Group Ltd, Oxen House Bay Ltd, Boldstart Ltd
Overseas Visits: 27 September 1992–2 October 1992, to Dubai and Abu Dhabi, as a guest of the Conservative Backbench Tourism Committee, as a guest of the Emirate Airlines; 3–9 April 1993, to Kenya, as a member of the Conservative Backbench Tourism Committee, as a guest of Lonrho

Comments: From declarations made to Companies House, Sykes is also a director of Oxen House Bay Ltd and Boldstart Ltd.

TAPSELL, Sir Peter

Constituency: Conservative, East Lindsey
Parliamentary Activities:
Select Committee Membership: None
Declared Interests:
Employment or Office: International Advisor to Nissho Iwai Corporation; Occasional Advisor to Nikko Securities Company.

TAYLOR, Ann

Constituency: Labour, Dewsbury
Parliamentary Activities: Shadow Education Secretary
Declared Interests: Director of Westminster Communications Group Ltd
Employment or Office: Advisor to the Assistant Masters and Mistresses Association; Clients: Foundation for Sports and Arts Commission for Racial Equality
Trade or Professions: Income from book *Choosing Our Future* 1992.
Financial Sponsorships, Gifts, etc.: Sponsored by the General, Municipal and Boilermakers Union.

TAYLOR, Ian

Constituency: Conservative, Esher
Parliamentary Activities: Parliamentary Private Secretary to William Waldegrave, Secretary of State for Public Service and Science
Declared Interests: Director of United Healthcare Finance Company (USA), Meadowbrook Healthcare Services Inc. (USA), American Community Schools Ltd, Glenesk School Ltd, (honorary), Job Ownership Ltd (honorary) Westminster Foundation for Democracy Ltd (honorary)
Employment or Office: Fentiman Consultants Ltd; Clients of Fentiman Consultants Ltd include: Commercial Union plc, Barclays de Zoete Wedd I.M.

Ltd, A. T. Hudson and Co. Ltd, Nextgen Ltd, Transatlantic Healthcare Ltd
Declarable Shareholdings: Fentiman Consultants Ltd
Overseas Visits: 19–22 August 1992, to Nice, France, as speaker at an international management conference, as a guest of Unisys Ltd.

TAYLOR, Rt.Hon. John

Constituency: Ulster Unionist, Strangford
Parliamentary Activities:
Select Committee Membership: None
Declared Interests: Director of West Ulster Estates Ltd (Chairman), Tontine Rooms Holding Co. Ltd (Chairman)
Trades or Professions: Civil Engineer; Publisher of the *Tyrone Courier*, the *Ulster Gazette*; Proprietor of Cerdac Business Systems in N. Ireland
Land and Property: Sites in the cities of Armagh and Belfast; Two cottages in Turkish Republic of Northern Cyprus; House in City of Westminster.
Declarable Shareholdings: Gosford Voluntary Housing Association Ltd; West Ulster Estates Ltd; Bramley Apple Restaurant Ltd; Tontine Rooms Holding Co. Ltd.

TAYLOR, John M

Constituency: Conservative, Solihull
Parliamentary Activities: Parliamentary Secretary in Lord Chancellor's Department
Declared Interests:
Trades or Professions: Solicitor (non-practising)
Overseas Visits: January 1992, to Hong Kong for one week. Return air flight and hotel bill were paid for by the Hong Kong Government

Comments: From declarations made to Companies House in London, Taylor is also a director of John Taylor Consultancies Ltd; Solihull Business Enterprise Ltd.

TAYLOR, Matthew

Constituency: Liberal Democrat, Truro
Parliamentary Activities:
Select Committee Membership: Commons Services (Broadcasting)
Declared Interests:
Trades or Professions: Occasional payment received for newspaper articles, television appearances, etc.
Overseas Visits: August 1992, 24 days travelling in United States to study Presidential Election, sponsored by the US Information Agency

Comments: From declarations made to Companies House in London, Taylor is also a director of Parliamentary Broadcasting Unit Ltd.

TAYLOR, Sir Teddy

Constituency: Conservative, Southend East
Parliamentary Activities:
Select Committee Membership: None
Declared Interests: Director of Shepherd Foods Ltd – non-executive director of company which is a small grocers chain operating within London only; Anmsvar Insurance Company – non-executive

director of UK branch of Temperance Insurance Co., based in Sweden
Employment or Office: Port of London Police Federation – Parliamentary Advisor to the Port of London Police who are now employed by the Tilbury Dock Co. – a small force of around 50 constables; Lawrence Building Co. – Advisor to this Glasgow-based building company; Parliamentary Advisor to the Association for Denture Prosthesis (an organisation seeking to promote the interests of specialists involved in the fitting of dentures)

Comments: From declarations made to Companies House in London, Taylor is also a director of Partridges of Sloane Street Ltd; Combined Capital Ltd.

TEMPLE-MORRIS, Peter

Constituency: Conservative, Leominster
Parliamentary Activities:
Select Committee Membership: None
Declared Interests: Director of J.K. Associates (Press Relations) Ltd
Employment or Office: Consultant to Unichem
Trades or Professions: Solicitor and Consultant to Payne Hicks Beach, Solicitors.
Overseas Visits: January 1992, to Japan as a guest of the Japanese Parliamentarians in support of the United Nations

Comments: From declarations made to Companies House in London, Temple-Morris is also a director of British Lebanese Association; Britain–Russia Centre.

THOMASON, Roy

Constituency: Conservative, Bromsgrove
Parliamentary Activities:
Select Committee Membership: Environment
Declared Interests:
Employment or Office: Consultant to Messrs Dyson, Bell, Martin, Solicitors and Parliamentary Agents
Trades or Professions: Receiving benefits as a former partner of Messrs Horden and George, Solicitors, Bournemouth and Wimborne, Dorset; Gift of presentational sword on opening offices of Avesta Sheffield Distributors Ltd
Land and Property: Part-owner of office buildings in Bournemouth and Wimborne
Overseas Visits: September 1993, to Germany, to participate in all–party study visit to look at environmental legislation in Germany and its impact on the chemical industry, as a guest of BASF.

THOMPSON, Sir Donald

Constituency: Conservative, Calder Valley
Parliamentary Activities:
Select Committee Membership: None
Declared Interests: Voluntary Chairman to the Animal Health Trust Special Appeal
Employment or Office: Consultant to Naomi C Arnold Consultancy; Advisor to the National Federation of Meat Traders; Advisor to British Agrochemicals Association; One of a cross-party team of advisors to British Nuclear Forum; Advisor to National Caravan Council
Trades or professions: Occasional journalism and broadcasting
Financial Sponsorships, Gifts, etc: 2 free European air tickets 29 April 1993; British Midland

Overseas Visits: 3–9 April 1993, to Hong Kong, as guest of Hongkong and Shanghai Bank.

THOMPSON, Jack

Constituency: Labour, Wansbeck
Parliamentary Activities: Opposition Spokesperson on Foreign Affairs
Declared Interests:
Financial Sponsorships, Gifts, etc.: National Union of Mineworkers.

THOMPSON, Patrick

Constituency: Conservative, Norwich North
Parliamentary Activities: Parliamentary Private Secretary to Brian Mawhinney, Health Minister
Declared Interests:
Employment or Office: Monthly fee received from the Institute of Electrical Engineers for regular articles in their magazine; Parliamentary Consultant to the Professional Association of Teachers (from 1.8.92)

Comments: From declarations made to Companies House in London, Thompson is also a director of Town Close House Educational Trust Ltd.

THORNTON, Sir Malcolm

Constituency: Conservative, Crosby
Parliamentary Activities:
Select Committee Membership: Chairman, Education
Declared Interests: Director of Keene Public Affairs Consultants Ltd
Employment or Office: Parliamentary Consultant to Building Employers Confederation; Parliamentary Consultant to Littlewoods Organisation plc; North West Water plc
Clients of Keene Public Affairs Consultants: Singapore Airlines; Tunstall Telecom and Computer Management Group Ltd

Comments: From declarations made to Companies House in London, Thornton is also a director of MRT Westminster Consultancy Services Ltd.

THURNHAM, Peter

Constituency: Conservative, Bolton North East
Parliamentary Activities:
Select Committee Membership: Social Security
Declared Interests: Director of Wathes Holdings Ltd., and Subsidiaries (9 of them).
Employment or Office: Consultant to the Electrical Contractors' Association
Trades or Professions: Occasional TV/ Radio appearance fees
Land and Property: Agricultural land and property in Cumbria
Declarable Shareholdings: Wathes Holdings Ltd and Subsidiaries
Overseas Visits: February 1992, to Romania, paid for by Romanian Relief Fund and Jubilee Campaign

Comments: Subsidiary Companies of Wathes Holdings Ltd include: Wathes Refrigeration Ltd; Wathes Air Conditioning Centre Ltd; Wathes Electrical N.W. Ltd; Wathes Computers Ltd; Wathes Ltd; T.H. Wathes and Co. Ltd; LCT Design Ltd;

Wathes Electrical Installations Ltd; Wathes Mechanical Services Ltd; Midland Dynamo Installations Ltd.

TIPPING, Paddy

Constituency: Labour, Sherwood
Parliamentary Activities:
Select Committee Membership: None
Declared Interests:
Employment or Office: Consultant to British Association of Colliery Management (unpaid).

TOWNEND, John

Constituency: Conservative, Bridlington
Parliamentary Activities:
Select Committee Membership: None
Declared Interests: Director of J. Townend and Sons (Hull) Ltd and subsidiary and associated companies; Surrey Building Society; AAH Holdings Ltd (from May 1989)
Trades or Professions: Member of Lloyd's

Comments: Mr Townend was very reluctant to talk about his business interests with the authors. He refused to say what AAH Holdings Ltd does and promptly put the telephone down. From declarations made to Companies House in London, Townend is a director of Clipper Cash and Carry Ltd; Merchant Vintners Company Ltd; Townend Catering Company Ltd; House of Townend Ltd; House of Townend (Northern) Ltd; Willerby Manor Hotels Ltd; Hull Bonding Company Ltd; John W. M. Turner (Driffield) Ltd; AAH plc (Wine Merchants); Townend Vintners Ltd; Cottingham King Street Holdings Ltd; Baronoff Vodka Company Ltd; Townend Wine Bars Ltd.

TOWNSEND, Cyril

Constituency: Conservative, Bexleyheath.
Parliamentary Activities:
Select Committee Membership: None
Declared Interests: Journalist and Broadcaster.

TRACEY, Richard

Constituency: Conservative, Surbiton
Parliamentary Activities:
Select Committee Membership: Selection
Declared Interests: Director of Ranelagh Ltd (non-executive) (from 1.7.92)
Employment or Office: Consultant to Tracey Communications
Trades or Professions: Barrister – not practising.

TREDINNICK, David

Constituency: Conservative, Bosworth
Parliamentary Activities:
Select Committee Membership: None
Declared Interests: Chairman of Anglo East European Trading Co. Ltd; Director of Future of Europe Trust (company limited by guarantee. Travel costs and incidental expenses only received); Ukraine Business Agency
Trades or Professions: Member of Lloyd's
Overseas Visits: April-May 1992, to Bulgaria, half of costs met by Future of Europe Trust

Comments: From declarations made to Companies House in London, Tredinnick is also a director of Slumbershades Ltd; East West Investments Ltd.

TREND, Michael

Constituency: Conservative, Windsor and Maidenhead
Parliamentary Activities:
Select Committee Membership: None
Declared Interests: None listed
Overseas Visits: 14–17 September 1992, to Stuttgart and Budapest, to attend the Third Anglo–German conference for parliamentarians at the invitation of the Konrad Adenauer Stiftung; 26 September–3 October 1992, to Hong Kong, accompanied by his wife, at the invitation of the Hong Kong Government; 16–24 Mar 93, to Japan, at invitation of Japanese Government.

TRIMBLE, David

Constituency: Ulster Unionist, Upper Bann
Parliamentary Activities:
Select Committee Membership: None
Declared Interests:
Trades or Professions: Non-practising member of the Bar of Northern Ireland
Declarable Shareholdings: Ulster Society (Publications) Ltd.

TROTTER, Neville

Constituency: Conservative, Tynemouth
Parliamentary Activities:
Select Committee Membership: Defence
Declared Interests: Director of Romag Holdings plc (from 12.3.91)
Employment or Office: Parliamentary Advisor to the British Marine Equipment Council; Parliamentary Advisor to the British Transport Police Federation; Consultant to the Bowring Group and to Go Ahead Northern; Consultant on energy matters to AMEC Offshore Ltd
Trades or Professions: Chartered Accountant; Consultant with Grant Thornton. Former partner in this firm with whom my connection commenced in 1948 on leaving school; Occasional lecturing at home and abroad including arrangements made by Cunard
Overseas Visits: A long-standing interest in transport matters results in occasional travel with various companies, both British and Foreign; February 1992, to the Gulf sponsored by Emirates; May 1992, travel between Newcastle and Amsterdam provided by Air UK; July 1992, visit to the Danish Civil Aviation Authority arranged by Thompson–CSF UK Ltd.

TURNER, Dennis

Constituency: Labour, Wolverhampton South East
Parliamentary Activities:
Select Committee Membership: Education
Declared Interests: Director of Springvale Co-operative Ltd; Springvale Enterprises Ltd; West Midlands Co-operative Finance Ltd (no remuneration)
Employment or Office: Advisor to the Club and Institute Union

Financial Sponsorships, Gifts, etc.: as a Parliamentary candidate by the Co-operative Party.
Declarable Shareholdings: Springvale Co-operative Ltd (£1 share).

TWINN Dr Ian

Constituency: Conservative, Edmonton
Parliamentary Activities: Parliamentary Private Secretary to Sir John Cope, Paymaster General (HM Treasury)
Declared Interests:
Employment or Office: Parliamentary Advisor to the Chartered Society of Physiotherapy; Consultant to TNT; Parliamentary Consultant to the British Surgical Trades Association; Parliamentary Consultant to CAPITB plc; Consultant to Atlantic Richfield Corporation (British) Ltd
Financial Sponsorships, Gifts, etc.: Free use of an electronic paging device from Pageboy Service (UK) Ltd
Overseas Visits: 3–5 February, to Washington DC, USA, to visit Parliamentarians and Government. Costs met by Friends of Cyprus Committee; 29 August–6 September 1992, sailing from and returning to Venice, with my family, accommodation aboard the *Azur* provided by Chandris Ltd.

TYLER, Paul

Constituency: Liberal Democrat, Cornwall North
Parliamentary Activities: an Opposition Spokesperson on Agricultural and Rural Affairs
Declared Interests: Director of Western Approaches Public Relations Ltd
Declarable Shareholdings: Gainpick Ltd T/A Oughs – The Unicorn Grocer; Western Approaches Public Relations Ltd; Bodmin and Wenford Railway plc.

VAUGHAN, Sir Gerard

Constituency: Conservative, Reading East
Parliamentary Activities:
Select Committee Membership: Science and Technology
Declared Interests: Director of Spahealth Ltd (a medical film company); HMT Hospitals Ltd (a wholly owned subsidiary of The Hospital Management Trust, a registered charity)
Trades or Professions: Member of Lloyd's; Consultants, lecturer, author
Declarable Shareholdings: Spahealth Ltd

Comments: From declarations made to Companies House in London, Vaughan is also a director of Rickmansworth Masonic School Services Ltd; Regionreturn Ltd; Spahealth Productions Ltd; G.D. Enterprises Ltd; RMIG Nominees.

VAZ, Keith

Constituency: Labour, Leicester East
Parliamentary Activities:
Select Committee Membership: None
Declared Interests:
Trades or Professions: Barrister
Financial Sponsorships, Gifts, etc.: Sponsored by UNISON (no money paid direct to him, £600 p.a. paid to Constituency Labour Party); Membership

of the St James Court Hotel Club, as a gift from the club; Sponsored by British Psychological Society; Donation from Control Securities plc in 1991 towards the cost of producing a report and bulletin for Asian Community into the work of the Immigration and Nationality Department
Overseas Visits: July 1992, to the Isle of Man to attend the first meeting of BCCI creditors, flight paid for by Vaz, no accommodation required; July 1992, to Paris for the Second Global Convention of People of Indian Origin, flight and accommodation paid for by Vaz; March 1993, to Gibraltar BCCI, paid for by him.

VIGGERS, Peter

Constituency: Conservative, Gosport
Parliamentary Activities:
Select Committee Memberships: Defence, Members' Interests
Declared Interests: Director of Nynex Cablecomms Solent Ltd; Nynex Cablecomms Surrey Ltd Nynex Cablecomms Wessex Ltd; Nynex Cablecomms Sussex Ltd; Nynex Cablecomms Bromley Ltd
Trades or Professions: Underwriting Member of Lloyd's; an Elected Member of the Council of Lloyd's
Financial Sponsorships, Gifts, etc.: Loan of Demonstration TV set with Fastext, by Ferguson Ltd
Overseas Visits: 14–23 September 1992, to Japan, as part of the Japanese Government's Visitors' Programme; to US as part of British–American Parliamentary Group.

WALDEGRAVE, Rt. Hon. William

Constituency: Conservative, Bristol West
Parliamentary Activities: Secretary of State for Public Service and Science
Declared Interests: None listed
Declarable Shareholdings: Waldegrave Farms Ltd

Comments: From declarations made to Companies House in London, Waldegrave is also a director of Waldegrave Farms Ltd.

WALDEN, George

Constituency: Conservative, Buckingham
Parliamentary Activities:
Select Committee Membership: None
Declared Interests: Consultant with Samuel Montagu and Co. Ltd.

WALKER, Bill

Constituency: Conservative, Tayside North
Parliamentary Activities:
Select Committee Membership: None
Declared Interests: Chairman, Walker Associates; Director, Stagecoach Malawi Ltd (from April 1989); Director, Stagecoach International Services Ltd (from April 1989)
Employment or Office: Royal Air Force Volunteer Reserve Commission (Squadron Leader); Parliamentary Advisor, British Holiday and Home Parks Association Ltd – minimal expenses only; Parliamentary Advisor, Society of Procurators Fiscal, Scotland – unpaid
Financial Sponsorships, Gifts, etc: Research services provided personally by Sir Albert McQuarrie

Declarable Shareholdings: Walker Associates (Management Design and Marketing), Stagecoach Holdings plc
Overseas Visits: 21–26 June 1992, to Jakarta, on inaugural flight between UK and Jakarta, as a guest of British Airways; 3–8 Febuary, to Cairo, Scout Confederation

Comments: Bill Walker takes his directorships very seriously. He vigorously defends MPs having outside commercial interests by arguing that they operate in a market place and have a monetary value. He told Granada TV's *World In Action*: 'I would have thought that any MP who has a market value in the outside world of a certain amount as a director and is paid a director's fee, then your constituents can say: "We have an MP who knows something about the real world. He has a worth."'
He also agrees that his colleagues should declare how much money they receive. 'I fully support it,' he said. 'I think once you say what you get paid, then that's your market worth, and I'm rather proud of my market worth.'

WALKER, Cecil

Constituency: Ulster Unionist, Belfast North
Parliamentary Activities:
Select Committee Membership: None
Declared Interests: None listed.

WALKER, Rt. Hon. Sir Harold

Constituency: Labour, Doncaster Central
Parliamentary Activities:
Select Committee Membership: None
Declared Interests:
Financial Sponsorships, Gifts, etc.: by the Amalgamated Union of Engineering Workers, who pay about two thirds of election expenses, and an annual sum to the Constituency Party towards the employment of a part-time agent (no personal payment or advantage, direct or indirect)

Comments: From declarations made to Companies House in London, Sir Harold is also a director of Doncaster Leisure Management Ltd.

WALLACE, James

Constituency: Liberal Democrat, Orkney and Shetland
Parliamentary Activities:
Select Committee Membership: None
Declared Interests:
Employment or Office: Parliamentary Advisor to Institute of Chartered Accountants of Scotland; Parliamentary Advisor to the Procurators Fiscal Society in Scotland (unpaid)
Trades or Professions: Member, Faculty of Advocates (ceased practice on election); Occasional Broadcasting.

WALLER, Gary

Constituency: Conservative, Keighley
Parliamentary Activities:
Select Committee Membership: Chairman, Commons Services (Information)
Declared Interests:
Employment or Office: Advisor to the Machine Tool Technologies Association
Overseas Visits: February 1992, to Pakistan

at the invitation of the Government of Azad Jammu and Kashmir.

WALLEY, Joan

Constituency: Labour, Stock-on-Trent North
Parliamentary Activities:
Opposition Spokesperson on Shipping and Environmental Issues
Declared Interests:
Financial Sponsorships, Gifts, etc.: Sponsored by the Confederation of Health Service Employees in form of donation to Constituency Labour Party; Loan of a fax machine from the Institute of Environmental Health Officers. Research expenses for 12 months received from NALGO to assist with frontbench responsibilities.

WARD, John

Constituency: Conservative, Poole
Parliamentary Activities:
Select Committee Membership: None
Declared Interests: None listed

Comments: From declarations made to Companies House in London, Ward is also a director of Anglo–Austrian Society; Taylor Woodrow (Premises) Ltd (until 30.5.92).

WARDELL, Gareth

Constituency: Labour, Gower
Parliamentary Activities:
Select Committee Membership: Chairman, Welsh Affairs
Declared Interests:
Financial Sponsorships, Gifts, etc.: Sponsored by the General, Municipal, Boilermakers and Allied Trades Union. (Average of £300 p.a. to Constituency Party – no personal benefit.)

Comments: From declarations made to Companies House in London, Wardell is also a director of Industry and Parliamentary Trust Ltd.

WARDLE, Charles

Constituency: Conservative, Bexhill and Battle
Parliamentary Activities: Parliamentary Under-Secretary at Home Office
Declared Interests: None listed.

WAREING, Bob

Constituency: Labour, Liverpool West Derby
Parliamentary Activities:
Select Committee Membership: Foreign Affairs
Declared Interests: None listed

Comments: From declarations made to Companies House in London, Wareing is also a director of Robert Wareing Ltd.

WATERSON, Nigel

Constituency: Conservative, Eastbourne
Parliamentary Activities:
Select Committee Membership: Statutory Instruments
Declared Interests:
Trades or Professions: Partner in firm of Solicitors, Messrs Waterson Hicks, London
Financial Sponsorships, Gifts, etc.: 12–14 March, Elveden Forest Holiday Village, as a guest of Centre Parcs.
Overseas Visits: 16–24 August 1992, to Washington, Houston and Florida. He received a per diem allowance from the British–American Parliamentary group. Internal flights and other expenses were paid by the United States Information agency; 27 September – 2 March 1992, to the United Arab Emirates as part of the Conservative Backbench Tourism Committee delegation, as the guest of the Emirates Airline; April 93, to Kenya, sponsored by Kenya National Tourist Office, Kenya Airways and Lonrho Hotels

Comments: From declarations made to Companies House in London, Waterson is also a director of Eastbourne Constitutional Club Ltd.

WATSON, Mike

Constituency: Labour, Glasgow Central
Parliamentary Activities:
Select Committee Membership: Parliamentary Commissioner for Administration (Ombudsman)
Declared Interests:
Financial Sponsorships, Gifts, etc.: Sponsored by Manufacturing, Science and Finance Union: sponsorship is paid direct to the constituency Labour Party
Overseas Visits: 6–10 January 1992, to German Lander (Berlin Brandenburg and Nord-Rhein/Westphalen), to study constitutional arrangements and electoral systems, as guest of the Friedrich Ebert Stiftung.

WATTS, John

Constituency: Conservative, Slough
Parliamentary Activities:
Select Committee Membership: Chairman, Treasury and Civil Service
Declared Interests:
Employment or Office: Parliamentary Advisor to the Institute of Actuaries; Advisor to Working Men's Club and Institute Union (CIU); Consultant to Wisdom Securities Ltd – Property developers; Consultant to British Bus plc
Trades or Professions: John Watts and Co., Chartered Accountants
Overseas Visits: April 1992, to Azad Kashmir and Pakistan as a guest of those Governments; August 1993 to New York, as a guest of Goldman Sachs and Co.

WELLS, Bowen

Constituency: Conservative, Hertford and Stortford
Parliamentary Activities: Parliamentary Private Secretary to Roger Freeman and Earl Caithness, Transport Ministers
Declared Interests: Non-executive Director of Belsize Holdings Inc
Employment or Office: Parliamentary Consultant to: International Distillers and Vintners Ltd; Geest plc

Comments: From declarations made to Companies House in London, Wells is also a director of Industry and Parliament Trust; Institute of Development Studies.

WELSH, Andrew

Constituency: Scottish National Party
Parliamentary Activities:
Select Committee Membership: Scottish Affairs
Declared Interests:
Trades or Profession: Occasional journalism and lecturing.

WHEELER, Rt.Hon. Sir John

Constituency: Conservative, Westminster North
Parliamentary Activities: Minister of State for Security in Northern Ireland
Declared Interests:
Trades or Professions: Member of Lloyd's
Overseas Visits: 3–9 January 1993, to Israel with Conservative Friends of Israel.

WHITNEY, Ray

Constituency: Conservative, Wycombe
Parliamentary Activities:
Select Committee Membership: None
Declared Interests: Chairman, Cable Corporation (from 18.1.89); Chairman, Local Government Network (from November 1992)
Employment or Office: Consultant to Fisons plc, Pharmaceutical Division

Comments: Whitney was one of three Tory MPs active in lobbying the Home Office over the cable TV aspects of the 1990 Broadcasting Bill. From declarations made to Companies House in London, Whitney is also a director of Foundation for Defence Studies.

WHITTINGDALE, John

Constituency: Conservative, Colchester South and Maldon
Parliamentary Activities:
Select Committee Membership: Health
Declared Interests: None listed.
Overseas Visits: 19–23 September 1993, to Cyprus, paid for by Friends of Cyprus.

WICKS, Malcolm

Constituency: Labour, Croydon North West
Parliamentary Activities:
Select Committee Membership: None
Declared Interests:
Trades of Professions: Occasional journalism/lectures

Comments: From declarations made to Companies House in London, Wicks is also a director of National Energy Foundation; New Ruskin House Croydon Club Ltd.

WIDDECOMBE, Ann

Constituency: Conservative, Maidstone
Parliamentary Activities: Parliamentary Under-Secretary for Employment
Declared Interests:

Employment or Office: Regular contributor to *Catholic Times*; Small and very occasional income from writing and broadcasting on Church matters.

WIGGIN, Sir Jerry

Constituency: Conservative, Weston-super-Mare
Parliamentary Activities:
Select Committee Membership: Chairman, Agriculture
Declared Interests:
Employment or Office: Consultant to British Sugar; Advisor to British Marine Industries Federation; Advisor to Weighing Federation; Consultant to Sears plc; Advisor to British Holiday and Home Parks Association; Consultant to the Security Industry Association
Trades or Professions: Member of Lloyd's (ceased underwriting 1.1.92)

Comments: In 1989 Wiggin asked the Agriculture Secretary John Gummer in a Commons question 'for a substantial contribution from the government' to be paid to the British Sugar Corporation. Wiggin was and remains a consultant to British Sugar which he described as 'that excellent British enterprise'.

WIGLEY, Dafydd

Constituency: Plaid Cymru, Caernarfon
Parliamentary Activities:
Select Committee Membership: None
Declared Interests: Director of Alpha Cysylltiadau Cyf (from October 1991)
Trades or Professions: Occasional television and radio items and articles in press and periodicals
Financial Sponsorships, Gifts, etc.: Research assistance provided by European Public Policy Advisers (UK) Ltd
Declarable Shareholdings: Caernarfon Town Football Club Ltd; Arianrhod Cyf; Padarn Power Company Ltd; Alpha Cysylltiadau Cyf
Clients: Diagnostic Products Corporation.

WILKINSON, John

Constituency: Conservative, Ruislip Northwood.
Parliamentary Activities:
Select Committee Membership: None
Declared Interests: Chairman, EMC (Communications) Ltd.
Trades or Professions: Marketing consultant, lecturer and author; Occasional journalism, radio and TV.
Overseas Visits: 7–10 March 1992, to Chile as a guest of Chilean Government
Declarable Shareholdings: EMC Communications Ltd
Clients: Thorn EMI Electronics Ltd. (parliamentary advice).

WILLETTS, David

Constituency: Conservative, Havant
Parliamentary Activities:
Select Committee Membership: Social Security
Declared Interests: Director of Retirement Security Ltd; Electra Innvotec Ltd; Sphere Drake Holdings Ltd
Employment or Office: Consultant to: TI Group plc; Healthcall UK Ltd; Kleinwort

Benson Securities Ltd
Trades or Professions: Author and freelance writer
Declarable Shareholdings: Retirement Security Ltd
Overseas Visits: 14–16 May 1993, to Italy, Konrad Adenauer Stiftung; 1993, to Stuttgart, Konrad Adenauer Stiftung; 15–16 January 1993, Germany
Comments: From declarations made to Companies House in London, Willetts is also a director of Electra Corporate Ventures Ltd; Social Market Foundation.

WILLIAMS, Rt. Hon. Alan

Constituency: Labour, Swansea West
Parliamentary Activities:
Select Committee Membership: Public Accounts
Declared Interests:
Employment or Office: Advisor to the Institute of Plant Engineers; Advisor to the Transport Salaried Staffs Association. No salary received. A payment is made to the constituency party
Trades or Professions: Occasional broadcasting fees.

WILLIAMS, Alan W.

Constituency: Labour, Carmarthen
Parliamentary Activities:
Select Committee Membership: Science and Technology
Declared Interests: None listed.

WILSHIRE, David

Constituency: Conservative, Spelthorne
Parliamentary Activities:
Select Committee Membership: None
Declared Interests:
Trades or Professions: Partner, Western Political Research Services
Overseas Visits: 5–11 January 1992, to USA. Travel was provided by United Airlines and accommodation by Rolls Royce, British Aerospace and Lockheed; October 1992, 3–day visit to Washington DC to press the US Government to authorise British Airways' proposed investment in US Air, paid for by British Airways; 6–7 January 1993, to Brussels, courtesy of British Airways; April 1993, to Cyprus, paid for by the Government of Northern Cyprus.

WILSON, Brian

Constituency: Labour, Cunninghame North
Parliamentary Activities: Opposition Spokesperson on Transport
Declared Interests: Director of West Highland Publishing Co. Ltd
Trades or Professions: Journalism
Declarable Shareholdings: West Highland Publishing Co. Ltd
Overseas Visits 27–30 June, to Colorado, Nuclear Dry Storage, Scottish Nuclear.

WINNICK, David

Constituency: Labour, Walsall North
Parliamentary Activities:
Select Committee Membership: Procedure
Declared Interests:

Trades or Professions: Occasional fees received for broadcasting or television interviews.
Financial Sponsorships, Gifts, etc.: Contribution by the General Municipal Boilermakers and Allied Trades Union to election expenses; payment of £300 annually between elections to Constituency Party.

WINTERTON, Ann

Constituency: Conservative, Congleton
Parliamentary Activities:
Select Committee Membership: Agriculture
Declared Interests: None listed
Overseas Visits: 3–10 April 1993, to Turkish Republic of National Cyprus as a member of an all-party Parliamentary Delegation as a guest of that Government.

WINTERTON, Nicholas

Constituency: Conservative, Macclesfield
Parliamentary Activities:
Select Committee Membership: None
Declared Interests: Director of Bridgewater Paper Company Ltd (non-executive) (from Febuary 1990); the Government Relations Unit; MSB Ltd (non-executive) (from 1.10.92)
Employment or Office: Parliamentary Advisor to the Construction Plant Hire Association; Parliamentary Advisor to Baird Textile Holdings Ltd; Parliamentary Advisor to Emerson International Ltd; Parliamentary Advisor to Tricoville Ltd (from Febuary 1993)
Trades or Professions: Fees from occasional broadcasting and speaking engagements
Clients (of the Government Relations Unit): The Society for the Promotion of Nutritional Therapy; Manufacturing and Construction Industries Alliance Ltd; EMAP; Sony Broadcast and Professional Ltd; Britt Allcroft Group; the Portman Group.

WISE, Audrey

Constituency: Labour, Preston
Parliamentary Activities:
Select Committee Membership: Health
Declared Interests:
Financial Sponsorships, Gifts, etc.: Sponsored by Union of Shop Distributive and Allied Workers. No payments or material benefits to me. Help to Constituency Party given, as per Hastings Agreement; President of USDAW (with an honorarium).

WOLFSON, Mark

Constituency: Conservative, Sevenoaks
Parliamentary Activities:
Select Committee Membership: None
Declared Interests: Independent Business Consultant, specialising in the management of human resources – occasional earnings only
Comments: For many years 'Business Consultant' was the only information Wolfson disclosed in the Register of Members' Interests. This was one of the most inadequate declarations ever provided to the Register. For it fails to indicate its clients, as stipulated in Rule 4, or the

companies that Wolfson 'consults' for and has represented. Only in 1994 did Wolfson add 'specialising in management of human resources'.

WOOD, Timothy

Constituency: Conservative, Stevenage
Parliamentary Activities: Government Whip
Declared Interests: None listed.

WORTHINGTON, Tony

Constituency: Labour, Clydebank and Milngavie
Parliamentary Activities: Opposition Spokesperson on Foreign Affairs
Declared Interests:
Employment or Office: Occasional income from articles, talks, television appearances
Financial Sponsorships, Gifts, etc.: Sponsored as a Member of Parliament by GMB Union, no personal benefit.

WRAY, Jimmy

Constituency: Labour, Glasgow Provan
Parliamentary Activities:
Select Committee Memberships: European Legislation, Social Security
Declared Interests:
Financial Sponsorhips, Gifts, etc.: Sponsored by Transport and General Workers' Union (no personal benefit).

WRIGHT, Tony

Constituency: Labour, Cannock and Burntwood
Parliamentary Activities:
Select Committee Membership: Parliamentary Commissioner for Administration (Ombudsman)
Declared Interests:
Trades or Professions: Occasional writing

Comments: From declarations made to Companies House in London, Wright is also a director of Political Quarterly Publishing Company Ltd.

YEO, Tim

Constituency: Conservative, Suffolk South
Parliamentary Activities:
Select Committee Membership: None
Declared Interests: None listed
Declarable Shareholdings: Anacol Holdings Ltd; General Securities Register Ltd

Comments: From declarations made to Companies House in London, Yeo is also a director of General Securities Register Ltd; D'Arcy Stand Ltd; No. 151 Properties Ltd; Anacol Holdings Ltd.

YOUNG, David

Constituency: Labour, Bolton South East
Parliamentary Activities:
Select Committee Membership: Employment
Declared Interests:
Financial Sponsorships Gifts, etc.: Sponsored by the Transport and General Worker's Union.

YOUNG, Rt. Hon. Sir George

Constituency: Conservative, Ealing Acton
Parliamentary Activities: Minister of State for Housing, Construction and Inner Cities
Declared Interests: None listed.

Section Two

Lords on the Boards – Senior Peers and their Business Interests

Unlike the House of Commons, there is no Register of Interests for Members of the House of Lords. Information about their business and financial interests is therefore not available to the public. Peers are obliged to declare their interests on the floor of the parliamentary chamber during debates and questions. But there are no rules governing lobbying and their commercial interests. The only guideline is that declaration in the Lords is 'a matter of honour' and governed by a 'gentlemen's agreement'.

There are 1,205 members of the Lords. They are made up 774 hereditory peers, 26 Bishops and 405 Life Peers. Each Member is entitled to a fee of £130 per day. This consists of £69 as an overnight allowance, £31 for subsistence and a £30 office allowance.

The Lords exert influence rather than exercise power. They examine legislation at committee stages but their ability to change bills is largely based on delaying tactics. By a combination of filibustering and astute cross-party coalitions, the Upper House can certainly give the Commons a hard time. Peers can table amendments, even as late as third readings, although these are often Government redrafts by Ministers. Essentially, their power is limited. They can revise and frustrate but they cannot reform and defeat. However, for vested interests the Lords are a very useful focal point for dissent, lobbying and propaganda.

We have done an analysis of former senior Cabinet Ministers, from both Labour and Conservative Governments in the past twenty years, who have been elevated to the Upper House. The following is a list of their directorships and consultancies:

LORD BARNETT

Chief Secretary to Treasury 1974–79. Cabinet Minister 1977–79

Directorships: Berstar Properties Ltd, Newcroft Ltd, Stockpack Ltd, British Screen Finance Ltd, Bodycote International plc, Stephens–Itex Safety Ltd, National Film Trustee Company Ltd, European Co-Production Fund Ltd, L. Marks Ltd, BBC Pension Fund Trust Ltd, National Film Development Fund, Global Soccer Management Ltd.

LORD CALLAGHAN

Prime Minister 1976–79

Directorships: Coleg Harlech.

LORD ENNALS

Social Services and Health Secretary 1976–79

Directorships: Anglia Television Telethon Trust Ltd, Independent Broadcasting Telethon Trust Ltd, Takare Plc.

LORD HOWE

Chancellor of the Exchequer 1979–83, Foreign Secretary 1983–89 and then Leader of the House of Commons and Deputy Prime Minister 1989–90

Directorships: Glaxo Holdings plc, BICC
Consultant or Advisor: Jones, Day, Reavis and Pogue (American law firm, advisor on international and European affairs), J.P. Morgan (member of the International Council).

LORD JENKIN

Social Services Secretary 1979–81, Industry Secretary 1981–83 and Environment Secretary 1983–85.

Directorships: Friends Provident Life (also Chairman), Target Finland Ltd
Consultant or Advisor: Andersen Consulting, Sumitomo Trust Bank, National Economic Research, Marsh and McLennan

LORD LAWSON

Chancellor of the Exchequer 1983–89.

Directorships: Central Europe Trust Financial Services Co. Ltd, Barclays Bank plc, Stafford Mansions Residents Association Ltd
Consultant or Advisor: Credit Anstalt (member of advisory board)
Comments: Lord Lawson joined Barclays Bank within three months of leaving the Treasury. He was hired to advise the clients of Barclays De Zoete Wedd, its investment and securities subsidiary.

LORD MOORE

Financial Secretary to Treasury 1983–86, Transport Secretary 1986–87, Social Services Secretary 1987–88 and Social Security Secretary 1988–89
Directorships: Credit Suisse Asset Management (also Chairman), Monitor (Europe) (also Chairman), Energy Savings Trust (also Chairman), Blue Circle, Monitor Inc, G-Tech Inc
Consultant or Advisor: Sir Alexander Gibb

LORD PARKINSON

Trade and Industry Secretary June to October 1983, Energy Secretary 1987–89 and Transport Secretary 1989–1990

Directorships: Great Queen Street Consultants, Jarvis Harpenden Holdings Ltd (also Chairman), Usbourne plc, Starmin plc (also Deputy Chairman), Starmin (Pension Trust) Ltd, Taskforce Communications Ltd, Chemical Dependency Centre Ltd, J.L. Manson Insurance Group Ltd, Midland Expressway Ltd, Dartford River Crossing Ltd, Dartford River Crossing Trustees Ltd, Eurorail Ltd, Dolphin Holdings Ltd (registered in Bermuda).

LORD PRIOR

Employment Secretary 1979–81 and Northern Ireland Secretary 1981–84

Directorships: General Electric Company (GEC) plc (also Chairman), Industry and Parliamentary Trust, East Anglian Radio plc, Alders Ltd, United Biscuits (Holdings) plc, South Pickenham Estate Co. Ltd
Consultant or Advisor: Tenneco (member of advisory board), AIG International (member of advisory board).

LORD PYM

Defence Secretary 1979–81, Leader of the House of Commons 1981–82 and Foreign Secretary 1982–83

Directorships: Cablevision Communications Co. Ltd, St Andrews (Ecumenical) Trust, Cablevision North Bedfordshire Ltd, Cablevision Bedfordshire Ltd, Philip N. Christie and Co. Ltd, Cablevision Communications Company of Hertfordshire.

LORD REES

Chief Secretary to the Treasury, 1983–85

Directorships: Lasmo plc (also Chairman), Leopold Joseph Holdings (also Deputy Chairman), General Cable, Cable Corporation, Quadrant Group, James Finlay plc.

LORD TEBBIT

Employment Secretary 1981–83 and Trade and Industry Secretary 1983–85

Directorships: BET plc, British Star min Telecommunications plc
Spectator (1928) Ltd, Sears plc

Comments: Lord Tebbit's most controversial appointment was his directorship of British Telecom plc. It was Tebbit, as Secretary of State for Trade and Industry, who privatised the company in 1984.

BARONESS THATCHER

Prime Minister 1979–90

Directorships: Margaret Thatcher Foundation Ltd
Consultant or Advisor: Philip Morris Group Inc.

Comments: Philip Morris are the American manufacturers of Marlboro cigarettes. This was a curious appointment for Baroness Thatcher, particularly as when she was Prime Minister she backed a campaign designed to halve the number of young smokers by 1993. She also received £3.5 million from HarperCollins for her memoirs and charges £27,000 per lecture.

LORD WALKER

Agriculture Secretary 1979–83, Energy Secretary 1983–1987 and Welsh Secretary 1987–90

Directorships: British Gas plc, Tate and Lyle plc, Worcester Group plc, European Smaller Companies plc, Robert Bosch Investment plc, Allianz (UK) Ltd, Cornhill Insurance plc, Thornton Asian Emerging Markets Investment Trust plc, CBC UK Ltd, Thornton Unit Managers Ltd, Taemit Finance Ltd, Thornton Management Ltd, Thornton Investment Management Ltd

Comments: Lord Walker's decision to join the board of British Gas plc was heavily criticised because he was the Secretary of State for Energy who privatised the corporation in 1986. Political opponents recalled that Walker had been criticised at the time of the British Gas sale for not breaking up its monopoly or replacing the management team. Walker countered by arguing that he had been hired for his knowledge of international oil and gas markets.

LORD WHITELAW

Home Secretary 1979–83, Leader of the House of Lords and Deputy Prime Minister 1983–88

Directorships: Carlton Club (London) Ltd, Carlton Trustees (London) Ltd, The Britain–Russia Centre, International Centre for Child Studies Ltd, Carlton Club Collection Ltd.

LORD YOUNG

Employment Secretary 1985–87 and Trade and Industry Secretary 1987–89

Directorships: Cable and Wireless plc (also Chairman), Kibo Foundation (UK) Ltd, Salomon Inc

Comments: As Secretary of State for Trade and Industry, Lord Young had dealt directly with Cable and Wireless plc as telecommunications is a highly regulated industry. 'His experience of negotiating at the highest level is a rare talent,' said Lord Sharp, Cable and Wireless's outgoing Chairman.

LORD YOUNGER

Scottish Secretary 1979–86 and Defence Secretary 1986–89

Directorships: Royal Bank of Scotland plc (Chairman), Royal Bank of Scotland Group plc, Siemens Plessey Electronic Systems Ltd (Chairman), Scottish Equitable Life Assurance Society, Scottish Equitable Policy Holders Trust Ltd, Edinburgh Festival Theatre Trading Ltd, Murray International Trust plc, Murray Income Trust plc, Murray Smaller Markets Trust plc, Edinburgh Festival Theatre Trust, Speed Ltd (Chairman), Quality Scotland Foundation Educational Trust, BCH Property Ltd, Edinburgh Festival Society, PIK Holdings Ltd, Murray Johnstone Holdings Ltd (Deputy Chairman).

Section Three

Members of the European Parliament and their Financial Interests

Your Euro MP is a strange political creature, perceived by many as someone who works in Brussels or Strasbourg doing God knows what and almost certainly nothing that directly has anything to do with the average voter.

This perception is, however, a false one and Euro MPs are not comfortable or happy with it. Like all politicians they bask in the light of publicity but the sad truth is that nobody in Britain cares greatly about them or knows what they do. This is reinforced by the low level of publicity given to Euro MPs by the two major parties. Euro MPs also tend to be shunned by national newspapers and the efforts on publicity by the London office of the European Parliament leans towards members of the regional press.

It would not be unreasonable to suggest that the vast majority of our voting public would not know who their Euro MP is or the name of their constituency.

Now this unhappy state of affairs cannot be blamed completely on the MPs. They provide excellent facilities for journalists in Strasbourg and Brussels and the spokespersons in these cities are ever eager to attend to press inquiries. They also produce a prodigious amount of paper and will cheerfully put you on a mailing list if you ask.

Not so long ago your Euro MP was someone who couldn't quite get into Westminster or was a Commons reject. Now it is no longer the case. Edwina Currie has expressed interest in a Euro constituency, as has Labour's Tony Banks.

The reasons for the change in the status of the Euro MP is simple. Maastricht gave them power.

The final agreement, signed in November 1993, will allow the Parliament more say in Community budget and legislation after the June 1994 elections in an extended Parliament.

Some clever officials in the Labour Party may have worked out that while they cannot get socialist legislation through the Tory Commons they can, with their European socialist colleagues, get it through Strasbourg. For it is a simple and unpalatable truth for many that Community law is also British law – and it must be enacted as such here.

And for those who do read the small print, opt-out clauses do not run indefinitely and decision-taking within the Community is broadly based on the votes of the majority of member states.

But what of the institution now called the European Parliament? It held its first election under universal suffrage in 1979. Before this, members were appointed by their own Governments.

At a very early stage political groupings had started to form and the socialist bloc is now the largest. There are around ten groups at present, from Greens to the far right.

The leaders of these groups, along with some fourteen vice-presidents, form the Bureau of Parliament and work with and advise the President; an inner cabinet, if you like, designed to run the Parliament for its members over matters such as budget and staffing and relations with other non-parliamentary groups such as the Commission and the Council of Ministers.

Parliament sits in Strasbourg in part session for one week in every month excepting August. Committee work is undertaken in Brussels and the secretariat is in Luxembourg.

Since Maastricht's signing, which makes all of us members of the European Union, the Parliament will become more effective as a tool for democratising the functions of an expanding Community. Its powers to summons officials and Ministers will be increased, its oversights on budgetry matters enhanced and its ability to criticise more widely taken.

What does your MP get by way of pay? Well, rather more than his domestic counterpart if you take in allowances and other fringe benefits.

British Euro MPs, like all others, have their basic salary tagged to the normal rate of pay for a domestic MP. The Commons last November voted themselves a 5.4 per cent increase above the rate of inflation, spread over some two years, so the Euro MPs enjoy this as well.

So to a basic salary of around £31,000 add another £25,000 for costs of postage, telephone and travel within the member state, plus subsistence allowances of £153 per day within the Community and £77 per day outside the Community, with the cost of overnight accommodation, as well as secretarial assistance of up to some £6,000 per month. Unlike the domestic MP, the Euro MP must actually pay for a secretary to claim this allowance. Finally there is the matter of some £800 per annum for the running of data-processing equipment. All of these figures are based on the exchange rate at 7 October 1993 in relationship to the ECU. Now there is also a mileage allowance of 56 pence per kilometre, but this cannot be quantified as an annual amount.

So in all, our Euro MP can expect to gross something like £80,000 per annum and this is taxed at the standard British rate. With a secretary thrown in for £24,000, they do very well indeed.

Our Euro MPs are pampered in other ways. Once elected they cannot be removed except with the consent of the Parliament. The rules of procedure (seventh edition) state simply that if a national government wants an MEP removed they must give good reason and show what laws may have been breached in that member's home country.

But if the European Parliament does not agree it will not lift immunity for its member. In cases where members have been removed it is usually at their own request because they wish to defend themselves against allegations in their own countries.

Is it easy to find out what your Euro MP does? No, it is in fact very difficult.

You could simply telephone your MEP and ask, but the answers may not be forthcoming. On the other hand you may never hear the end of it.

Apologists for the Parliament and its workings point out that it really is a European Parliament and therefore properly the bulk of information on it should come from its institutions. The information section that handles this is called the Directorate-General for Research, based in Luxembourg.

But what ordinary curious British voter wants to ring around Strasbourg, Brussels or Luxembourg to get some simple answers? Not many.

Why not instead just ring up the European Parliament office in London and ask away there? Well, it simply won't work.

The London office has a staff of twelve which has not been increased since 1979. It has a small library and an overworked librarian. If you want to find out what issues your MEP has raised in the European Parliament there are documents on debates called the Official Journal but unlike our Commons no index of Speeches that can be cross-referenced to the member. That information is available on a computer not accessible to the public. This computer is called EPOQUE.

EPOQUE can list the keynote contents of speeches or questions and cross-index them for you but you cannot easily get into it.

The office in London can access it, so can others in the UK.

You might instead be provided with a booklet called *Accessing European Parliament Documentation*. It is a worthy publication but its contents are somewhat depressing. It is not user friendly and you might feel that this would deter the casual inquirer. It is published by the Directorate-General for Research. We were given our copy by the London office.

Sadly nowhere in this guide is there an explanation as to how you could find out about the activities of your MEP's interests outside Parliament simply because this information is, for all practical purposes, hidden and not accessible, firstly on computer and secondly to the public at large.

What you are entitled to know is what outside interests your Euro MP has. Like the UK there is a register of members' interests. Unlike the UK it is never published and no copy exists in Britain. One copy exists in Brussels, another in Luxembourg and the main registry is in Strasbourg. Euro MPs tend to enter their interests on joining the Parliament and then forget about it. But not all.

Now although the rules state that the register is open to public inspection in practice it is not. When Parliament sits in Strasbourg the bureaucrats have decided that the copies in Brussels and Luxembourg cannot be made available for inspection. This foolish and boorish rule is said to have been made by the Bureau. When we asked to see this edict we were told to write to the Secretary-General of the Parliament and ask for it.

Our Euro MP declarations hero must be Mr Brian Cassidy who represents Dorset East and Hampshire West for the Conservatives. Mr Cassidy has cheerfully filled his declaration with a wide variety of activities and we commend his candour to his fellow MEPs.

Under the Rules of Procedure on page 105, annex 1, it states clearly: 'each member shall be required to make a detailed declaration of his professional activities' and: 'Members shall also list any other paid functions or activities in so far as these are relevant.' And finally: 'This register shall be made open to the public for inspection.'

When we first searched the 'public' registry in July last year in Brussels, we found that in the preceding twelve months only four other applications to view it had been made. Possibly this is because of the obstructions placed in the way by the inconvenience of travel, as well as cost.

If the register is in practice to be open to the public then it must surely follow that the register must be reasonably accessible in published form. When we asked Dr Martyn Bond, who heads the European Parliament's office in London, why no register of members' interests was published he said: 'If the European Parliament decides it will be published, then it will be published. But there have been no arguments or proposals for this to happen. You have to remember that this is a new Parliament and things take time.'

We pressed him further when we suggested that the ordinary British voter would have considerable difficulty in finding out what their Euro MP actually did on their behalf, he responded by saying: 'That is a fatuous and simplistic argument. It [the register] is openly available in Brussels. For the register to be published and distributed throughout the UK would be very difficult. It would be a hefty document and very expensive to produce. There are all kinds of potential problems in terms of how many cities it is distributed in and in which constituencies.'

Well these suggestions are not 'fatuous.' The simple truth is that any member of the public will have to go to some considerable difficulty in finding out what their MEP does with his or her time, what legislation they do or do not support, and whose interests they promote when they accept outside consultancies or directorships of companies.

The register is not easily available for inspection: appointments have to be made to view it as the staff have numerous other duties to perform.

In fact the register fails in many respects. The entries in Brussels do not tie in exactly with those in Strasbourg, which may be explained by members simply adding to their original declaration as opposed to making a new, updated one as the need arises.

To say the register is 'open' to the public, as Dr Bond had asserted, is indeed fatuous, considering the difficulties encountered when trying to find and search it. On average there are only about twenty requests each year for inspection of the register in both Brussels and Strasbourg. In a community with over 360 million voters it is abundantly clear that the access offered to the material on members' interests falls little short of scandalous.

The number of MEPs is not great. Already there is another List of Members which is published every June. It shows their addresses, political affiliations and committees on which they sit. It comes out in all languages. It would be simple to add just a few lines to every entry to cover outside interests in this existing publication. The fact that it does not, and no other publication exists covering this basic information, hardly supports the theory of open government, something the European Parliament attempts to pride itself on.

There is however a Committee on Procedure which has before it a draft report which may help to clear up some of these matters. No one we spoke to has seen it or is aware of its exact contents.

To suggest, as Dr Bond has, that to rectify these shortcomings is a difficult task is nonsense.

It is strange, is it not, that the first publication to list these activities is one written by British journalists and not by the bureaucrats within the European Parliament who are charged with European Union.

But let's not blame the bureaucrats only. Euro MPs have a responsibility for openness in their dealings both in and out of Parliament. Everyone suffers when they fail to overhaul and reform this appalling system of mismanaged information that is vital to voter understanding of the work put in by Euro MPs who should, after all, be the most accountable civil servants of all.

ADAM, Gordon Johnston

D.O.B.: 28.3.34.
Occupation: Unlisted
Constituency: Labour, Northumbria
Parliamentary Activities: Member of the group of the Party of European Socialists; Vice-Chairman of the Committee on Energy Research and Technology; Substitute member of the Committee on Agriculture, Fisheries and Rural Development; Substitute member of the Committee on Fisheries; Member of the delegation for relations with the member states of ASEAN and the ASEAN Interparliamentary organisation (AIPO) and the Republic of Korea; Substitute member of the delegation for relations with the Republics of the Commonwealth of Independant States
Declaration Date: 18.7.89
Declared Interests: None
Comments: From declarations made to Companies House in London, Adam is a director of Tyne Threatre Trust Ltd and The Newcastle Free Festival.

BALFE, Richard Andrew

D.O.B.: 14.5.44
Occupation: Writer, broadcaster and lecturer
Constituency: Labour, London South Inner
Parliamentary Activities: Member of the European Socialist Party; Substitute member of the Committee on External Economic Relations; Substitute member of the Committee of the rules of Procedure, the verification of Credentials and Immunities; Vice-Chairman for the Sub-Committee on Security and Disarmament; Member of the delegation to the EC–Turkey Joint Parliamentary Committee; Substitute member of the delegation for relations with Japan
Declaration Date: 18.7.89
Declared Interests: Chairman of the Co-operative Society South-East branch; Member of the regional Committee of the Co-operative Wholesale Society; European advisor – Co-operative Wholesale Society and subsidaries; Chairman of the Co-operative Wholesale Society Political Committee.
Comments: Balfe is also a fellow of the Royal Statistical Society. From information obtained from Companies House in London, Balfe is also a director of Cambridge House and Talbot Ltd and European Shadow Communications Agency Ltd. Both directorships were taken up in 1991.

BARTON, Roger

D.O.B.: 6.1.45
Occupation: Unlisted
Constituency: Labour, Sheffield
Parliamentary Activities: Member of the Committee on Economic and Monetary Affairs and Industrial Policy; Substitute member of the Committee on Foreign Affairs and Security; Substitute member of the Committee on Petitions; Member of the delegation for relations with Israel; Substitute member of the delegation to the EC–Turkey Joint Parliamentary Committee
Declaration Date: 26.7.89
Declared Interests: None.

BEAZLEY, Christopher

D.O.B.: 5.9.53
Occupation: Unlisted
Constituency: Conservative, Cornwall and Plymouth
Parliamentary Activities: Member of the group of European Peoples Party (PPE) – the Christian Democratic Group; Member of the Committee on Civil Liberties and Internal Affairs; Substitute member of the Committee of Regional Policy, Regional Planning and Relations with Regional and Local Authorities; Vice-Chairman of the delegation for relations with Estonia, Latvia and Lithvania

BEAZLEY, Peter George

D.O.B.: 9.6.22
Occupation: Unlisted
Constituency: Conservative, Bedford South
Declaration Date: 12.7.89
Parliamentary Activities: Member of the PPE; Member of the Committee on Economic and Monetary Affairs and Industrial Policy; Substitute member of the Committee on External Economic Relations; Member of the delegation for relations with the member states of ASEAN and the ASEAN Interparliamentary Organisation (AIPO) and the Republic of Korea; Substitute member of the delegation to the EC–European Economic Joint Parliamentary Committee
Declared Interests: The Brewers Society contributes a small annual amount to his constituency association.

BETHELL, The Lord Nicholas William

D.O.B.: 19.7.38
Occupation: Freelance writer and journalist
Constituency: Conservative, London North West
Parliamentary Activities: Member of the PPE; Member of the Committee on Foreign Affairs and Security; Substitute member of the Committee on Civil Liberties and Internal Affairs; Vice-chairman for the Sub-Committee on Human Rights; Vice Chairman for the delegation for relations with the Republic of the Commonwealth of Independant States; Substitute member of the delegation for relations with Poland.
Declaration Date: 19.7.89
Declared Interests: Underwriting Member of Lloyd's of London; an Advisor to the Police Federation in the UK.

BIRD, John Alfred William

D.O.B.: 6.2.26
Occupation: Unlisted
Constituency: Labour, Midlands West
Parliamentary Activities: Member of the Party Socialist European; Member of the Committee on Development and Co-operation; Substitute member of the Committee on External Economic Relations; Member of the delegation to the EC–Malta Joint Parliamentary Committee; Substitute member of the delegation to the EC–Austria Joint Parliamentary Committee
Declaration Date: 25.7.89
Declared Interests: None shown
Comments: From declarations made to Companies House in London, Bird is shown as a director of Temple Services Ltd of Wolverhampton which provides managed workshops for small businesses. This appointment was taken up on 10.8.91.

He will be retiring after the June 1994 Euro elections.

BOWE, David Robert

D.O.B.: 19.7.55
Occupation: Unlisted
Constituency: Labour, Cleveland and Yorkshire North
Parliamentary Activities: Member of the PSE; Member of the Committee on the Environment, Public Health and Consumer Protection; Substitute member of the Committee on Energy, Reasearch and Technology; Member of the delegation for relations with Japan; Substitute member of the delegation for relations with the Czech Republic and the Slovak Republic
Declaration Date: 15.7.89
Declared Interests: Member of the National Union of Teachers, UK; Member of the National Union of Public Employees, UK.

BUCHAN, Janey O'Neil

D.O.B.: 30.4.26
Occupation: Unlisted
Constituency: Labour, Glasgow
Parliamentary Activities: Member of the PSE; Member of the Committee on Development and Co-operation; Substitute member of the Committee on Culture, Youth Education and the Media; Substitute member of the delegation for relations with Israel
Declaration date: 14.7.89
Declared Interests: None shown.
Comments: Ms Buchan retires after the Euro elections in June 1994.

CATHERWOOD, Sir Fred

D.O.B.: 30.1.25
Occupation: Unlisted
Constituency: Conservative, Cambridgeshire and Bedforshire North
Parliamentary Activities: Member of the PPE; Vice-Chairman of the Committee on Foreign Affairs and Security; Substitute member of the Committee on Economic and Monetary Affairs and Industrial Policy; Member of the delegation for relations with Canada; Substitute member of the delegation for relations with the United States
Declaration date: 19.7.89
Declared interests: Director Goodyear GB Ltd; Occasional articles and books published
Comments: From declarations made to Companies House London, Sir Fred was appointed a director of the Evangelical Alliance Ltd on January 1992.

COATES, Kenneth

D.O.B.: 16.9.30
Occupation: Author
Constituency: Labour, Nottingham
Parliamentary Activities: Member of PSE; Member of the Committee on Foreign Affairs and Security; Substitute member of the Committee on Development and Co-operation; Chairman of the Sub-Committee on Human Rights; Member of the delegation for relations with the Republics of the Commonwealth of Independant States (CIS); Substitute member of the delegation for relations with Estonia, Latvia and Lithuania
Declaration Date: 17.7.89
Declared Interests: Royalties from books; Honorary university post: Reader in Adult

Education, Nottingham University
Comments: From declarations made to Companies House in London, Coates is also a director of the Bertand Russell Peace Foundation Limited, a company formed to publish the writings of Bertrand Russell and to support peace movements around the world; Furtina Ltd, a non-trading company holding the archives of Bertrand Russell; Europa Nottingham Limited, a company formed by Coates to run his European Parliamentary office.

COLLINS, Kenneth Darlingston

D.O.B.: 12.8.39
Occupation: Unlisted
Constituency: Labour, Strathclyde East
Parliamentary Activities: Member of the PSE; Chairman of the Committee on the Environment, Public Health and Consumer Protection; Substitute member of the Committee on Economic and Monetary Affairs and Industrial Policy; Member of the delegation for relations with the Czech Republic and the Slovak Republic; Substitute member of the delegation for relations with Hungary
Declaration Date: 14.7.89
Declared Interests: Paid consultant to European Public Policy advisors; Consultant to ERGO Communications Ltd; Director of the Institute for European Environmental Policy, London; Member of the Advisory Board of *Water Law* journal; Member of the Advisory Committee on European Public Policy Unit, University of Warwick; European Advisor to NALGO, EETPU, ACTT, BECTV (all British trade unions); Honorary senior research fellow Department of Geography, University of Lancaster; Board Member, Friends of the Earth (Scotland)

CRAMPTON, Peter Duncan

D.O.B.: 10.6.32
Occupation: Unlisted
Constituency: Labour, Humberside
Parliamentary Activities: Member of PSE; Vice-Chairman of the Committee on Foreign Affairs and Security, Substitute member of the Committee on Civil Liberties and Internal Affairs; Member of the Sub-Committee on Security and Disarmament; Member of the delegation for relations with the People's Republic of China; Substitute member of the delegation for relations with Iceland
Declaration Date: 8.9.93
Declared Interests: Visit to Turkey in November 1992 paid for by the Turkish Government; Visit to Taiwan in September 1993 paid for by the Taiwanese Government.

CRAWLEY, Christine Mary

D.O.B.: 9.1.50
Occupation: Unlisted
Constituency: Labour, Birmingham East
Parliamentary Activities: Member of PSE; Member of the Committee on Civil Liberties and Internal Affairs; Chairman of the Committee on Women's Rights; Substitute member of the Committee on Economic and Monetary Affairs and Industrial Policy; Member of the delegation for relations with Estonia, Latvia and Lithuania
Declaration Date: 16.7.89
Declared Interests: None shown.

DALY, Margaret Elisabeth

D.O.B.: 26.1.38
Occupation: Unlisted
Constituency: Conservative, Somerset and Dorset West
Parliamentary Activities: Member of the PPE; Member of the Committee on Development and Co-operation; Substitute member for the Committee on Agriculture, Fisheries and Rural Development; Substitute member of the committee on Women's Rights; Substitute member of the delegation to the EC–Turkey Joint Parliamentary Committee
Declaration Date: 13.7.89
Declared Interests: Director of Cophall Associates Ltd; JPB Associates Ltd; Somerset local radio; Consultant to the Banking Insurance and Finance Union; Companies House in London note that Ms Daly is also shown as the secretary of Cophall Associates Ltd.

DAVID, Wayne

D.O.B.: 1.7.57
Occupation: Unlisted
Constituency: Labour, South Wales
Parliamentary Activities: Member of PSE; Vice-Chairman of the Committee on Regional Policy, Regional Planning and Relations with Regional and Local Authorities; Member of the Committee on Institutional Affairs; Substitute member of the Committee on Budgets; Member of the delegation to the EC–Austria Joint Parliamentary Committee; Member of the delegation to the EC European Economic Area Joint Parliamentary Committee
Declaration Date: 17.7.89
Declared interests: None shown
Comments: From declarations made to Companies House in London, David is also a director of Valley and Vale Community Arts Limited. He is also shown as a director of European Shadow Communications Agency Limited, an alternative company set up by Labour MPs to present European issues from a Labour perspective.

DONNELLY, Alan John

D.O.B.: 16.7.57
Occupation: Unlisted
Constituency: Labour, Tyne and Wear
Parliamentary Activities: Member of the PSE; Member of the Committee on Economic and Monetary Affairs; Substitute member of the Committee on Regional Policy, Regional Planning and Relations with Regional and Local Authorities; Member of the Sub-Committee on Monetary Affairs; Chairman of the delegation for relations with the United States; Substitute member of the delegation to the EC–Sweden Joint Parliamentary Committee
Declaration Date: 13.7.89
Declared Interests: Director of Unity Trust Bank plc; Central Finance manager of the GMB until September 1989. Since 1992 the American–European Community Association has paid for an assistant to work in Donnelly's Brussels office.
Comments: From declarations made to Companies House in London, Donnelly is also a director of European Shadow Communications Agency Limited, an alternative company set up by Labour MPs to present European issues from a Labour perspective.

ELLES, James E. M.

D.O.B.: 3.9.49
Occupation: Unlisted
Constituency: Conservative, Oxford and Buckinghamshire
Parliamentary Activities: Member of the Committee on Budgets; Substitute member of the Committee on Budgetary Control; Member of the delegation for relations with Australia and New Zealand; Substitute member of the delegation for relations with Japan
Declaration Date: 16.7.89
Declared Interests: None shown

ELLIOT, Michael Norman

D.O.B.: 3.6.32
Occupation: Unlisted
Constituency: Conservative: London West
Parliamentary Activities: Member of PSE; Member of the Committee on Culture, Youth Education and the Media; Substitute member of the Committee on Civil Liberties and Internal Affairs; Member of the delegation to the EC–Finland Joint Parliamentary Committee; Substitute member of the delegation to the EC Economic area Joint Parliamentary Committee
Declaration Date: 15.7.89
Declared Interests: None shown.

EWING, Winifred M.

D.O.B.: 10.7.29
Occupation: Unlisted
Constituency: Scottish National Party member for Highlands and Islands
Parliamentary Activities: Member of ARC (Rainbow group in the European Parliament); Member of the Committee for Development and Co-operation; Substitute member of the Committee on Agriculture, Fisheries and Rural Development; Member of the Sub-Committee on Fisheries; Substitute member of the delegation for relations with Estonia, Latvia and Lithuania
Declaration Date: 23.10.90
Declared Interests: Member of the Law Society, Scotland
Comments: From declarations made to Companies House in London, Ewing is also a director of Cedargrove Property Company Limited, a non-trading company.

FALCONER, Alexander C.

D.O.B.: 1.4.40
Occupation: Unlisted
Constituency: Labour, Mid Scotland and Fyfe
Parliamentary Activities: Member of PSE; Member of the Committee on Regional Policy, Regional Planning and Relations with Regional and Local Authorities; Substitute member of the Committee on Legal Affairs and Citizens' Rights; Member of the delegation for relations with the countries of South America; Substitute member of the delegation to the EC–Norway Joint Parliamentary Committee
Declaration Date: 14.7.89
Declared Interests: Shareholder in Peoples Press Publications; Publishers of the *Morning Star* daily newspaper.

FORD, James Glyn

D.O.B.: 28.1.50
Occupation: Author
Constituency: Labour, Greater Manchester East
Parliamentary Activities: Member of PSE; Member of the Committee on Energy, Research and Technology; Member of the Committee on Institutional Affairs; Substitute member of the Committee on Foreign Affairs and Security; Substitute member of the Committee on the Rules and Procedure, the Verification of Credentials and Immunities; Substitute member of the sub-committee on Security and Disarmament; Vice-Chairman of the delegation for relations with Japan
Declaration Date: 14.7.89
Declared Interests: Occasional journalistic and media work; Honorary Senior Research Fellow, Department of Science and Technology, University of Manchester (unpaid); Chairman of Tameside Business Technology Centre Management Committee (unpaid); Member of the Management Committee, Chinese Information Centre; Member of the Institute of Professional Geologists
Comments: Ford was formerly leader of Labour MPs to the European Parliament. From declarations made to Companies House in London, Ford is also a director of European Shadow Communications Agency Limited, an alternative company set up by Labour MPs to present European issues from a Labour perspective.

GREEN, Pauline

D.O.B.: 8.12.48 (Malta)
Occupation: Unlisted
Constituency: Labour, London North
Parliamentary Activities: Member of PSE; Member of the Committee on the Environment, Public Health and Consumer Protection; Substitute member of the Committee on Agriculture, Fisheries and Rural Development; Substitute member of the Committee on Women's Rights; Member of the delegation to the EC–Cyprus Joint Parliamentary Committee; Substitute member of the delegation to the EC–Malta Joint Parliamentary Committee
Declaration Date: 24.10.93
Declared Interests: Vice-President, Institute of Environmental Health Officers (honorary); Vice-President of the Institute of Trading Standards Officers (honorary); Sponsored by the Co-operative Party; Member of the Parliamentary group of Union of Shop Distributive and Allied Workers
Comments: From declarations made to Companies House in London, Green is shown as a director of European Shadow Communications Agency Limited, an alternative company set up by Labour MPs to present European issues from a Labour perspective. She was elected leader of the Labour Group in the European Parliament which has 45 MEPs. They all in turn belong to the Party of European Socialists, the largest group in the Parliament.

HARRISON, Lyndon Henry Arthur

D.O.B.: 28.9.47
Occupation: Unlisted
Constituency: Labour, Cheshire West
Parliamentary Activities: Member of PSE; Member of the Committee on Economic and Monetary Affairs and Industrial Policy; Member of the Committee on the Rules of Procedure, the Verification of Credentials and Immunities; Substitute member of the

Committee of Regional Planning and Relations with Regional and Local Authorities; Substitute member of the Sub-Committee on Monetary Affairs; Member of the delegation for relations with the member states of ASEAN and the ASEAN Interparliamentary organisation (AIPO) and the Republic of Korea; Substitute member of the delegation for relations with the United States
Declaration Date: 15.7.89
Declared Interests: Cheshire CHI ISF UK (paid attendance allowance); Member of the Cheshire Country Council.

HINDLEY, Michael John

D.O.B.: 11.4.47
Occupation: None Listed
Constituency: Lancashire East, Labour
Parliamentary Activities: Member of Committee of External Economic Relations; Substitute member of Committee of Civil Liberties and Internal Affairs; Member of delegation for relations with the People's Republic of China
Declaration Date: 17.7.89
Declared Interests: None shown.

HOON, Geoffrey William

D.O.B.: 6.12.53
Occupation: Barrister
Constituency: Labour, Derbyshire
Parliamentary Activities: Member of PSE; Member of the Committee on Legal Affairs and Citizens' Rights; Member of the Committee on Economic and Monetary Affairs and Industrial Policy; Member of the delegation for relations with the Gulf States; Member of the delegation for relations with the countries of Central America and Mexico
Declaration Date: 16.7.89
Declared Interests: None shown
Comments: Hoon is standing down in the June 1993 elections.

HOWELL, Paul Frederic

D.O.B.: 17.1.51
Occupation: Farmer
Constituency: Conservative, Norfolk
Parliamentary Activities: Member of PPE; Member of the Committee of Regional Policy, Regional Planning and Relations with Regional and Local Authorities; Substitute member of the Committee on Agriculture, Fisheries and Regional Development; Member of the Sub-Committee on Fisheries; Member of the delegation for relations with the Republics of the Commonwealth of Independent States; Substitute member of the delegation for relations with the countries of Central America and Mexico
Declaration Date: 15.5.91
Declared Interests: Consultant to the European Regional Airlines Association
Comments: From declarations made to Companies House in London, Howell is also a director of Nuffield–Russia Trust, a charitable company formed to promote agricultural research in Russia.

HUME, John

D.O.B.: 18.1.37
Occupation: Member of Parliament
Constituency: Social Democratic and Labour, Northern Ireland
Parliamentary Activities: Member of PSE; Member of the Committee on Regional Policy, Regional Planning and Relations with Regional and Local Authorities; Substitute member of the Committee on Agriculture, Fisheries and Rural Development
Declaration Date: 14.9.89
Declared Interests: None listed.

HUGHES, Stephen S.

D.O.B.: 19.8.52
Occupation: Unlisted
Constituency: Labour, Durham
Parliamentary Activities: Member of PSE; Member of the Committee on Social Affairs, Employment and the Working Environment; Substitute member of the Committee on the Environment, Public Health and Consumer Protection; Substitute member of the Committee on the Rules of Procedure, the Verification of Credentials and Immunities; Substitute member of the Sub-Committee on Security and Disarmament; Member of the delegation for relations with Japan; Substitute member of the delegation for relations with Switzerland
Declaration Date: 17.7.89
Declared Interests: None shown.

INGLEWOOD, The Lord William Richard Fletcher V.

D.O.B.: 37.7.51
Occupation: Barrister, Landowner.
Constituency: Conservative, Cumbria and Lancashire North
Parliamentary Activities: Member of PPE; Member of the Committee on Legal Affairs and Citizens' Rights; Substitute member of the Committee on Civil Liberties and Internal Affairs; Member of the delegation to the EC–Turkey Joint Parliamentary Committee; Substitute Member of the delegation for relations with the People's Republic of China
Declaration Date: 20.7.89
Declared Interests: Director of the Pheasant Inn (Bassenthwaite Lake) Ltd
Comments: From declarations made to Companies House in London, Inglewood is also a director of 111 Alderney Street (1981) Ltd, a residental freehold owning company. He is also shown as a director of The Calvert Trust (Challenge for the Disabled). Former interests include a directorship of General Environmental Options Limited, from which he resigned 19.12.92.

JACKSON, Caroline Frances

D.O.B.: 5.11.46
Occupation: Unlisted
Constituency: Conservative, Wiltshire
Parliamentary Activities: Member of PPE; Member of the Committee on Social Affairs, Employment and the Working Environment; Member of the Committee on the Environment, Public Health and Consumer Protection; Member of the delegation for relations with the People's Republic of China; Substitute member of the delegation for relations with Canada

Declaration Date: 26.7.89
Declared Interests: Consultant to Merck, Sharp and Domme, Mars Company, Market Access International, Brewers Society, Historic Houses Association; Board member of Peugeot Talbot (UK) Ltd
Comments: From declarations made to Companies House in London, Jackson is also a director of the Institute for European Environmental Policy, London. She is also shown as a director of Peugot Talbot Motor Company plc.

JACKSON, Christopher Murray

D.O.B.: 24.5.35
Occupation: Unlisted
Constituancy: Conservative, Kent East
Parliamentary Activities: Member of PPE; Member of the Committee on Economic and Monetary Affairs and Industrial Policy; Substitute member of the Committee on Development and Co-operation; Substitute member of the Sub-Committee on Monetary Affairs; Substitute member of the delegation for relations with the Republics of the Commonwealth of Independant States (CIS); Substitute member of the delegation for relations with the countries of South America
Declaration Date: 14.11.93
Declared Interests: Director of Westminster Communications Ltd (director's fee paid); Occasional fees from articles a media appearances; Underwriting Member of Lloyd's of London; Clarendon House Residents Maintenance Society Ltd
Comments: Was formerly a director of the now disolved Kent European Youth Association.

KELLET-BOWMAN, Edward Thomas

D.O.B.: 25.2.31
Occupation: Business and Management Consultant
Constituency: Conservative, Hampshire Central
Declaration Date: 24.7.89
Declared Interests: Director of Padern Education Trust Ltd
Comments: In August 1990 Kellet-Bowman visited South Africa as a guest of the Electricity Supply Commission (ESKOM), the South African Foundation and the Urban Foundation. Kellet-Bowman was de-selected in January 1994 and replaced by Graham Mather, a right-wing anti-European. Mather was at one time employed at the Institute of Directors.

LOMAS, Alfred

D.O.B.: 30.4.28
Occupation: Unlisted
Constituency: Labour, London North East
Parliamentary Activities: Member of PSE; Member of the Committee on Development and Co-operation; Substitute Member of the Committee on Foreign Affairs and Security; Substitute member of the Committee on Industrial Affairs; Substitute member of the delegation for relations with the People's Republic of China
Declaration Date: 14.7.89
Declared Interests: None shown
Comments: From declarations made to Companies House in London, Lomas is also a director of Pioneer Theatres Limited.

MARTIN, David W.

Vice-President of the Socialist Group
D.O.B.: 26.8.54
Occupation: Unlisted
Constituency: Labour, Lothians
Parliamentary Activities: Member of PSE; Member of the Committee on External Economic Relations; Member of the Committee on Institutional Affairs; Substitute member of the Committee on Legal Affairs and Citizens' Rights; Member of the delegation for relations with Australia and New Zealand; Substitute member of the delegation to the EC–Cyprus Joint Parliamentary Committee
Declaration Date: 14.7.89
Declared Interests: Occasional income from television and journalism
Comments: From declarations made to Companies House in London, Martin is also a director of The John Wheatley Centre, also St Andrew Animal Fund Ltd.

McMAHON, Hugh Robert

D.O.B.: 17.6.38
Occupation: Unlisted
Constituency: Labour, Strathclyde West
Parliamentary Activities: Vice-Chairman of the Committee of Social Affairs, Employment and the Working Environment; Substitute member of the Committee on the Environment, Public Health and Consumer Protection; Substitute member of the Committee on Budgetary Control; Member of the delegation to the EC–Sweden Joint Parliamentary Committee; Substitute member of the delegation to the EC Economic Area Joint Parliamentary Committee; Substitute member of the delegation for relations with Ireland
Declaration Date: 14.7.89
Declared Interests: None shown.

MEGAHY, Thomas

D.O.B.: 16.7.29
Occupation: Unlisted
Constituency: Labour, Yorkshire South West
Parliamentary Activities: Member of PSE; Member of the Committee on Social Affairs, Employment and the Working Environment; Substitute member of the Committee on Transport and Tourism; Member of the delegation for relations with Hungary; Substitute member of the delegation for relations with Canada
Declaration Date: 26.10.93
Declared Interests: None shown

MOORHOUSE, James

D.O.B.: 1.1.24 (Copenhagen)
Occupation: Unlisted
Constituency: Conservative, London South East
Parliamentary Activities: Member of PPE; Member of the Committee on External Economic Relations; Substitute member of the Committee on Transport and Tourism; Member of the delegation for relations with Japan; Substitute member of the delegation for relations with Australia and New Zealand
Declaration Date: 16.7.89
Declared Interests: Consultant to Marketing, Commercial and Trade Policy; Director of Project International, London; Consultant to Raitt Orr and Associates, Government and Public Relations Advisors,

London; Partner in Aviation and Tourism Consultants International, London and Advocacy Partnership, Public Affairs Consultants, London

McCUBBIN, Henry

D.O.B.: 15.7.42
Occupation: Unlisted
Constituency: Labour, North East Scotland
Parliamentary Activities: Member of PSE; Member of the Committee on Agriculture, Fisheries and Rural Development; Member of the Committee on the Rules of Procedure, the Verification of Credentials and Immunities; Substitute member of the Committee on Social Affairs, Employment and the Working Environment; Member of the Sub-Committee on Fisheries; Member of the delegation for relations with Albania, Bulgaria and Rumania; Substitute member of the delegation for relations with the countries of South America
Declaration Date: 13.7.89
Declared Interests: None listed
Comments: From declarations made to Companies House in London, McCubb is also a director of Dundee Repertory Theatre Limited.

McGOWAN, Michael

D.O.B.: 19.5.40
Occupation: Unlisted
Constituency: Labour, Leeds
Parliamentary Activities: Member of PSE; Member of the Committee on Development and Co-operation; Substitute member of the Committee on Foreign Affairs and Security; Substitute member of the delegation for relations with Poland
Declaration Date: 14.9.89
Declared Interests: None shown

McINTOSH, Ann Caroline Ballingall

D.O.B.: 20.9.54
Occupation: Advocate (non-practising)
Constituency: Conservative, Essex North East
Parliamentary Activities: Member of PPE; Member of the Committee on Transport and Tourism; Member of the Committee on the Rules of Procedure, the Verification of Credentials and Immunities; Substitute member of the Committee on Legal Affairs and Citizen's Rights; Substitute member of the Committee on Social Affairs, Employment and the Working Environment; Member of the Delegation to the EC–Norway Joint Parliamentary Committee; Substitute member of the delegation for relations with the Czech Republic and the Slovak Republic
Declaration Date: 14.7.89 (original)
Declared Interests: 1–4 December 1990, McIntosh went to the United States as a reporter on external relations in the field of Civil Aviation. The event was organised by American Airlines for members of the Transport Committee. Authorisation was given for this trip with the proviso that McIntosh would not be accompanied by an official; 25–27 February 1990, fact-finding mission as a reporter on air transport to Dallas, Texas and Tulsa, Oklahoma; 29 October–2 November 1990: Speaking tour to the United States for the English Speaking Union
Declared: 6.6.91. European Parliamentary Advisor to Hill and Knowlton, public affairs consultants.

McMILLAN-SCOTT, Edward

D.O.B.: 15.8.49
Occupation: Public Affairs Consultant
Constituency: Conservative, York
Parliamentary Activities: Member of PPE; Member of the Committee on Foreign Affairs and Security; Substitute member of the Committee on Petitions; Member of the Sub-Committee on Security and Disarmament; Member of the delegation for relations with Poland; Substitute member of the delegation for relations with the Republics of former Yugoslavia
Declaration Date: 24.7.89
Declared Interests: None listed.

MORRIS, David Richard

D.O.B.: 28.1.30
Occupation: Unlisted
Constituency: Labour, Mid and West Wales
Parliamentary Activities: Member of PSE; Member of the Committee on Agriculture, Fisheries and Rural Development; Substitute member of the Committee on the Environment, Public Health and Consumer Protection; Substitute member of the delegation for relations with the Gulf States
Declaration Date: 7.7.89
Declared Interests: None listed.

NEWENS, Arthur Stanley

D.O.B.: 4.2.30
Occupation: Unlisted
Constituency: Labour, London Central
Parliamentary Activities: Member of PSE; Member of the Committee on Foreign Affairs and Security; Substitute member of the Committee on Development and Co-operation; Member of the Sub-Committee on Human Rights; Member of the delegation for relations with the countries of South Asia and the South Asian Association for Regional Co-operation (SAARC); Substitute member of the delegation for relations with the Republics of former Yugoslavia
Declaration Date: 18.7.89
Declared Interests: Occasional fees for broadcasting; Sponsored by the Co-operative Movement for Electoral Purposes but not in receipt of any personal financial allowance
Comments: From declarations made to Companies House in London, Newens is also a director of Outset Limited, a registered charity that aims to train the mentally and physically handicapped in the use of computers.

NEWMAN, Edward

D.O.B.: 14.5.53
Occupation: Unlisted
Constituency: Labour, Greater Manchester Central
Parliamentary Activities: Member of PSE. Member of the Committee on Civil Liberties and Internal Affairs; Member of the Committee on Petitions; Substitute member of the Committee on Social Affairs, Employment and the Working Environment; Member of the delegation to the EC–Austria Joint Parliamentary Committee; Substitute member of the delegation for relations with Switzerland
Declaration Date: 17.7.89
Declared Interests: Member, formerly elected official of, and European advisor to, the Union of Communication Workers; Although receiving no personal payment

from the Union, they sponsor Newman by financially subsidising the Labour Party within his European constituency
Comments: From declarations made to Companies House in London, Newman is also a director of Pebblehill Limited, a management and service company, with an annual turnover of around £30,000.

NEWTON-DUNN, William Francis

D.O.B.: 3.10.41
Occupation: Unlisted
Constituency: Conservative, Lincolnshire
Parliamentary Activities: Member of PPE; Member of the Committee on Petitions; Substitute member of the Committee on Foreign Affairs and Security; Substitute member of the Committee on Institutional Affairs; Member of the delegation for relations with the countries of South America; Substitute member of the delegation for relations with Hungary
Declaration Date: 26.7.89
Declared Interests: None listed.

NICHOLSON, James

D.O.B.: 29.1.45
Occupation: Farmer, District Councillor
Constituency: Ulster Unionist Party, Northern Ireland
Parliamentary Activities: Member of PPE; Member of the Committee on Regional Policy, Regional Planning and Relations with Regional and Local Authorities; Substitute member of the Committee on Agriculture, Fisheries and Rural Development; Member of the Sub-Committee on Fisheries; Member of the delegation for relations with Australia and New Zealand; Substitute member of the delegation for relations with Israel
Declaration Date: 15.7.89
Declared Interests: None listed.

ODDY, Christine

D.O.B.: 20.9.55
Occupation: Marker, Law Society Business and Insolvency Law
Constituency: Labour, Midlands Central
Parliamentary Activities: Member of PSE; Member of the Comittee on Legal Affairs and Citizens' Rights; Substitute member of the Committee on Social Affairs, Employment and the Working Environment; Substitute member of the Committee on Women's Rights; Substitute member of the Sub-Committee on Human Rights; Member of the delegation for relations with the countries of Central America and Mexico
Declaration Date: 20.7.89
Declared Interests: None listed

O'HAGAN, The Lord Charles Townley Strachey

D.O.B.: 6.9.45
Occupation: Unlisted
Constituency: Conservative, Devon
Parliamentary Activities: Member of PPE; Member of the Committee on Social Affairs, Employment and the Working Environment; Member of the Committee on Women's Rights; Substitute member of the Committee on Development and Co-operation; Member of the delegation for relations with the countries of South Asia

and the South Asian Association for Regional Co-operation (SAARC); Substitute member of the delegation for relations with the countries of Central America and Mexico
Declaration Date: 10.9.9
Declared Interests: Member of the House of Lords; Consultant to International Employers Ltd as Chairman; Study group of two works councils
Comments: From declarations made to Companies House in London, O'Hagan is also a director of Articus Research and Design Ltd, Hereditary Property Consultants; Also he is a director of The European Community Chamber Orchestra. Lord O'Hagan will be retiring from the European Parliament in June 1994.

PAISLEY, The Reverend Ian

D.O.B.: 6.4.26
Occupation: Protestant Minister, British Member of Parliament
Constituency: Democratic Unionist Party, Northern Ireland
Parliamentary Activities: Paisley is not attached to any political group within the European Parliament; Member of the Committee on Agriculture, Fisheries and Rural Development; Member of the delegation to the EC–Cyprus Joint Parliamentary Committee
Declaration Date: 16.8.89
Declared Interests: None listed.

PATTERSON, George Benjamin

D.O.B.: 21.4.39
Occupation: Unlisted
Constituency: Conservative, Kent West
Parliamentary Activities: Member of PPE; Vice-Chairman of the Committee on Economic and Monetary Affairs and Industrial Policy; Member of the Committee on Petitions; Substitute member of the Committee on Energy, Research and Technology; Substitute member of the Committee on the Rules of Procedure, the Verification of Credentials and Immunities; Member of the Sub-Committee on Monetary Affairs; Member of the delegation for relations with the countries of Central America and Mexico; Substitute member of the delegation for relations with the Mashreq countries
Declaration Date: 15.7.89
Declared Interests: Director of Wiltenbridge Ltd; Consultant to Countrywide Political Communications Ltd, London
Comments: From declarations made to Companies House in London, Patterson is also a director of The Dyslexia Institute, London. His resignation on 29 December 1991 from Wiltenbridge Limited appears in documents at Companies House but is not recorded in the register of members' interests.

PLUMB, The Lord Henry

D.O.B.: 27.3.25
Occupation: Unlisted
Constituency: Conservative, Cotswolds
Parliamentary Activities: Member of PPE; Member of the Committee on Agriculture, Fisheries and Rural Development; Substitute member of the Committee on Culture, Youth Education and the Media;

Member of the delegation for relations with Hungary; Substitute member of the delegation to the EC–Malta Joint Parliamentary Committee
Declaration Date: 18.7.89
Declared Interests: Non-Executive director of Lloyds Bank plc; United Biscuits plc; Fisons plc; Angora International
Comments: From declarations made to Companies House in London, Plumb is also a director of Nuffield Russia Trust, a charitable company formed to promote agricultural research in Russia. He is also a director of the International Agricultural Training Programme.

POLLACK, Anita Jean

D.O.B.: 3.6.46 (Australia)
Occupation: Unlisted
Constituency: Labour, London South West
Parliamentary Activities: Member of PSE; Member of the Committee on the Environment, Public Health and Consumer Protection; Member of the Committee on Women's Rights; Substitute member of the Committee on Energy, Research and Technology; Chairman of the delegation for relations with the countries of South Asia and the South Asian Association for Regional Cooperation (SAARC); Substitute member of the delegation for relations with the Member States of ASEAN and the ASEAN Interparliamentary Organisation (AIPO) and the Republic of Korea
Declaration Date: 15.7.89
Declared Interests: None listed.

PRAG, Derek

D.O.B.: 6.8.23
Occupation: Unlisted
Constituency: Conservative, Hertfordshire
Parliamentary Activities: Member of PPE; Member of the Committee on Transport and Tourism; Vice-Chairman of the Committee on Institutional Affairs; Substitute member of the Committee on Foreign Affairs and Security; Member of the Sub-Committee on Security and Disarmament; Member of the delegation for relations with Israel; Substitute member of the delegation for relations with the Member States of ASEAN and the ASEAN Inter-parliamentary Organisation (AIPO) and the Republic of Korea
Declaration Date: 14.7.89
Declared Interests: None listed.

PRICE, Peter Nicholas

D.O.B.: 19.2.42
Occupation: Solicitor (not in day-to-day practice)
Constituency: Conservative, London South East
Parliamentary Activities: Member of PPE; Member of the Committee on External Economic Relations; Member of the Committee on Budgetary Control; Substitute member of the Committee on Budgets; Member of the delegation for relations with the United States
Declaration Date: 13.7.89 (original)
Declared Interests: Consultant to Sir Owen Williams and Partners, Consulting Engineers; Consultant to the British Printing Industries Federation
Declared 26.6.90: European Parliamentary Consultant to the National Association of Local Government Officers (NALGO), London

Declared 5.8.91 (Amended): Director of Bureau Veritas Quality International Ltd
Declared 25.8.92: Consultancy with Slingsby, Farmiloe and Greenfield Solicitors
Former Business Interests: 29.6.90–1.9.92: Consultancy with Coopers and Lybrand Europe; 3.9.90–1.9.92: European consultant to Payne, Hicks and Beach, Solicitors.

PROUT, Sir Christopher J.

D.O.B.: 1.1.42
Occupation: Member of Chambers (barrister)
Constituency: Conservative, Shropshire and Stafford
Parliamentary Activities: Member of PPE; Member of the Committee on the Rules of Procedure, the Verification of Credentials and Immunities; Substitute member of the Committee on Legal Affairs and Citizens' Rights; Substitute member of the Committee on Institutional Affairs; Member of the delegation to the EC–Malta Joint Parliamentary Committee; Substitute member of the delegation to the EC–Austria Joint Parliamentary Committee
Declaration Date: 21.10.91
Declared Interests: None listed.

RAWLINGS, Patricia E.

D.O.B.: 27.1.39
Occupation: Unlisted
Constituency: Conservative, Essex South West
Parliamentary Activities: Member of PPE; Member of the Committee on Culture, Youth Education and the Media; Substitute member of the Committee on Foreign Affairs and Security; Substitute member of the Sub-Committee on Human Rights; Member of the delegation for relations with Albania, Bulgaria and Romania; Substitute member of the delegation for relations with the United States
Declaration Date: 19.7.89
Declared Interests: Director of Nigel Greenwood Inc., the English Chamber Orchestra and Music Society and Video Classification Council (British Film Board of Censors). All these directorships are unpaid
Comments: From declarations made to Companies House in London, Rawlings is also a former director of Friends of Bulgaria. She resigned this directorship on 19 August 1992.

READ, Imelda Mary

D.O.B.: 8.1.39
Occupation: Unlisted
Constituency: Labour, Leicester
Parliamentary Activities: Member of PSE; Member of the Committee on Economic and Monetary Affairs and Industrial Policy; Substitute member of the Committee on Agriculture, Fisheries and Rural Development; Substitute member of the Committee on Women's Rights; Member of the delegation for relations with the countries of South Asia and the South Asian Association for Regional Co-operation (SAARC); Substitute member of the delegation for relations with the Member States of ASEAN and the ASEAN Interparliamentary Organisation (AIPO) and the Republic of Korea
Declaration Date: 16.7.89
Declared Interests: None listed.

SCOTT-HOPKINS, Sir James

D.O.B.: 29.11.21
Occupation: Unlisted
Constituency: Conservative, Hereford and Worcester
Parliamentary Activities: Member of PPE; Member of the Committee on the Environment, Public Health and Consumer Protection; Substitute member of the Committee on Agriculture, Fisheries and Rural Development; Chairman of the delegation to the EC–Cyprus Joint Parliamentary Committee; Substitute member of the delegation for relations with the countries of South America
Declaration Date: 14.7.89
Declared Interests: None listed
Comments: From declarations made to Companies House in London, Scott-Hopkins is also a director of Greenway Housing plc, now dissolved; Greenway Social Housing Limited; the Akron Trust Limited, an organisation, now dissolved, that dealt with drug dependancy. Scott-Hopkins will be retiring from the European Parliament in June 1994.

SEAL, Barry H.

D.O.B.: 28.10.37
Occupation: Unlisted
Constituency: Labour, Yorkshire West
Parliamentary Activities: Member of PSE; Member of the Committee on Economic and Monetary Affairs and Industrial Policy; Substitute member of the Committee on Transport and Tourism; Substitute member of the Committee on Budgetary Control; Member of the delegation for relations with the United States; Substitute member of the delegation for relations with Estonia, Latvia and Lithuania
Declaration Date: 15.7.89
Declared Interests: Advisor to the National Communications Union (UK)
Comments: From declarations made to Companies House in London, Seal is also a director and secretary of Jurgair Ltd, a non-trading company formed to manage a privately owned aeroplane.

SELIGMAN, Madron Richard

D.O.B.: 10.11.18
Occupation: Unlisted
Constituency: Conservative, Sussex West
Parliamentary Activities: Member of PPE; Member of the Committee on Energy, Research and Technology; Substitute member of the Committee on the Environment, Public Health and Consumer Protection; Member of the delegation to the EC–Finland Joint Parliamentary Committee; Substitute member of the delegation for relations with Israel
Declaration Date: 14.7.89
Declared Interests: Consultant to Racal UK; Chairman of the Incinerator Company
Comments: From declarations made to Companies House in London, Seligman is also a director of Ifield Golf Club Limited. Seligman with be retiring from the European Parliament in June 1994.

SIMMONDS, Richard J.

D.O.B.: 2.8.44
Occupation: Farmer, Consultant Surveyor
Constituency: Conservative, Wight and Hampshire East
Parliamentary Activities: Member of PPE; Member of the Committee on Agriculture,

Fisheries and Rural Development; Substitute member of the Committee on the Environment, Public Health and Consumer Protection; Substitute member of the committee on Budgetary Control; Member of the delegation for relations with the countries of South America; Substitute member of the delegation for relations with the countries of South Asia and the South Asian Association for Regional Co-operation (SAARC)
Declaration Date: 15.5.90
Declared Interests: Consultant to Estée Lauder International Inc.
Comments: Until 19 January 1993 Simmonds was a consultant to Greenland Reclamation Limited.

SIMPSON, Anthony M. H.

D.O.B.: 28.10.35
Occupation: Legal Consultant
Constituency: Conservative, Northamptonshire
Parliamentary Activities: Member of PPE; Member of the Committee on Legal Affairs and Citizens' Rights; Substitute member of the Committee on Development and Co-operation; Substitute member of the Committee on the Rules of Procedure, the Verification of Credentials and Immunities; Member of the delegation for relations with the countries of Central America and Mexico
Declaration Date: 20.7.89
Declared Interests: None listed.

SIMPSON, Brian

D.O.B.: 6.2.53
Occupation: Unlisted
Constituency: Labour, Cheshire East
Parliamentary Activities: Member of PSE; Member of the Committee on Transport and Tourism; Substitute member of the Committee on Budgets; Vice-Chairman of the delegation for relations with the Republics of former Yugoslavia; Substitute member of the delegation for relations with Australia and New Zealand
Declaration Date: 13.7.89
Declared Interests: Board of Directors: Warrington Borough Transport (unpaid)
Declared 5.8.1991 (Additional): 3,000 shares in the Great Central Railway plc, UK
Comments: From declarations made to Companies House in London, Simpson is also a director of Coachlines of Warrington Limited, a coach hire company.

SMITH, Alex

D.O.B.: 2.12.43
Occupation: Unlisted
Constituency: Labour, South of Scotland
Parliamentary Activities: Member of PSE; Member of the Committee on Budgets; Substitute member of the Committee on Regional Policy, Regional Planning and Relations with Regional and Local Authorities; Member of the delegation for relations with the countries of South America; Substitute member of the delegation for relations with the Republics of the Commonwealth of Independant States (CIS)
Declaration Date: 14.7.89
Declared Interests: None listed.

SMITH, Llewellyn Thomas

D.O.B.: 16.4.44
Occupation: Unlisted
Constituency: Labour, South East Wales
Parliamentary Activities: Member of PSE; Member of the Committee on Energy, Research and Technology; Substitute member of the Committee on the Environment, Public Health and Consumer Protection; Member of the delegation to the EC–Norway Joint Parliamentary Committee; Substitute member of the delegation for relations with the member States of ASEAN and the ASEAN Inter-parliamentary Organisation (AIPO) and the Republic of Korea
Declaration Date: 16.7.89
Declared Interests: None listed
Comments: From declarations made to Companies House in London, Smith is also a director of Theatre in Education (Gwent) Ltd. Smith will be standing down from the European Parliament in June 1994.

SPENCER, Thomas Newnham Bayley

D.O.B.: 10.4.48
Occupation: Unlisted
Constituency: Conservative, Surrey West
Parliamentary Activities: Member of PPE; Member of the Committee on the Environment, Public Health and Consumer Protection; Member of the Committee on Institutional Affairs; Substitute member of the Committee on External Economic Relations; Member of the delegation to the EC–European Economic Area Joint Parliamentary Committee; Vice-Chairman of the delegation for relations with the Czech Republic and the Slovak Republic; Substitute member of the delegation to the EC–Sweden Joint Parliamentary Committee
Declaration Date: 14.7.89
Declared Interests: Occasional unpaid lectures at Oxford and other universities; Unpaid member of the management board of the European Centre for Public Affairs; Director of Public Focus Limited

STEVENS, John Christopher Courtney

D.O.B.: 23.5.55 (Washington DC, USA)
Occupation: Unlisted
Constituency: Conservative, Thames Valley
Parliamentary Activities: Member of PPE; Substitute member of the Committee on Economic and Monetary Affairs and Industrial Policy; Substitute member of the Committee on Social Affairs, Employment and the Working Environment; Member of the delegation for relations with the Republics of former Yugoslavia
Declaration Date: 21.7.89
Declared Interests: Investment Dealer with RIT Capital Partners Limited
Further Declaration 29.1.92: RIT Capital Futures Partnership, a partnership between RITCP Futures Ltd (a wholly owned indirect subsidiary of RIT Capital Partners plc) with an 80 per cent interest, and J.C. Stevens and Company Ltd, with a 20 per cent interest. The company deals in international bonds which may include bonds issued by governments within the EEC
Comments: From declarations made to Companies House in London, Stevens declared that he resigned as director of RIT Capital Partners Securities Limited on 31 March 1993.

STEVENSON, George William

D.O.B.: 30.8.38
Occupation: Unlisted
Constituency: Labour, Stafford East
Parliamentary Activities: Member of PSE; Member of the Committee on Agriculture, Fisheries and Rural Development; Substitute member of the Committee on Budgets; Member of the delegation for relations with Poland; Substitute member of the delegation for relations with the countries of South Asia and the South Asian Assosiation for Regional Cooperation (SAARC)
Declaration Date: 21.7.89
Declared Interests: None listed
Comments: From declarations made to Companies House in London, Stevenson is also a director of 55 Chester Way Limited, a land holding company. Stevenson will be standing down from the European Parliament in June 1994, and hopes to become a British MP.

STEWART, Kenneth Albert

D.O.B.: 28.7.25
Occupation: Unlisted
Constituency: Labour, Merseyside West
Parliamentary Activities: Member of PSE; Member of the Committee on Transport and Tourism; Substitute member of the Committee on the Environment, Public Health and Consumer Protection; Substitute member of the Committee on Petitions; Member of the delegation for relations with Australia and New Zealand; Substitute member of the delegation to the EC–Austria Joint Parliamentary Committee
Declaration Date: 15.7.89
Declared Interests: Member of the Union of Construction Allied Trades and Technicians.

STEWART-CLARK, Sir Jack

Vice-President of the Conservative Group
D.O.B.: 17.9.29
Occupation: Unlisted
Constituency: Conservative, Sussex East
Parliamentary Activities: Member of PPE; Member of the Committee on Culture, Youth Education and the Media; Substitute member of the Committee on the Environment, Public Health and Consumer Protection; Member of the delegation for relations with the Mashreq countries; Substitute member of the delegation to the EC–Cyprus Joint Parliamentary Committee
Declaration Date: 15.7.89
Declared Interests: Non-executive director of: Low Bonar plc, Dundee, Scotland, A.T. Kearney Limited, London, a subsidiary of A.T. Kearney Inc. Chicago (Management Consultants), Pioneer Concrete Holdings Ltd, London, a subsidiary of Pioneer Australia; manufacturers of construction industry materials; Advisor to Philips Electronics Limited, London.

TITLEY, Gary

DOB: 19.1.50
Occupation: Unlisted
Constituency: Labour, Greater Manchester West
Parliamentary Activities: Member of PSE; Member of the Committee on Foreign Affairs and Security; Substitute member of the Committee on External Economic Relations; Substitute member of the Committee on Petitions; Substitute member of the Sub-Committee on Security and Disarmament; Chairman of the delegation to the EC–Finland Joint Parliamentary Committee; Chairman of the delegation to the EC–European Economic Area Joint

Parliamentary Committee; Substitute member of the delegation for relations with the countries of South America
Declaration Date: 9.9.93
Declared Interests: Visit to Taiwan paid for by the Taiwanese Government 30 Aug–4 Sept 1993; Irregular ad-hoc support from the Graphical Print Media Union in UK.

TOMLINSON, John Edward

DOB: 1.8.39
Occupation: Unlisted
Constituency: Labour, Birmingham West
Parliamentary Activities: Member of PSE; Member of the Committee on Budgets; Member of the Committee on Budgetary Control; Substitute member of the Committee on Legal Affairs and Citizens' Rights; Member of the delegation to the EC–Sweden Joint Parliamentary Committee; Substitute member of the delegation for relations with the countries of South Asia and the South Asian Association for Regional Co-operation (SAARC)
Declaration Date: 14.7.89
Declared Interests: None listed
Comments: From declarations made to Companies House in London, Tomlinson is a director of Industry and Parliament Trust, an educational charity that aims to foster a better understanding between Parliament and industry.

TONGUE, Carole

DOB: 14.10.55 (Lausanne, Switzerland)
Occupation: Unlisted
Constituency: Labour, London East
Parliamentary Activities: Member of PSE; Member of the Committee on Social Affairs, Employment and the Working Environment; Member of the Committee on Women's Rights; Substitute member of the Committee on Economic and Monetary Affairs and Industrial Policy; Member of the delegation for relations with the Republics of the Commonwealth of Independent States (CIS); Substitute member of the delegation for relations with the United States
Declaration Date: 20.7.89
Declared Interests: None listed.
Comments: From declarations made to Companies House in London, Tongue is a director of European Movement (British Council) Ltd; the Westminster Foundation For Democracy Ltd, an interparliamentary group which advocates the Westminster model of democracy; the Centre For Alternative Industrial and Technological Studies. Tongue was also a director of the Association For Prevention Of Addiction, from which she resigned on 6 July 1992.

TURNER, Amedee Edward

D.O.B.: 26.3.29
Occupation: Barrister
Constituency: Conservative, Suffolk
Parliamentary Activities: Member of PPE; Member of the Committee on Development and Co-operation; Chairman of the Committee on Civil Liberties and Internal Affairs; Substitute member of the Committee on Energy, Research and Technology; Substitute member of the delegation for relations with the Gulf States
Declaration Date: 24.7.89
Declared Interests: None listed.

WELSH, Michael J.

D.O.B.: 22.5.42
Occupation: Unlisted
Constituency: Conservative, Lancashire Central
Parliamentary Activities: Member of PPE; Member of the Committee on Agriculture, Fisheries and Rural Development; Member of the Committee on Regional Policy, Regional Planning and Relations with Regional and Local Authorities; Substitute member of the Sub-Committee on Fisheries; Member of the delegation to the EC–Austria Joint Parliamentary Committee; Member of the delegation to the EC–European Economic Area Joint Parliamentary Committee; Substitute member of the delegation for relations with Albania, Bulgaria and Romania
Declaration Date: 14.7.89
Declared Interests: Unpaid committee member of Eaves Brook Housing Association, Preston; Welsh was also a non-executive director of BET Environmental Services plc (formerly Initial plc). He resigned on 19 November 1989.

WEST, Norman

D.O.B.: 26.11.35
Occupation: Unlisted
Constituency: Labour, Yorkshire South
Parliamentary Activities: Member of PSE; Member of the Committee on Energy, Research and Technology; Substitute member of the Committee on the Environment, Public Health and Consumer Protection; Member of the delegation for relations with the countries of Central America and Mexico; Substitute member of the delegation for relations with Albania, Bulgaria and Romania
Declaration Date: 14.7.89
Declared Interests: None listed.

WHITE, Ian

D.O.B.: 8.4.45
Occupation: Unlisted
Constituency: Labour, Bristol
Parliamentary Activities: Member of PSE; Member of the Committee on the Environment, Public Health and Consumer Protection; Substitute member of the Committee on Social Affairs, Employment and the Working Environment; Substitute member of the Committee on Institutional Affairs; Vice-Chairman of the delegation for relations with Switzerland
Declaration Date: 17.7.89
Declared Interests: Partner in McCarthy and White Solicitors, Bristol.

WILSON, Anthony Joseph

D.O.B.: 6.7.37
Occupation: Unlisted
Constituency: Labour, South Wales
Parliamentary Activities: Member of PSE; Member of the Committee on Agriculture, Fisheries and Rural Development; Member of the Committee on Petitions; Substitute member of the Committee on Social Affairs, Employment and the Working Environment; Vice-Chairman of the delegation for relations with Canada; Substitute member of the delegation for relations with the Maghreb countries and the Arab Maghreb Union
Declaration Date: 24.7.89
Declared Interests: None listed.

WYNN, Terence

D.O.B.: 27.6.46
Occupation: Unlisted
Constituency: Labour, Merseyside East
Parliamentary Activities: Member of PSE. Member of the Committee on Budgets; Member of the Committee on Budgetary Control; Substitute member of the Committee on Development and Co-operation; Substitute member of the delegation to the EC–Malta Joint Parliamentary Committee
Declaration date: 14.7.89
Declared Interests: None listed.

Section Four

Reverse Directory – MPs' and MEPs' Commercial Interests Divided into Categories, and Brief Profiles of the Lobbies

Accountants

The accountancy profession and lobby has done very well out of the short-lived booms experienced by the City in recent years. Apart from the increased demand for their services, accountancy firms have also diversified into management consultancy, investment counselling and corporate finance. Hence they are always on the prowl for clients and MPs are well-placed to provide introductions. MPs are also able to obtain useful information from government departments by putting down parliamentary written and oral questions to Ministers and securing the data privately from official sources.

Accountants are not immune from some discreet lobbying of the Treasury and Department of Trade and Industry. One of the campaigns closest to their hearts is to change the law to ensure accountancy firms only have a 'limited liability' when companies collapse. This would enable them to avoid legal action for negligence – or worse from angry creditors.

AMESS, DAVID (Basildon) – Director of Accountancy Ltd

FORMAN, NIGEL (Carshalton and Wallington) – Advisor to the Institute of Chartered Accountants

GRYLLS, SIR MICHAEL (North West Surrey) – Consultant to Association of Authorised Public Accountants

HEATH, SIR EDWARD (Old Bexley and Sidcup) – Member of Public Review Board of Arthur Andersen and Co.

HORDERN, SIR PETER (Horsham) – Consultant to Pannell, Kerr, Forster

KNOX, DAVID (Staffordshire, Moorlands) – Advisor to the Chartered Institute of Management Accountants

McGRADY, EDDIE (South Down) – Chartered Accountant

STERN, MICHAEL (Bristol North West) – Consultant to Cohen Arnold and Co., chartered accountants

TROTTER, NEVILLE (Tynemouth) – Chartered accountant; Consultant to Grant Thornton

WALLACE, JAMES (Orkney and Shetland) – Advisor to Institute of Chartered Accountants of Scotland.

Agriculture and Farmers

It has been argued that the farming lobby is one of the most successful because, except perhaps the nuclear industry, it is one of the most heavily subsidised and pampered of all trades and professions.

An example of the farming lobby's influence and guile was just after the 1992 budget. The then Chancellor, Norman Lamont, announced that all small firms with a turnover of over £500,000 would not have to pay inheritance tax. This was welcomed by small businessmen. But their pleasure turned to anger when they discovered that farmers began setting up companies and calling their land a business. As the earnings of most farms do not exceed £500,000 they were able to avoid paying inheritance tax. The small business lobby protested but all to no avail.

However the farmers do not always get their own way. They have been frustrated in recent years by not being awarded what they see as adequate compensation for the effects of the Chernobyl nuclear disaster on their land. Still, it helps when the Secretary of State for Agriculture is a farmer, as happened with Michael Jopling between 1983 and 1987.

ANCRAM, MICHAEL (Devizes) – Director and Shareholder in Portzim Ltd and a partnership in a tenanted farm

BANKS, ROBERT (Harrogate) – Owner of a small farm

BEGGS, ROY (East Antrim) – Owner of small farms and approximately 60 acres in County Antrim

BOSWELL, TIM (Daventry) – Self-employed partner in Lower Aynho Grounds Farm, the family farming business

BUDGEN, NICHOLAS (Wolverhampton South West) – Farmer in Staffordshire

CARLISLE, KENNETH (Lincoln) – Owner of a farm at Wyken Hall Farm, Stanton, Bury St Edmunds

CLAPPISON, JAMES (Hertsmere) – Farmer

CLIFTON-BROWN, GEOFFREY (Cirencester and Tewkesbury) – Director of GRCB Farming Company, a private unlimited farming company; Also owner of agricultural holdings in Norfolk and Gloucestershire

DAFIS, CYNOG (Ceredigion and Pembroke North) – Owner of 32 acres of agricultural land

HAMILTON, ARCHIE (Epsom and Ewell) – Owner of Bramley Park Farm

HEATHCOAT-AMORY, DAVID (Wells) – Farm in Scotland

HOME ROBERTSON, JOHN (East Lothian) – Owner of Paxton South Mains and Overhowden farms in Berwickshire

NICHOLSON, JAMES (Ulster*) – Farmer
HOWELL, PAUL (Norfolk*) – Farmer
HOWELL, RALPH (North Norfolk) – Owner of farms in Norfolk
JOPLING, MICHAEL (Westmorland and Lonsdale) – Farmer
MARTIN, DAVID (Portsmouth South) – Partner in ADP and E Farmers; He has a shared interest in three hectares of orchard-pasture in North Brittany
MONRO, SIR HECTOR (Dumfries) – Farmer
OPPENHEIM, PHILLIP (Amber Valley) – Owner of a 240 acre farm (no net income)
PAICE, JAMES (South East Cambridgeshire) – Director of United Framlingham Farmers Ltd
ROSS, WILLIAM (East Londonderry) – Farmer
RYDER, RICHARD (Mid Norfolk) – Shareholder in Great Bradley Farms Company
SAINSBURY, TIM (Hove) – Owner of two farms
SIMMONS, RICHARD (Wight and Hampshire East*) – Farmer
SYKES, JOHN (Scarborough) – Director and shareholder of Farnley Estates Ltd
WALDEGRAVE, WILLIAM (Bristol West) – Director and shareholder of Waldegrave Farms Ltd.

Aviation

Lobbying of and by MPs in the aviation industry is particularly vigorous because it is such a highly regulated industry. Decisions by Governments and the Civil Aviation Authority (CAA) on allocation of routes can make a real commercial difference for airlines. For example, British Airways conducted an intense lobbying campaign against a CAA report in 1984 which recommended the transfer of some of BA's most profitable routes to its rival, British Caledonian. Although Nicholas Ridley, the Transport Secretary, supported the plan, BA was able to change the Government's mind and Ridley backed down. This was achieved largely by a heavy lobbying operation of Conservative backbenchers.

Airlines only occasionally place MPs on the payroll. BA hired Michael Portillo as a consultant for a year between 1986 and 1987. British Caledonian retained Sir Robert McCrindle for several years, while Anthony Steen has represented the smaller airlines. A more common tactic by the aviation lobby is the overseas freebie (or 'facility trip' as described by BA) for MPs. This is ostensibly for them to launch and promote new flights but in many cases the free trips are used to butter up MPs.

BANKS, MATTHEW (Southport) – Consultant to Emirates Airlines
DEVA, (NIRJ Brentford and Isleworth) – Director Designate of Fitzroy Aviation Ltd
HOWARTH, ALAN (Stratford-on-Avon) – Consultant to Richard Branson and Virgin Atlantic Airways
HOWELL, PAUL (Norfolk*) – Consultant to European Regional Airlines Association
MOORHOUSE, JAMES (London South East*) – Partner in Aviation and Tourism Consultants International

* MEPs

PORTER, BARRY (Wirral South) – Consultant to Airline Maintenance Association
SEAL, BARRY (Yorkshire West*) – Director of Jurgair Ltd (non-trading company formed to manage a privately-owned aeroplane)
STEEN, ANTHONY (South Hams) – Advisor to Airlines of Great Britain (plus regular travel on a number of airlines in connection with airline work in the UK and Europe; He also receives occasional free air travel for immediate family in the UK and Europe).
THORNTON, SIR MALCOLM (Crosby) – Consultant to Singapore Airlines

Brewers and Alcohol

Like aviation, the alcohol industry can be directly affected by government decisions – and not just at budget times. Extending the licensing hours has been the main issue which has been advocated by MPs who are consultants to brewers and associations representing publicans and spirits. Others include the payment of excise duty and under-age drinking.

The 'Big Six' Brewers (Bass, Grand Metropolitan, Whitbread, Allied Lyons, Scottish and Newcastle and Courage, represented by the Brewers Society) are a very powerful lobby. Not only do some of them have MPs on the payroll but they are also closely wedded to the Conservative Establishment by making regular donations to the Party. Unlike the tobacco lobby, the brewers have preserved and protected their power, the extension of the licensing hours being their main achievement.

BURNS, SIMON (Chelmsford) – Consultant to Allied Lyons
CHANNON, PAUL (Southend West) – Shareholder in Guinness plc
COLVIN, MICHAEL (Romsey and Waterside) – Advisor to Federation of Retail Licensed Trade (Northern Ireland)
COUCHMAN, JAMES (Gillingham) – Advisor to the Gin and Vodka Association
GALE, ROGER (North Thanet) – Consultant to Scottish and Newcastle Breweries plc
JACKSON, CAROLINE (Wiltshire*) – Consultant to the Brewers Society
JONES, MARTYN (South West Clwyd) – Advisor to the Brewers Society (payment is net of tax and deductions are paid to the Labour Party at local, regional and national level)
LENNOX-BOYD, MARK (Morecambe and Lunescale) – Shareholder in The Iveagh Trustees Ltd (Guinness management company); Duke Seabridge Ltd (Guinness investment company); Guinness plc
MILLS, IAIN (Meriden) – Advisor to the Small Independent Brewers Association
RIDDICK, GRAHAM (Colne Valley) – Advisor to the Brewers Society
SIMS, ROGER (Chislehurst) – Advisor to the Scotch Whisky Association
TOWNEND, JOHN (Bridlington) – Director of J. Townend and Sons
WELLS, BOWEN (Hertford and Stortford) – Consultant to International Distillers and Vintners Ltd.

* MEPs

The City

The potential for MPs to make money in the City is enormous. If they are strategically placed, the opportunities for making easy money on the stock market are immense.

MPs have also taken advantage of the 1980s craze for takeovers and mergers which created enormous opportunities for stockbrokers, merchant banks and investment fund managers. Some MPs have acted not just as consultants but also client introductory agents and brokers. This is an activity which other MPs, even those who have consultancies, find distasteful. 'I think acting as an agent like that and taking a commission is quite wrong,' one Conservative MP told the authors.

AINSWORTH, PETER (East Surrey) – Consultant to S.G. Warburg Group plc
DAVIES, QUENTIN (Stamford) – Consultant to Natwest Securities Ltd
DONNELLY, ALAN (Tyne and Wear*) – Director of Unity Trust Bank plc
DYKES, HUGH (Harrow East) – Member of International Stock Exchange
FISHBURN, DUDLEY (Kensington) – Consultant to J.P. Morgan; Director of HFC plc
GAREL-JONES, TRISTAN (Watford) – Advisor to Union Bank of Switzerland
GRANT, SIR ANTHONY (South West Cambridgeshire) – Advisor to Barclays Bank plc
HAMILTON, ARCHIE (Epsom and Ewell) – Consultant to Merrill Lynch International Ltd
HIGGINS, TERENCE, (Worthing) – Advisor to KPMG Peat Marwick
HOWELL, DAVID (Guildford) – Advisor to Swiss Bank Corporation (UK)
JOPLING, MICHAEL (Westmorland and Lonsdale) – Consultant to Union Bank of Switzerland
KING, TOM (Bridgewater) – Director of Electra Investment Trust plc
MARSHALL, JOHN (Hendon South) – Stockbroker with London Wall Equities
MITCHELL, ANDREW (Gedling) – Advisor to Lazard Brothers and Co. Ltd
PLUMB, LORD HENRY (Cotswolds*) – Director of Lloyds Bank plc
RENTON, TIM (Mid Sussex) – Consultant to Robert Fleming Holdings Ltd
Robinson, Mark (Somerton) – Director of Leopold Joseph and Sons Ltd
SPRING, RICHARD (Bury St Edmunds) – Director of Abbey Regent Global Fund; Consultant to Xerox Furman Selz; Consultant to Malabar Capital Ltd
STANLEY, SIR JOHN (Tonbridge and Malling) – Consultant to Fidelity Investment Management Ltd
STEVENS, JOHN (Thames Valley*) – Investment dealer for RIT Capital Partners Ltd
TAPSELL, SIR PETER (East Lindsey) – Advisor to Nikko Securities Company
TAYLOR, IAN (Esher) – Consultant to Barclays De Zoete Wedd IM, Ltd
WALDEN, GEORGE (Buckingham) – Consultant to Samuel Montagu and Co. Ltd

* MEPs

Defence

For a defence company to have a well-placed MP on its books is invaluable. Contracts for military equipment awarded by the Ministry of Defence are worth millions of pounds and so backing from an influential MP with the right connections can be invaluable.

Many MPs with defence consultancies, like Sir Geoffrey Johnson-Smith, have asked rhetorical questions and made speeches in the Commons opposing cuts in defence expenditure. The real potential for a conflict of interests is if an MP with a consultancy is on the Select Committee for Defence. This is, apart from the Public Accounts Committee, perhaps the most important unit of government accountability because it monitors a budget of approximately £21 billion.

Defence Committee members are in a unique position because they receive classified material on the progress of major defence projects and confidential briefings on the failure rates of military equipment. This clearly gives them an advantage over not just fellow backbenchers but even businessmen in the trade. Very useful.

ASHDOWN, PADDY (Yeovil) – Shareholder in Westland plc
DEVA, NIRJ (Brentford and Isleworth) – Consultant to Electronic Data Systems Corporation
HAMILTON, SIR ARCHIE (Epsom and Ewall) – Consultant to Litton Industries Inc.
HASELHURST, ALAN (Saffron Walden) – Consultant to British Aerospace, Rolls Royce and Racal
MARSHALL, SIR MICHAEL (Arundel) – Consultant to British Aerospace plc; and to Williams Holdings plc
MELLOR, DAVID (Putney) – Consultant to Racal Tacticom Ltd
ONSLOW, SIR CRANLEY (Woking) – Consultant to Bristow Helicopters
PATTIE, SIR GEOFFREY (Chertsey and Walton) – Chairman and Director of GEC Marconi; and Director of Fairey Group plc
RUMBOLD, DAME ANGELA (Mitcham and Morden) – Consultant to Hunting Engineering
SELIGMAN, RICHARD (Sussex West*) – Consultant to Racal UK
STEPHEN, MICHAEL (Shoreham) – Consultant to Electronic Data Systems (UK) Ltd
WILKINSON, JOHN (Ruislip Northwood) – Consultant to Thorn EMI Electronics Ltd.

Drugs and the Chemical Industry

The pharmaceutical industry is one of the most profitable sectors of the British economy, with estimates of annual profits of £130 and £150 million on sales to the NHS. As the Government plays a direct regulatory role in the industry, lobbying and the use of MPs is very important. For the Department of Health and its appointed agents can decide which drugs doctors are permitted to use on the NHS, for which drugs to give

* MEPs

licences, levels of profit the companies make from them and how long the pharmaceutical firms can retain the exclusive marketing of the drugs.

Consequently, high quality, exclusive information from MPs can be invaluable. Most MPs with consultancies restrict themselves to ensuring the drugs industry's case is heard and asking parliamentary questions. But occasionally they will go into battle as they did in their unsuccessful attempt to stop the Government's 'limited list' of proscribed drugs in the mid-1980s.

The chemical industry is not quite so financially lucrative, but they are just as active because they are also much affected by legislation, particularly on pollution control and waste disposal.

BATISTE, SPENCER (Elmet) – Consultant to Magellan Medical Communications
BEITH, ALAN (Berwick-upon-Tweed) – Consultant to Magellan Medical Communications
BELL, STUART (Middlesbrough) – Advisor to Merck, Sharp and Dohme
BELLINGHAM, HENRY (North West Norfolk) – Director of Lothian plc
CASSIDY, BRIAN (Dorset East and Hampshire West*) – Consultant to Union Carbide NV Antwerp
COUCHMAN, JAMES (Gillingham) – Advisor to Pfizer Ltd
CUNNINGHAM, JOHN (Copeland) – Advisor to Albright and Wilson UK; and to Hays Chemicals
GALE, ROGER (North Thanet) – Consultant to Rhone Poulenc Rorer; and to Organon UK Ltd
GOODSON-WICKES, CHARLES (Wimbledon) – Advisor to Upjohn Ltd
GRYLLS, SIR MICHAEL (North West Surrey) – Consultant to Sanofi Winthrop Ltd
HASELHURST, ALAN (Saffron Walden) – Advisor to Albright and Wilson UK Ltd
JACKSON, CAROLINE (Wiltshire*) – Consultant to Merck, Sharp and Dohme
MCNAIR-WILSON, SIR PATRICK (New Forest) – Consultant to Rhone Poulenc plc
PLUMB, LORD HENRY (Cotswolds*) – Director of Fisons plc
SHEERMAN, BARRY (Huddersfield) – Consultant to Monsanto Europe plc
SMITH, SIR DUDLEY (Warwick and Leamington) – Consultant to SmithKline Beecham plc; and to F.H. Faulding UK Ltd.

Electronics and Information Technology

Regulated by the Department of Trade and Industry, the telecommunications and electronics business is increasingly competitive. The growing rivalry between British Telecom and Mercury Communications, wholly owned by Cable and Wireless plc, has made decisions by the DTI potentially crucial to their business. For the DTI award licences to companies worth millions in potential sales revenue. For example, in 1989 Lord Young, Trade and Industry Secretary, decided that Mercury should have a licence to act as Personal Communication Network operators (i.e. sell mobile phones).

* MEPs

This was bitterly resented by BT who complained of 'favouritism'. The DTI also monitors competition policy and ownership very closely. Consequently, lobbying is very important in the new hi-tech industry.

BUTCHER, JOHN (Coventry South West) – Chairman and Director of Texas Instruments Ltd; Chairman and Director of Images Soft Ltd
CASSIDY, BRIAN (Dorset East and Hampshire West*) – Director of Nynex UK Telephone and Cable Holding Company Ltd; Advisor to Nynex Network Systems
COOMBS, SIMON (Swindon) – Consultant to British Telecom
GRYLLS, SIR MICHAEL (North West Surrey) – Consultant to Charter Consolidated
HORDERN, SIR PETER (Horsham) – Director of T.R. Technology plc
MARSHALL, SIR MICHAEL (Arundel) – Consultant to Cable and Wireless plc; and to General Offshore Corporation
ONSLOW, SIR CRANLEY (Woking) – Chairman and Director of Redifon Holdings Ltd; Consultant to Generics Holdings Corporation
PORTER, BARRY (Wirral South) – Parliamentary Advisor to Wang (UK) Ltd
ROBINSON, GEOFFREY (Coventry North West) – Director and shareholder of Transfer Technology Group plc
SELIGMAN, RICHARD (Sussex West*) – Consultant to Racal UK
STAFFORD-CLARK, SIR JACK (Sussex East*) – Advisor to Phillips Electronics Ltd.

Engineering

In the harsh new world of the service economy and hi-tech, manufacturing industry has not found the Government very responsive to their needs. The best they can hope for are grants from the Department of Trade and Industry. For in recent years most Ministers believe industrial and engineering companies should be left alone in the market place, unfettered by government regulation. As one former Secretary of State for Trade and Industry famously commented when he first arrived in the office: 'What is this Department for?' That has changed to some extent under Michael Heseltine, but any MP lobbying Whitehall for an engineering or industrial company is in for a hard time.

BIFFEN, JOHN (North Shropshire) – Director of Glynwed International plc; and of J. Bibby and Sons plc, a subsidiary of Barlow Rand
BLACKBURN, JOHN (Dudley West) – Director and shareholder of Shoalway Engineering Ltd (non-remunerated)
COOMBS, ANTHONY (Wyre Forest) – Shareholder in Metalrax Holdings plc
DEVA, NIRJ (Brentford and Isleworth) – Consultant to KHD (GB) Ltd; and to TECHPRO Ltd

* MEPs

DICKENS, GEOFFREY (Littleborough and Saddleworth) – Director of Cunnington and Cooper Ltd and FEL Ltd
FOWLER, SIR NORMAN (Sutton Goldfield) – Director of Evered Bardon plc
FRENCH, DOUGLAS (Gloucester) – Director and shareholder of P.W. Merkle Ltd
KINNOCK, NEIL (Islwyn) – Director of Caparo plc
PATTIE, SIR GEOFFREY (Chertsey and Walton) – Consultant to Knight Piesold
SHEPHERD, COLIN (Hereford) – Director of Haigh Group Ltd; and Haigh Engineering Co. Ltd
THURNHAM, PETER (Bolton North East) – Director of Wathes Holdings Ltd and subsidiary companies
WILLETTS, DAVID (Havants) – Director of TI Group plc.

Food

One of the most vigorous and impassioned bouts of lobbying of recent years (on both sides of the argument) has been over Sunday shopping. For one MP, Graham Bright, it became rather embarrassing as he was a consultant to Safeway Food Stores who breached Sunday trading laws. It did not help that he was also Parliamentary Private Secretary to the Prime Minister, John Major.

The Sugar lobby has been the most active in recent years. At one stage in 1990 Tate and Lyle retained two Tory MPs, Sir William Clark and David Davis, as consultants and Peter Walker, former Agriculture Secretary, as a director. Tate and Lyle were also able to call on Tory MP Michael Shersby, who was the parliamentary advisor to the Sugar Bureau.

AINSWORTH, PETER (East Surrey) – Director of JLI Group plc
BRIGHT, GRAHAM (Luton South) – Chairman and Director of Cumberland Foods Ltd; and of Dietary Foods Ltd; Advisor to Safeway Food Stores Ltd
BURNS, SIMON (Chelmsford) – Consultant to Mc Donalds
FENNER, DAME PEGGY (Medway) – Parliamentary and Legislative Consultant to British Frozen Food Federation (includes a lunch in the House of Commons!)
FOX, SIR MARCUS (Shipley) – Director of Yorkshire Food Group plc
JACKSON, CAROLINE (Wiltshire*) – Consultant to the Mars Company
PLUMB, LORD HENRY (Cotswolds*) – Director of United Biscuits plc
SAINSBURY, TIM (Hove) – Shareholder of J. Sainsbury plc
SHEPHERD, RICHARD (Aldridge–Brownhills) – Director of Partridges of Sloane Street Ltd and Shepherd Foods (London) Ltd
SHERSBY, MICHAEL (Uxbridge) – Advisor to the Sugar Bureau
SMITH, SIR DUDLEY (Warwick and Leamington) – Consultant to the Procordia Group of Sweden
TAYLOR, SIR TEDDY (Southend East) – Director of Shepherd Foods (London) Ltd
WIGGIN, JERRY (Weston-Super-Mare) – Consultant to British Sugar.

* MEPs

Foreign Affairs

MPs have always looked abroad for lucrative consultancies, one-off payments and free holidays. In turn, foreign agencies and companies see it as a useful investment to have well-placed backbenchers on their pay-roll. The Arab lobby is particularly active and influential. Its most notorious member was the former Tory MP John Browne. In 1990 he was forced to resign after an inquiry found he had not declared some of his commercial clients, largely from the Middle East (he was paid £57,000 in 1982 for producing one report for the Saudi Arabian Monetary Agency).

BAKER, KENNETH (Mole Valley) – Director of Torrey Investments Inc.
BANKS, MATTHEW (Southport) – Consultant to Sheikh Ahmed
BIN SAEED AL-MAKTOUM
CARRINGTON, MATTHEW (Fulham) – Advisor to the Saudi International Bank
DEVA, NIRJ (Brentford and Isleworth) – Director of Ceylon and Foreign Trades Ltd; Consultant to Cyprus Turkish Association
EMERY, SIR PETER (Honiton) – Shareholder in Axion Ltd (advises on joint venture projects)
HEATH, SIR EDWARD (Old Bexley and Sidcup) – Advisor to the China Investment and Development Fund Ltd and to Kleinwort Benson China Management Ltd
MACLENNAN, ROBERT (Caithness and Sutherland) – Director of Atlantic Tele-Network Inc
MELLOR, DAVID (Putney) – Consultant to the Middle East Broadcasting Centre; Investcorp; and GL Holdings (Bermuda) Ltd
SIMMONDS, RICHARD (Wight and Hampshire East*) – Consultant to Estée Lauder International Inc.
STEPHEN, MICHAEL (Shoreham) – Consultant to the Cyprus Turkish Association
TAYLOR, IAN (Esher) – Director of United Healthcare Finance Company (USA); and Meadowbrook Healthcare Services Inc (USA).

Insurance

The insurance companies comprise one of the most powerful and influential sectors of the economy. In 1992 the total premium income of the top 'Non-Life' insurance giants amounted to £18.9 billion. For the top ten Life corporations the premium income was £19.1 billion. In the total Life Insurance Fund there is about £130 billion. Consequently, these companies are sitting on unparalleled cash for investment purposes. As they also control the Pension Funds, their financial and corporate power is immense. 'They could be more powerful than the Cabinet,' the former Prime Minister Harold Wilson once told the author Anthony Sampson.

* MEPs

For many years the insurance industry has been a curiously private and self-contained world. But they have become more assertive recently, particularly when investigating companies in which they are investors. They have also been lobbying the Treasury over permanent health insurance and private pension schemes.

BUTTERFILL, JOHN (Bournemouth West) – Consultant to British Insurance and Investment Brokers Association
FOX, SIR MARCUS (Shipley) – Consultant to Standard Life
GILBERT, JOHN (Dudley East) – International Advisor to Jardine Insurance Brokers International Ltd
GILLAN, CHERYL (Chesham and Amersham) – Director of Bankers Insurance Co. Ltd
GRANT, SIR ANTHONY (South West Cambridgeshire) – Advisor to Bowring UK Ltd
GREENWAY, JOHN (Ryedale) – Director and shareholder of Greenway Middleton and Co. Ltd (insurance brokers); Consultant to Institute of Insurance Brokers
HOWELL, DAVID (Guildford) – Director of Jardine Insurance Brokers plc
JENKIN, BERNARD (Colchester North) – Advisor to the Legal and General Group plc
JOHNSON-SMITH, SIR GEOFFREY (Wealden) – Consultant to Eagle Star Group
JONES, GWILYM (Cardiff North) – Director of Bowring Wales Ltd
TAYLOR, IAN (Esher) – Consultant to the Commercial Union plc
TAYLOR, SIR TEDDY (Southend East) – Director of Anmsvar Insurance Company (UK branch of Temperance Insurance Co. based in Sweden)
TROTTER, NEVILLE (Tynemouth) – Consultant to the Bowring Group.

Labour MPs

BELL, STUART (Middlesbrough) – Advisor to Merck, Sharp and Dohme
BOYES, ROLAND (Houghton and Washington) – Advisor to the Retail Motor industry
BRAY, JEREMY (Motherwell South) – Consultant to Society of Telecom Executives
CLWYD, ANN (Cynon Valley) – Advisor to Society of Telecom Executives
CUNNINGHAM, JOHN (Copeland) – Advisor to Albright and Wilson (UK) Ltd; Leather Chemicals; and Centurion Press Ltd
FISHER, MARK (Stoke-on-Trent) – Consultant to the National Union of Teachers
GILBERT, JOHN (Dudley East) – Director of John Gilbert and Associates; Edmund Nuttall Ltd; Kyle Stewart Ltd; Advisor to Jardine Insurance Brokers International Ltd
GOLDING, LLIN (Newcastle-under-Lyme) – Advisor to National Market Traders Association
HOEY, KATE (Vauxhall) – Member of Advisory Board of London Weekend Television
HOGG, NORMAN (Cumbernauld and Kilsyth) – Director of Kelvin Central Buses Ltd;

Consultant to National and Local Government Officers Association; Advisor to the Bus and Coach Council
JANNER, GREVILLE (Leicester West) – Director of Ladbroke plc; Director and shareholder of JSB Group
JONES, BARRY (Alyn and Deeside) – Consultant to National Union of Teachers
MOWLAM, MARJORIE (Redcar) – Consultant to Banking, Insurance and Finance Union
MURPHY, PAUL (Torfaen) – Consultant to National Association of Teachers in Further and Higher Education
OAKES, GORDON (Halton) – Consultant to 3M United Kingdom Ltd
RAYNSFORD, NICK (Greenwich) – Director of Raynsford, Dallison Associates Ltd
ROBERTSON, GEORGE (Hamilton) – Advisor to Halton–Gill Associates
ROBINSON, GEOFFREY (Coventry North West) – Director of Agie UK Ltd; Director and shareholder of Transfer Technology Group plc
SNAPE, PETER (West Bromwich East) – Director of West Midlands Travel plc
STRAW, JACK (Blackburn) – Advisor to the Association of University Teachers
WILLIAMS, ALAN (Swansea West) – Advisor to the Institute of Plant Engineers.

Lawyers

The legal profession is one of the most disorganised and incoherent lobbies, the main reason being the mutual mistrust and often antagonism between solicitors and barristers. The classic example was the proposal to allow solicitors to stand at the bar without the use of a barrister. This was bitterly opposed by the barristers but they were defeated, although solicitors can act on their own in some cases. There was another row when solicitors wanted to advertise. But again the barristers lost. Consequently, the lawyer lobby is quite weak. On the other hand, the fact that there are 47 MPs who are solicitors and barristers is a potential sleeping army. But perhaps the most overriding characteristic of MPs as lawyers is how they take advantage of the Commons' late start to the day by using the mornings to carry on their business.

ALEXANDER, RICHARD (Newark) – Solicitor
ANDERSON, DONALD (Swansea East) – Barrister
ARBUTHNOT, JAMES (Wanstead and Woodford) – Barrister (non-practising)
ASHBY, DAVID (North West Leicestershire) – Barrister
BAKER, NICHOLAS (North Dorset) – Solicitor, partner in Frere Cholmeley
BATISTE, SPENCER (Elmet) – Solicitor, partner in Dibb Lupton Broomhead
BELL, STUART (Middlesbrough) – Barrister
BELLINGHAM, HENRY (North West Norfolk) – Barrister
BERMINGHAM, GERALD (St Helens South) – Barrister

BLAIR, TONY (Sedgefield) – Barrister (no longer practising)
BOATENG, PAUL (Brent South) – Barrister
BONSOR, SIR NICHOLAS (Upminster) – Barrister, Inner Temple (non-practising)
BOOTH, HARTLEY (Finchley) – Solicitor, consultant to Berwin Leighton
BUDGEN, NICHOLAS (Wolverhampton South West) – Barrister (practising in the Midlands and London)
BUTLER, PETER (Milton Keynes North East) – Solicitor, consultant with Linnells
CAMPBELL, MENZIES (North East Fife) – Queen's Counsel
CARLILE, ALEX (Montgomery) – Queen's Counsel
CASH, WILLIAM (Stafford) – Solicitor, William Cash and Co.
CLAPPISON, JAMES (Hertsmere) – Barrister
CORSTON, JEAN (Bristol East) – Barrister
DARLING, ALISTAIR (Edinburgh Central) – Advocate
DAVIES, DENZIL (Llanelli) – Barrister
DEVLIN, TIM (Stockton South) – Barrister (non-practising)
DEWAR, DONALD (Glasgow, Garscadden) – Solicitor, partner of Ross Harper and Murphy
DOUGLAS-HAMILTON, LORD JAMES (Edinburgh West) – Scots advocate
DYKES, HUGH (Harrow East) – Consultant to Rogers and Wells (US law firm)
EVANS, JONATHAN (Brecon and Radnor) – Solicitor, Leo Abse and Cohen
EVANS, ROGER (Monmouth) – Barrister
FAIRBAIRN, SIR NICHOLAS (Perth and Kinross) – Queen's Counsel
FISHBURN, DUDLEY (Kensington) – Consultant to Sheerman and Sterling (US law firm)
FRASER, JOHN (Norwood) – Solicitor, Lewis Silkin
FRENCH, DOUGLAS (Gloucester) – Barrister (non-practising)
GARNIER, EDWARD (Harborough) – Barrister
GOODSON-WICKES, CHARLES (Wimbledon) – Barrister (non-practising)
HAMILTON, NEIL (Tatton) – Barrister (does not practise)
HAXES, JERRY (Harlow) – Barrister
HEALD, OLIVER (North Hertfordshire) – Barrister (practising in Cambridge and London)
HOON, GEOFFREY (Derbyshire*) – Barrister
HOWARD, MICHAEL (Folkestone and Hythe) – Queen's Counsel (ceased practising on 2 September 1985)
HUGHES, SIMON (Southwark and Bermondsey) – Barrister
HUNT, DAVID (Wirral West) – Solicitor, partner in Beachcroft Stanleys
INGLEWOOD, LORD WILLIAM (Cumbria and Lancashire North*) – Barrister
JANNER, GREVILLE (Leicester West) – Queen's Counsel
JONES, IEUAN (Ynys Mon) – Solicitor
KELLETT-BOWMAN, DAME ELAINE (Lancaster) – Barrister (no longer practising)

* MEPs

KIRKHOPE, TIMOTHY (Leeds North East) – Solicitor, consultant with R.V. Clerey and Co.
LAWRENCE, SIR IVAN (Burton) – Queen's Counsel
LEIGH, EDWARD (Gainsborough and Horncastle) – Barrister (non-practising)
LLWYD, ELFYN (Meirionnydd Nant Conwy) – Solicitor, consultant with Guthrie, Jones and Jones
LYELL, SIR NICHOLAS (Mid Bedfordshire) – Queen's Counsel
MACLENNAN, ROBERT (Caithness and Sutherland) – Barrister, employed by Britannica as a consultant
MALONE, GERALD (Winchester) – Solicitor. Consultant to three law firms: Norton Rose, Peterkins and McGrigor Donald
McINTOSH, ANN (Essex North East*) – Advocate (non-practising)
MORRIS, JOHN (Aberavon) – Queen's Counsel
NICHOLLS, PATRICK (Teignbridge) – Solicitor, partner in Dunn and Baker
OAKES, GORDON (Halton) – Solicitor (not in practice)
O'BRIEN, MICHAEL (North Warwickshire) – Self-employed solicitor in criminal law (non-practising)
PORTER, BARRY (Wirral South) – Solicitor with Fanshaw, Porter and Hazelhurst
POWELL, WILLIAM (Corby) – Barrister (non-practising)
PRICE, PETER (London South East*) – Solicitor, consultant with Slingsby, Farmiloe and Greenfield
PROUT, SIR CHRISTOPHER (Shropshire and Stafford*) – Member of Chambers
SPROAT, IAIN (Harwich) – Consultant to Wragge and Co.
STEEN, ANTHONY (South Hams) – Barrister (non-practising)
STREETER, GARY (Plymouth Sutton) – Solicitor, partner at Foot and Bowden
SUMBERG, DAVID (Bury South) – Solicitor, consultant to Jacques and Lewis
SWEENEY, WALTER (Vale of Glamorgan) – Solicitor, consultant with Gordon Kemp and Co.
TEMPLE-MORRIS, PETER (Leominster) – Solicitor and consultant to Payne Hicks Beach
THOMASON, ROY (Bromsgrove) – Consultant to Dyson, Bell, Martin, solicitors and parliamentary agents
TURNER, AMEDEE EDWARD (Suffolk*) – Barrister
VAZ, KEITH (Leicester East) – Barrister
WHITE, IAN (Bristol*) – Solicitor with McCarthy and White

Lloyd's – Members of the Lloyd's Insurance Market

Despite being beset by allegations of incompetence and fraud, Lloyd's of London, one of the world's biggest insurance markets, remains blissfully free of Government regulation.

* MEPs

This has been largely due to MPs who are Lloyd's Members ambushing any attempt at legislation. In 1980 the Society of Lloyd's pre-empted the prospect of regulation by introducing their own private Bill. One of the sponsors was Sir Anthony Royle, then a Tory MP and a director of a major insurance broking firm at Lloyd's, who said: 'It is right that, where possible, our major institutions should police themselves and not involve the government.'

More recently, the 44 MPs who are Lloyd's Members, including four Cabinet Ministers, faced a direct conflict of interests over the 1992 Finance Bill. Key clauses of that Act provided tax assistance to Members yet the MPs were allowed to vote for those measures.

This ability to avoid regulation and for MPs to use their position to look after their own interests has been the benchmark for Lloyd's, despite the chaos and debts.

The following are Lloyd's Members:

ALLASON, RUPERT (Torbay)
ARBUTHNOT, JAMES (Wanstead and Woodford)
ASHBY, DAVID (North-West Leicestershire)
BAKER, NICHOLAS (North Dorset)
BATISTE, SPENCER (Elmet)
BELLINGHAM, HENRY (North West Norfolk)
BETHELL, LORD NICHOLAS (London North West*)
BODY, SIR RICHARD (Holland with Boston)
BONSOR, SIR NICHOLAS (Upminster)
BOOTH, HARTLEY (Finchley)
BROOKE, PETER (City of London and Westminster South)
CHURCHILL, WINSTON (Davyhulme)
CLAPPISON, JAMES (Hertsmere)
COLVIN, MICHAEL (Romsey and Waterside)
EVENNETT, DAVID (Erith and Crayford)
FABER, DAVID (Westbury)
FOWLER, SIR NORMAN (Sutton Coldfield)
GOODLAD ALASTAIR, (Eddisbury)
HAMILTON, ARCHIE (Epsom and Ewell)
HEATH, SIR EDWARD (Old Bexley and Sidcup)
HOWARTH, ALAN (Startford-on-Avon)
HOWELL, RALPH (North Norfolk)
HUNT, DAVID (Wirral West)
JACKSON, CHRISTOPHER (Kent East*)
JOPLING, MICHAEL (Westmorland and Lonsdale)
KELLETT-BOWMAN, DAME ELAINE (Lancaster)
KNAPMAN, ROGER (Stroud)
LANG, IAN (Galloway and Upper Nithsdale)

* MEPs

LLOYD, PETER (Fareham)
LYELL, SIR NICHOLAS (Mid Bedfordshire)
MARLAND, PAUL (West Gloucestershire)
MARSHALL, SIR MICHAEL (Arundel)
NEEDHAM, RICHARD (North Wiltshire)
OPPENHEIM, PHILLIP (Amber Valley)
PAWSEY, JAMES (Rugby and Kenilworth)
RENTON, TIMOTHY (Mid Sussex)
RIDDICK, GRAHAM (Colne Valley)
SHEPHERD, RICHARD (Aldridge–Brownhills)
STEEN, ANTHONY (South Hams)
TOWNEND, JOHN (Bridlington)
TREDINNICK, DAVID (Bosworth)
VAUGHAN, SIR GERARD (Reading East)
VIGGERS, PETER (Gosport)
WHEELER, SIR JOHN (Westminster North)

Management Consultants

Management consultancy was one of the fastest growing businesses of the 1980s. By the end of the decade, total revenue for these companies had risen from about £100 million to £463 million. The Government itself contributed to their growth by contracting out work from the civil service and the full-scale privatisation of industry. And so, as potential clients for management consultants were Government departments, MPs are important assets in helping to secure valuable Whitehall contacts.

Accountancy firms also specialise in management consultancy. That was why in 1988 Tim Smith, a Tory MP and consultant to Price Waterhouse, asked no less than eighteen government departments parliamentary questions for detailed information on management consultancy contracts. The answers disclosed the nature of the contracts, the successful companies, their assignments and the government expenditure involved.

This is not so much a lobby but a group of MPs advising clients and searching for new business and customers.

BANKS, MATTHEW (Southport) – Director of LBJ Ltd
BROWNING, ANGELA (Tiverton) – Self-employed management consultant
ELLETSON, HAROLD (Blackpool North) – Director of Harold Elletson Ltd
FRENCH, DOUGLAS (Gloucester) – Consultant to Alexander Consulting Group
HAYES, JERRY (Harlow) – Consultant to Hornagold and Hills
KELLETT-BOWMAN, EDWARD (Hampshire Central*) – Freelance Management Consultant
PORTER, BARRY (Wirral South) – Director of Impac plc

* MEPs

SMITH, SIR DUDLEY (Warwick and Leamington) – Partner in Dudley Smith Management Consultancy
SPINK, ROBERT (Castle Point) – Self-employed Management Consultant
STEEN, ANTHONY (South Hams) – Advisor to Waggett and Co.
STEWART-CLARK, SIR JACK (Sussex East*) – Director of A.T. Kearney Ltd, Subsidiary of A.T. Kearney Inc. of Chicago
TAYLOR, IAN (Esher) – Consultant to A.T. Hudson and Co. Ltd

The Media – Advertising, Television and Marketing

MPs love being on television. But they also seem to like advising and lobbying for ITV and cable companies. MPs retained by ITV firms tend to be vociferous when the franchises become available. They were particularly critical of the 1991 franchise system of the highest bidder. But otherwise any lobbying is very low key.

The cable TV MPs are a different breed. They are much more assertive in representing their clients' interest at the Home Office, largely because it is an emerging and growing industry. During the 1990 Broadcasting Bill David Mellor, the Minister responsible, acknowledged the behind-the-scenes lobbying by MPs Sir Peter Blaker, Peter Viggers and Ray Whitney, all of whom were directors of cable TV companies. They asked him 'to reconsider some aspects of the bill' which might damage 'some of the investment that is ready to carry the cable revolution forward'. Mellor agreed and 'the Industry' was placated.

AMESS, DAVID (Basildon) – Consultant to GGK
BANKS, ROBERT (Harrogate) – Director of foote, Cone and Belding
BOOTH, HARTLEY (Finchley) – Director of Canford Audio plc
BROWNING, ANGELA (Tiverton) – Advisor to Institute of Sales and Marketing Management
COE, SEBASTIAN (Falmouth and Camborne) – Director of Comodale Ltd
COLVIN, MICHAEL (Romsey and Waterside) – Advisor to Meridian Broadcasting Ltd
DEVA, NIRJ (Brentford and Isleworth) – Director of First European Communications Corporation Ltd (advertising)
FABRICANT, MICHAEL (Mid Staffordshire) – Technical and Marketing Consultant to the BBC
FOWLER, SIR NORMAN (Sutton Coldfield) – Director of Midland Independent Newspapers Ltd
GREENWAY, JOHN (Ryedale) – Advisor to Yorkshire Television plc
HOEY, KATE (Vauxhall) – Member of the advisory board of London Weekend Television
LENNOX-BOYD, Mark (Morecombe and Lunesdale) – Shareholder in Mintel International Group Ltd

* MEPs

MALONE, GERALD (Winchester) – Consultant to Grampian Television plc
MOATE, POGER (Faversham) – Consultant for Woollams, Moira, Gaskin, O'Malley
STEEL, SIR DAVID (Tweedale, Ettrick and Lauderdale) – Director of Border Television
WILKINSON, JOHN (Ruislip Northwood) – Director, Chairman and shareholder of European Marketing Consultants Communications Ltd; Director of the International Partnership Group Inc

Oil

The Government's relationship with the oil lobby has usually been determined by the huge significance of North Sea oil. In the 1980s the subsequent revenue was crucial and so the Government was dependent on financing and technology from the 'Seven Sisters'. For the oil corporations the target was the Department of Energy which granted licences to develop the North Sea, and the Treasury over the petroleum revenue tax.

Potentially, the power and wealth of the foreign oil companies is enormous. In 1991, Shell's revenue was over £59 billion, British Petroleum accumulated £41 billion and Esso £5.4 billion. This is comparable even to national governments. As Tony Benn, the former Secretary of State for Energy, reflected: 'I learned that relations between governments and oil companies were rather like treaty negotiations.'

DUNCAN, ALAN (Rutland and Melton) – Owner of Harcourt Consultants, trading as an oil broker
HORDERN, SIR PETER (Horsham) – Director of Fina plc
MALONE, GERALD (Winchester) – Consultant to Texaco Ltd
MONTGOMERY, SIR FERGUS (Altrincham and Sale) – Director of Select Resources plc
OTTAWAY, RICHARD (Croydon South) – Director of Coastal States Holdings (UK) Ltd
STEEL, SIR DAVID (Tweedale, Ettrick and Lauderdale) – Director of Heritage Oil and Gas Ltd
SYKES, JOHN (Scarborough) – Director of Shaws Petroleum Ltd
TWIN, IAN (Edmonton) – Consultant to Atlantic Richfield Corporation (UK)

Political and Parliamentary Lobbying Companies

Political and parliamentary lobbying is one of the fastest growing industries. There are over 50 lobbying companies with an estimated turnover of over £10 million and business is increasingly retaining political consultancies for 'Government Work'. Essentially, they act as conduits between the worlds of commerce and government.

They provide a variety of services for their clients. They lobby Ministers and officials in Government departments on specific issues, provide research material, promote the client through the media and offer strategic advice. And what better way of getting on the inside track than placing an MP on the payroll?

One of the most controversial aspects of the relationship between MPs and lobbying firms are secret commission fees. These have been paid when a backbencher introduces new clients. Ian Greer Associates paid three such fees to Sir Michael Grylls and also payments to two other MPs whom the lobbyist refused to name. None of these payments was declared.

CAMPBELL, MENZIES (North East Fife) – Director of the Westminster Communications Group

CASSIDY, BRIAN (Dorset East and Hampshire West*) – Consultant to Rowland Public Affairs

COLLINS, KENNETH (Strathclyde East*) – Consultant to European Public Policy Advisors

CORMACK, PATRICK (South Staffordshire) – Consultant to Parliamentary Communications Ltd

DAVIES, QUENTIN (Stamford and Spalding) – Director of Dewe Rogerson Consultants Ltd

DEVA, NIRJ (Brentford and Isleworth) – Director of Parliamentary and Public Affairs International Ltd

FRY, PETER (Wellingborough) – Consultant to Westminster Advisors Ltd

GARDINER, SIR GEORGE (Reigate) – Public Affairs Consultant

GRYLLS, SIR MICHAEL (North West Surrey) – Introduces clients for Ian Greer Associates and in return has received commission payments. He did not declare those clients.

HASELHURST, ALAN (Saffron Walden) – Consultant to Barrington Jay and Company

JACKSON, CAROLINE (Wiltshire*) – Consultant to Market Access International

JACKSON, CHRISTOPHER (Kent East*) – Director of Westminster Communications Ltd

JOPLING, MICHAEL (Westmorland and Lonsdale) – Consultant to Hill and Knowlton (UK) Ltd

McINTOSH, ANN (Essex North East*) – European Advisor to Hill and Knowlton

McMILLAN-SCOTT, EDWARD (York*) – Public Affairs Consultant

MELLOR, DAVID (Putney) – Consultant to Shandwick plc

MOORHOUSE, JAMES (London South East*) – Consultant to Raitt, Orr and Associates; Partner of Advocacy Partnership (public affairs consultants)

PATTERSON, GEORGE (Kent West*) – Consultant to Countrywide Political Communications Ltd

* MEPs

RUMBOLD, DAME ANGELA (Mitcham and Morden) – Executive Director of Decision Makers Ltd
SPEED, SIR KEITH (Ashford) – Director and shareholder of Westminster Communications Ltd
STEPHEN, MICHAEL (Shoreham) – Consultant and shareholder of Parliamentary and Public Affairs International Ltd
TAYLOR, ANN (Dewsbury) – Director of the Westminster Communications Group Ltd
THORNTON, SIR MALCOLM (Crosby) – Director of Keene Public Affairs Consultants Ltd; Director of MRT Westminster Consultancy Services Ltd
WINTERTON, NICHOLAS (Macclesfield) – Director of the Government Relations Unit

Private Business Consultancy Firms

One device that some MPs employ when they start cultivating commercial interests is to set up their own private limited companies. These firms do not own or make anything. Usually there are one or two other directors, often the wife or husband, and shareholders. They are purely a front and channel for clients.

This is not such a problem if the MPs declare their clients. But many of them do not. One reason why the MP John Browne fell from grace was that he did not declare all the clients of his company, Falcon Finance Management Ltd. Some MPs do not even declare a company. Mark Wolfson merely states 'Business Consultant', a meaningless disclosure.

Most MPs who are consultants to lobbying companies now declare their clients. There is no reason why the same should not apply to private or family consultancy companies.

EVANS, DAVID (Welwyn Hatfield) – Director and shareholder of Leapsquare Ltd
GILBERT, JOHN (Dudley East) – Shareholder in John Gilbert and Associates
GILLAN, CHERYL (Chesham and Amersham) – Director and Joint Owner of Leeming Consultants Ltd
GOODSON-WICKES, CHARLES (Wimbledon) – Director of Medarc Ltd
GORST, JOHN (Hendon North) – Director of John Gorst and Associates
GRYLLS, SIR MICHAEL (North West Survey) – Director of Armstrong Consulting Services Ltd
MORRIS, MICHAEL (Northampton South) – Director of Modern Personnel Ltd
TAYLOR, IAN (Esher) – Director of Fentiman Consultants Ltd
WALDEN, GEORGE (Buckingham) – Director of Ashchurch Enterprises
WALKER, BILL (North Tayside) – Chairman and director of Walker Associates
WOLFSON, MARK (Sevenoaks) – Business Consultant. Does not declare any clients.

Privatisation

Privatisation has created more business and financial opportunities for MPs than anything else. The contracts, franchises, clients and commissions resulting from the selling off of state industries have proved an irresistible temptation for backbenchers keen on cultivating lucrative bits on the side, so to speak.

For a company to win the franchise or contract or for a merchant bank or stockbroker to be appointed as advisors on the privatisation, it is obviously a huge advantage to have inside government information. Hence the MP on the payroll.

Then there are the MPs who become consultants or directors of companies which have just been privatised, something which some of them had enthusiastically advocated in the Commons or in the media.

ASPINWALL, JACK (Wansdyke) – Consultant to British Gas plc
BOWDEN, ANDREW (Brighton Kemptown) – Consultant to Southern Water plc
BRUCE, IAN (South Dorset) – Consultant to Southern Electricity plc
CAMPBELL, MENZIES (North East Fife) – Consultant to British Gas plc and British Railways Board
FOWLER, SIR NORMAN (Sutton Coldfield) – Director of National Freight Corporation (NFC) plc
FOX, SIR MARCUS (Shipley) – Consultant to British Gas plc
GALLIE, PHILIP (Ayr) – Parliamentary Liaison Consultant to Scottish Power plc (he also has use of a company car and private health care provided by Scottish Power plc)
GAREL-JONES, TRISTAN (Watford) – Consultant to Britsh Gas plc
GOODSON-WICKES, CHARLES (Wimbledon) – Director of Nestor plc
HARGREAVES, ANDREW (Birmingham Hall Green) – Consultant to Midlands Electricity plc
HASELHURST, ALAN (Saffron Walden) – Consultant to National Power plc
HAWKINS, NICHOLAS (Blackpool South) – Consultant to North West Water plc (unpaid)
JOPLING, MICHAEL (Westmorland) Consultant to Railtrack
RATHBONE, TIM (Lewes) – Consultant to South East Electricity Board (SEEBOARD) plc
SHAW, SIR GILES (Pudsey) – Director of Yorkshire Water plc and British Steel plc
SPEED, SIR KEITH (Ashford) – Consultant to British Gas plc
THORNTON, SIR MALCOLM (Crosby) – Consultant to North West Water plc
WALKER, BILL (North Tayside) – Director of Stagecoach International Services Ltd
WILLETTS, DAVID (Havants) – Director of Healthcall UK Ltd

Property

BOWDEN, ANDREW (Brighton) – Consultant to Wyncote Group plc
BUTTERFILL, JOHN (Bournemouth West) – Director of Conservation Investments Ltd and Foxwell Securities Ltd
EMERY, SIR PETER (Honiton) – Director of Winglaw Group Ltd
HILL, JAMES (Southampton Test) – Director of Clanfield Properties Ltd
INGLEWOOD, LORD WILLIAM (Cumbria and Lancashire North*) – Director of 111 Alderney Street (1981) Ltd (residential freehold-owning company)
JOHNSON-SMITH, SIR GEOFFREY (Wealdon) – Director of Glengate Holdings plc (commercial and industrial property)
JOPLING, MICHAEL (Westmorland and Lonsdale) – Shareholder in Ryeland Properties Ltd
MARLOW, TONY (Northampton North) – Shareholder in Toddingtons Ltd
NICHOLLS, PATRICK (Teignbridge) – Consultant to Howard de Walden Estates Ltd
O'HAGAN, LORD CHARLES (Devon*) – Director of Articus Research and Design Ltd (hereditory property consultants)
ONSLOW, SIR CRANLEY (Woking) – Director of Elmdale Investments Ltd
PAWSEY, JAMES (Rugby and Kenilworth) – Shareholder of Corinium Ltd
SYKES, JOHN (Scarborough) – Shareholder of Boldstart Ltd
WATTS, JOHN (Slough) – Consultant to Wisdom Securities Ltd
WINTERTON, NICHOLAS Macclesfield – Advisor to Emerson International Ltd

Public Relations Firms

MPs can be extremely useful to PR companies. Well-known or senior MPs can almost guarantee media coverage. A speech in the House of Commons is automatically on the public record and quite often reported in the press. MPs can also host receptions and launch PR events. These will be more successful purely because the person is an MP. Indeed this category is a classic case of MPs making money out of Parliament. After all, few of them are or were specialised public relations professionals.

This section is also shrouded in secrecy. Most of these MPs on the books of PR companies have not declared the clients for whom they are working. As most of them are not members of any professional PR association, there is no way the public can find out the identity of the clients. It is a similar situation to MPs setting up private limited companies.

CARLISLE, JOHN (Luton North) – Consultant to Barry Simmons PR Ltd
COLLINS, KENNETH (Strathclyde East*) – Consultant to ERGO Communications
DURANT, SIR ANTHONY (Reading West) – Advisor to Shire Hall Communications
FISHBURN, DUDLEY (Kensington) – Consultant to Fishburn, Hedges, Boys, Williams Ltd (corporate communications)

* MEPs

GOODSON-WICKES, CHARLES (Wimbledon) – Consultant to Chelgate Ltd
HAWKINS, NICHOLAS (Blackpool South) – Director of Revelfree Ltd (corporate advisers)
JOHNSON-SMITH, SIR GEOFFREY (Wealden) – Director of Taylor Alden Ltd
LUFF, PETER (Worcester) – Consultant to Lowe Bell Consultants Ltd
MONTGOMERY, SIR FERGUS (Altrincham and Sale) – Consultant to Welbeck PR
PAWSEY, JAMES (Rugby and Kenilworth) – Director of Ranelagh Ltd
SHAW, DAVID (Dover) – Director of Sabrelance Ltd (corporate communications)
SMITH, SIR DUDLEY (Warwick and Leamington) – Consultant to Pielle and Co.
STEEN, ANTHONY (South Hams) – Consultant to the Communication Group plc
SUMBERG, DAVID (Bury South) – Consultant to Consensus (Scotland) Ltd (currently unpaid)
TEMPLE-MORRIS, PETER (Leominster) – Director of J. K. Associates (PR) Ltd
THOMPSON, SIR DONALD (Calder Valley) – Advisor to Naomi C. Arnold Consultancy
TRACEY, RICHARD (Surbiton) – Director of Ranelagh Ltd
TYLER, PAUL (North Cornwall) – Managing Director and shareholder of Western Approaches PR Ltd
WINTERTON, NICHOLAS (Macclesfield) – Director of MSB Ltd

Road, Motor and Construction Industry

The road and construction lobby is often seen as very powerful. But the two deep recessions of the past ten years have hit them harder than perhaps any other industry. In the Commons the Transport and Environment Select Committees are important, but of more significance is the powerful All-Party Road Study Group which has been funded by the Roads Campaign Council and Shandwick Consultants, the political lobbying company.

There are two main issues on which they have been lobbying hard recently. Firstly, the roads programme and the government-funded roads budget. Secondly, the Private Finance Initiative. Both these projects are co-ordinated by the Department of the Environment. But road and construction are a lobbyist's nightmare. For there are no less than nine Departments of State to deal with.

BURNS, SIMON (Chelmsford) – Consultant to Toyota
CATHERWOOD, FRED (Cambridgeshire and Bedfordshire North*) – Director of Goodyear GB Ltd
CORMACK, PATRICK, (South Staffordshire) – Consultant to Linford and Bridgeman
DEVA, NIRJ (Brentford and Isleworth) – Consultant to Laing International Ltd
FOX, SIR MARCUS (Shipley) – Consultant to Shepherd (Construction) Ltd and Buildres Merchant Federation
GOODSON-WICKES, CHARLES (Wimbledon) – Director of Eve Group

* MEPs

GREENWAY, HARRY (Ealing North) – Consultant to Taylor Woodrow plc. Also has use of a company car provided by Taylor Woodrow plc
GRYLLS, SIR MICHAEL (North West Surrey) – Director of Cape plc
HAMPSON, KEITH (Leeds North West) – Consultant to White Young Consulting; Advisor to Yorkshire and Humberside Building Employers Confederation
HOWELL, DAVID (Guildford) – Director of Trafalgar House plc
NEUBERT, SIR MICHAEL (Romford) – Advisor to Federation of Master Builders
NICHOLLS, PATRICK (Teignbridge) – Consultant to Hill and Smith Holdings plc
NICHOLSON, DAVID (Taunton) – Advisor on taxation to Building Employers Confederation
PORTER, BARRY (Wirral South) – Director of Planning International Ltd
RENTON, TIM (Mid Sussex) – Director of City Renaissance plc (associate company of Tarmac plc)
SHEPHERD, COLIN (Hereford) – Advisor to Balfour Beatty Ltd
STEWART-CLARK, SIR JACK (Sussex East*) – Director of Pioneer Concrete Holdings Ltd, subsidiary of Pioneer Australia
THORNTON, SIR MALCOLM (Crosby) – Consultant to Building Employers Confederation

Transport

The enticing characteristic of the transport lobby is that MPs are often offered a substantial amount of 'hospitality', either in the shape of free overseas visits or 'entertainment' within the UK. Of course, most MPs and companies say these are 'fact-finding missions' or that they work very hard during the trips. But the leisure time quite often outweighs the work.

MPs with commercial interests in the transport industry seem to be barefaced as well about also being members of the Commons Select Committee on Transport. This automatically creates a conflict of interests for the Member because the Committee will often be investigating issues that directly affect the company which is paying him or her. For many years the Transport Select Committee was packed with MPs with transport business connections.

CARLISLE, JOHN (Luton South) – Director of Bletchley Motors Group plc
EVANS, DAVID (Welwyn Hatfield) – Consultant to the Retail Motor Industry Federation
FOWLER, SIR NORMAN (Sutton Coldfield) – Director of National Freight Consortium plc (NFC)
GRYLLS, SIR MICHAEL (North West Surrey) – Consultant to Freight Complex Development and Management Ltd
HIGGINS, TERENCE (Worthing) – Consultant to Lex Service Group plc

* MEPs

HUNTING: HOW YOUR MP VOTED

There were three separate votes on the Hunting Bill.
Option 1 was for self-regulation; Option 2 was for statutory licensing;
Option 3 (carried) was for a ban on hunting with dogs.
F: For; A: Against; —: abstained or absent

	1	2	3
Abbott, Diane (L, Hackney N)	A	A	F
Adams, Gerry (SF, Belfast W)	-	-	-
Adams, Irene (L, Paisley N)	A	A	F
Ainger, Nick (L, Carmarthen W)	A	A	F
Ainsworth, Peter (C, E Surrey)	F	F	A
Ainsworth, Robert (L, Cov NE)	A	A	F
Alexander, Douglas (L, Paisley S)	A	A	F
Allan, Richard (L, Sheff Hallam)	A	A	F
Allen, Graham (L, Nottingham N)	A	A	F
Amess, David (C, Southend W)	A	A	F
Ancram, Michael (C, Devizes)	F	F	A
Anderson, Donald (L, Swnsea E)	-	-	-
Anderson, Janet (L, Rossendale)	A	A	F
Arbuthnot, James (C, NE Hants)	F	F	A
Armstrong, Hilary (L, NW Durhm)	A	A	F
Ashdown, Paddy (LD, Yeovil)	-	F	A
Ashton, Joe (L, Bassetlaw)	A	A	F
Atherton, Ms Candy (L, Falmth)	A	A	F
Atkins, Ms Charlotte (L, Staf Mr)	A	A	F
Atkinson, David (C, B'mouth E)	A	A	F
Atkinson, Peter (C, Hexham)	F	F	A
Austin, John (L, Erith)	A	A	F
Bailey, Adrian (L, W Brom W)	A	A	F
Baker, Norman (LD, Lewes)	A	A	F
Baldry, Tony (C, Banbury)	F	F	A
Ballard, Jackie (LD, Taunton)	A	A	F
Banks, Tony (L, West Ham)	A	A	F
Barnes, Harry (L, NE Derbys)	A	A	F
Barron, Kevin (L, Rother Valley)	A	A	F
Battle, John (L, Leeds W)	-	-	-
Bayley, Hugh (L, City of York)	A	A	F
Beard, Nigel (L, Bexleyheath)	A	A	F
Beckett, Margaret (L, Derby S)	A	A	F
Begg, Miss Anne (L, Aberdn S)	A	A	F
Beggs, Roy (UUP, E Antrim)	F	F	A
Beith, Alan (LD, Berwick)	F	F	A
Bell, Martin (Ind, Tatton)	F	F	A
Bell, Stuart (L, Middlesbrough)	A	A	F
Benn, Hilary (L, Leeds C)	A	A	F
Benn, Tony (L, Chesterfield)	A	A	F
Bennett, Andrew (L, Denton)	A	A	F
Benton, Joe (L, Bootle)	A	A	F
Bercow, John (C, Buckingham)	F	F	A
Beresford, Sir Paul (C, Mole Vlly)	F	F	A
Bermingham, Gerald (L, St Hln S)	A	A	F
Berry, Roger (L, Kingswood)	A	A	F
Best, Harold (L, Leeds NW)	A	A	F
Betts, Clive (L, Sheff Attercliffe)	A	A	F
Blackman, Mrs Liz (L, Erewash)	A	A	F
Blair, Tony (L, Sedgefield)	-	-	-
Blears, Hazel (L, Salford)	A	A	F
Blizzard, Bob (L, Waveney)	A	A	F
Blunkett, David (L, Sheff Bright)	A	F	F
Blunt, Crispin (C, Reigate)	F	F	A
Boateng, Paul (L, Brent S)	A	A	F
Body, Sir Richard (C, Boston)	F	F	A

	1	2	3
Corston, Jean (L, Bristol E)	A	A	F
Cotter, Brian (LD, W-s-Mare)	A	A	F
Cousins, Jim (L, N Tyne C)	A	A	F
Cox, Tom (L, Tooting)	A	A	F
Cran, James (C, Beverley)	F	F	A
Cranston, Ross (L, Dudley N)	A	A	F
Crausby, David (L, Bolton N E)	A	A	F
Cryer, Ann (L, Keighley)	-	-	-
Cryer, John (L, Hornchurch)	A	A	F
Cummings, John (L, Easington)	A	A	F
Cunliffe, Lawrence (L, Leigh)	-	-	-
Cunningham, Dr Jack (L, Cpld)	-	-	-
Cunningham, Jim (L, Coventry S)	A	A	F
Cunningham, Roseanna (SNP, Prh)	-	-	-
Curry, David (C, Skipton)	F	F	A
Curtis-Thomas, Claire (L, Crosby)	A	A	F
Dalyell, Tam (L, Linlithgow)	-	-	-
Darling, Alistair (L, Edin C)	A	A	F
Darvill, Keith (L, Upminster)	A	A	F
Davey, Edward (LD, Kingston)	A	A	F
Davey, Valerie (L, Bristol)	A	A	F
Davidson, Ian (L, Glas Pollok)	A	A	F
Davies, Denzil (L, Llanelli)	A	A	F
Davies, Geraint (L, Croydon C)	A	A	F
Davies, Quentin (C, Grantham)	F	F	A
Davies, Ron (L, Caerphilly)	A	A	F
Davis, David (C, Haltemprice)	F	F	A
Davis, Terry (L, Birm, Hodge Hill)	A	A	F
Dawson, Hilton (L, Lanc & Wyre)	A	A	F
Day, Stephen (C, Cheadle)	A	A	F
Dean, Janet (L, Burton)	A	A	F
Denham, John (L, Soton, Itchen)	A	A	F
Dismore, Andrew (L, Hendon)	A	A	F
Dobbin, Jim (L, Heywood)	A	A	F
Dobson, Frank (L, Holborn)	A	A	F
Donaldson, Jeffrey (UUP, Lg V)	-	-	-
Donohoe, Brian (L, Cnnnghm S)	A	A	F
Doran, Frank (L, Aberdeen C)	A	A	F
Dorrell, Stephen (C, Charnwd)	F	F	A
Dowd, Jim (L, Lewisham W)	A	A	F
Drew, David (L, Stroud)	A	A	F
Drown, Julia (L, S Swindon)	A	A	F
Duncan, Alan (C, Rutland)	F	F	A
Duncan Smith, Iain (C, Cingfrd)	F	F	A
Dunwoody, Gwyneth (L, Crewe)	A	F	A
Eagle, Angela (L, Wallasey)	A	A	F
Eagle, Maria (L, L'pool, Garston)	A	A	F
Edwards, Huw (L, Monmouth)	A	A	F
Efford, Clive (L, Eltham)	A	A	F
Ellman, Louise (L, L'pool, Rvrsd)	A	A	F

	1	2	3
Healey, John (L, Wentworth)	A	-	F
Heath, David (LD, Somerton)	A	F	-
Heath, Sir Edward (C, O Bexley)	-	-	-
Heathcoat-Amory, David (C, Wls)	F	F	A
Henderson, Doug (L, N Tyne N)	A	A	F
Henderson, Ivan (L, Harwich)	A	A	F
Hendrick, Mark (L, Preston)	A	A	F
Hepburn, Stephen (L, Jarrow)	A	A	F
Heppell, John (L, Nottingham E)	A	A	F
Heseltine, Michael (C, Henley)	-	-	-
Hesford, Stephen (L, Wirral W)	A	A	F
Hewitt, Patricia (L, Leicester W)	-	-	-
Hill, Keith (L, Streatham)	-	-	-
Hinchliffe, David (L, Wakefield)	A	A	F
Hodge, Margaret (L, Barking)	A	A	F
Hoey, Kate (L, Vauxhall)	-	F	A
Hogg, Douglas (C, Sleaford)	F	F	A
Home Robertson, John (L, E Lth)	-	-	-
Hood, Jimmy (L, Clydesdale)	A	A	F
Hoon, Geoff (L, Ashfield)	A	A	F
Hope, Phil (L, Corby)	A	A	F
Hopkins, Kelvin (L, Luton N)	A	A	F
Horam, John (C, Orpington)	F	F	A
Howard, Michael (C, Folkestone)	F	-	A
Howarth, Alan (L, Newport E)	A	A	F
Howarth, George (L, Knowsley N)	A	A	F
Howarth, Gerald (C, Aldershot)	F	F	A
Howells, Dr Kim (L, Pontypridd)	A	A	F
Hoyle, Lindsay (L, Chorley)	A	A	F
Hughes, Beverley (L, Stretford)	A	A	F
Hughes, Kevin (L, Doncaster N)	A	A	F
Hughes, Simon (LD, N Sthwrk)	-	-	F
Humble, Joan (L, Blackpool N)	A	A	F
Hume, John (SDLP, Foyle)	-	-	-
Hunter, Andrew (C, Basingstoke)	F	F	A
Hurst, Alan (L, Braintree)	A	A	F
Hutton, John (L, Barrow & Frnss)	A	A	F
Iddon, Dr Brian (L, Bolton S E)	A	A	F
Illsley, Eric (L, Barnsley C)	-	-	-
Ingram, Adam (L, E Kilbride)	-	-	-
Jack, Michael (C, Fylde)	-	F	A
Jackson, Glenda (L, Hampstead)	A	A	F
Jackson, Helen (L, Sheff Hillsbr)	A	A	F
Jackson, Robert (C, Wantage)	F	F	A
Jamieson, David (L, Plymth Dvpt)	A	A	F
Jenkin, Bernard (C, N Essex)	F	F	A
Jenkins, Brian (L, Tamworth)	A	A	F
Johnson, Alan (L, K Hull W)	-	-	-
Johnson, Melanie (L, W Hatfield)	A	A	F
Johnson Smith, Sir G (C, Wldn)	F	F	A

	1	2	3
Mackay, Andrew (C, Bracknell)	F	F	A
McKenna, Mrs R (L, Cumbernauld)	-	-	-
Mackinlay, Andrew (L, Thurrock)	A	A	F
MacLean, David (C, Penrith)	F	F	A
McLeish, Henry B (L, C Fife)	-	-	-
Maclennan, Robert (LD, Cthnss)	-	F	A
McLoughlin, Patrick (C, W Derby)	F	F	A
McNamara, Kevin (L, K Hull N)	A	A	F
McNulty, Tony (L, Harrow E)	A	A	F
MacShane, Denis (L, Rothrham)	A	A	F
Mactaggart, Fiona (L, Slough)	A	A	F
McWalter, Tony (L, H Hempstd)	A	A	F
McWilliam, John (L, Blaydon)	A	A	F
Madel, Sir David (C, S W Beds)	-	-	-
Maginnis, Ken (UU, Fmg/S Tyrn)	-	-	-
Mahon, Mrs Alice (L, Halifax)	-	-	-
Major, John CH (C, Huntingdon)	-	-	-
Malins, Humfrey (C, Woking)	F	F	A
Mallaber, Judy (L, Amber Valley)	A	A	F
Mallon, Seamus (SDLP, N&Armgh)	-	-	-
Mandelson, Peter (L, Hartlepool)	-	-	-
Maples, John (C, S-on-Avon)	F	F	A
Marek, Dr John (L, Wrexham)	A	A	F
Marsden, Gordon (L, Blackpl S)	-	-	-
Marsden, Paul (L, Shrewsbury)	-	-	-
Marshall, David (L, Gls Shettleston)	A	A	F
Marshall, Jim (L, Leicester S)	A	A	F
Marshall-Andrews, R QC (L, Mdway)	A	A	F
Martlew, Eric (L, Carlisle)	A	A	F
Mates, Michael (C, E Hants)	F	F	A
Maude, Francis (C, Horsham)	F	F	A
Mawhinney, Sir Brian (C, NW Cam)	F	F	A
Maxton, John (L, Glas Cathcart)	A	A	F
May, Mrs Theresa (C, Maidenhd)	F	F	A
Meacher, Ml (L, Old W and Rtn)	A	-	F
Meale, Alan (L, Mansfield)	A	A	F
Merron, Ms Gillian (L, Lincoln)	A	A	F
Michael, Alun (L, Cardiff S)	A	A	F
Michie, Bill (L, Sheffield, Heeley)	A	A	F
Michie, Mrs Ray (LD, Argyll/Bute)	-	-	-
Milburn, Alan (L, Darlington)	A	A	F
Miller, Andrew (L, Ellesmere Pt)	A	A	F
Mitchell, Austin (L, Gt Grimsby)	A	F	-
Moffatt, Laura (L, Crawley)	A	A	F
Moonie, Dr Lewis (L, Kirkcaldy)	A	A	F
Moore, Michael (LD, Tweeddale)	F	F	A
Moran, Ms Margaret (L, Luton S)	A	A	F
Morgan, Alasdair (SNP, Gallowy)	-	-	-
Morgan, Ms Julie (L, Cardiff N)	A	A	F
Morgan, Rhodri (L, Cardiff W)	-	-	-
Morley, Elliot (L, Scunthorpe)	A	A	F
Morris, Estelle (L, B'ham, Yardly)	A	A	F
Morris, Sir John QC (L, Aberavn)	-	-	-
Moss, Malcolm (C, NE Cambs)	F	F	A
Mountford, Ms Kali (L, Colne Vly)	A	A	F
Mowlam, Dr Marjorie (L, Redcar)	A	A	F
Mudie, George (L, Leeds E)	A	A	F

	1	2	3
Salter, Martin (L, Reading W)	A	A	F
Sanders, Adrian (LD, Torbay)	A	A	F
Sarwar, Mohammad (L, Gl Gvan)	A	A	F
Savidge, Malcolm (L, Abrdn N)	-	-	-
Sawford, Phil (L, Kettering)	A	A	F
Sayeed, Jonathan (C, Mid Beds)	F	F	A
Sedgemore, Brian (L, Hckney S)	A	A	F
Shaw, Jonathon (L, Chatham)	A	A	F
Sheerman, Barry (L, Huddersfld)	A	F	-
Sheldon, Robert (L, Ashton Lyne)	A	A	F
Shephard, Gillian (C, SW Norflk)	F	F	A
Shepherd, Richard (C, A-Brwnhls)	F	F	A
Shipley, Ms Debra (L, Stbrdge)	A	A	F
Short, Clare (L, B'ham, Ladywd)	-	-	-
Simpson, Alan (L, Nottingham S)	A	A	F
Simpson, Keith (C, Mid Norfolk)	F	F	A
Singh, Marsha (L, Bradford W)	A	A	F
Skinner, Dennis (L, Bolsover)	A	A	F
Smith, Andrew (L, Oxford E)	A	A	F
Smith, Angela (L, Basildon)	A	A	F
Smith, Chris (L, Islington S)	A	A	F
Smith, Miss Geraldine (L, Mcmb)	A	A	F
Smith, Ms Jacqui (L, Redditch)	A	A	F
Smith, John (L, Vale of Glam)	A	A	F
Smith, Llew (L, Blaenau Gwent)	A	A	F
Smith, Sir Robert (LD W Abrdn)	F	F	A
Smyth, Rev W Martin (UU, Blfst S)	F	F	A
Snape, Peter (L, West Brom)	A	A	F
Soames, Hon Nicholas (C, M Susx)	F	F	A
Soley, Clive (L, Ealing, Acton)	A	A	F
Southworth, Ms Helen (L, Wrgtn S)	A	A	F
Spellar, John (L, Warley)	A	A	F
Spelman, Mrs Caroline (C, Mrdn)	F	F	A
Spicer, Sir Michael (C, W Worcs)	F	F	A
Spring, Richard (C, W Suffolk)	F	F	A
Squire, Ms Rachel (L, Dnfrln W)	A	A	F
Stanley, Sir John (C, Tnbrdge)	-	-	-
Starkey, Dr P (L, M Kyns S W)	-	-	-
Steen, Anthony (C, Totnes)	F	F	A
Steinberg, Gerry (L, Durham C)	A	A	F
Stevenson, George (L, S-o-Trnt S)	A	A	F
Stewart, David (L, Inverness E)	A	A	F
Stewart, Ian (L, Eccles)	A	A	F
Stinchcombe, Paul (L, Wlngbrgh)	A	A	F
Stoate, Dr Howard (L, Dartford)	A	A	F
Strang, Dr Gavin (L, Ednbrgh E)	-	-	-
Straw, Jack (L, Blackburn)	A	F	A
Streeter, Gary (C, S W Devon)	F	F	A
Stringer, Graham (L, Mcr Blckly)	A	A	F
Stuart, Ms Gisela (L, B, Edgbstn)	A	A	F
Stunell, Andrew (LD, Hzl Grove)	A	A	F
Sutcliffe, Gerry (L, Bradford S)	A	A	F
Swayne, Desmond (C, N Frst W)	F	F	A
Swinney, John (SNP, N Tayside	-	-	-
Syms, Robert (C, Poole)	F	F	A
Tapsell, Sir Peter (C, Louth)	F	F	A
Taylor, Mrs Ann (L, Dewsbury)	A	A	F

Tory payback that is over

By Roland Watson
Chief Political Correspondent

SIMON WALKE

UNTIL his £1 million cheque arrived at Conservative Central Office yesterday, Stuart Wheeler had made considerably more money from Tory woes than he had spent on helping the party.

In the 1997 general election, he won £30,000 by betting correctly that the party would end up with 160-odd seats.

Measured against his previous donations to Tory coffers, there is no comparison. He remembers vaguely giving £250 last July. And before that, he "possibly" handed over £50. He voted Liberal Democrat at the last election as an anti-Labour tactical vote.

Mr Wheeler struggles to recall why he decided to become the biggest personal donor in British politics. The decider seems to have been the news of three £2 million donations

AWAY

12

DREAMWORKS PICTURES AND TWENTIETH CENTURY FOX PRESENT AN IMAGEMOVERS / PLAYTONE PRODUCTION A ROBERT ZEMECKIS FILM

TOM HANKS HELEN HUNT "CAST AWAY" NICK SEARCY MUSIC COMPOSED AND CONDUCTED BY ALAN SILVESTRI COSTUME DESIGNER JOANNA JOHNSTON EDITED BY ARTHUR SCHMIDT

PRODUCTION DESIGNER RICK CARTER DIRECTOR OF PHOTOGRAPHY DON BURGESS, A S C EXECUTIVE PRODUCER JOAN BRADSHAW PRODUCED BY STEVE STARKEY TOM HANKS ROBERT ZEMECKIS JACK RAPKE

united international pictures

WRITTEN BY WILLIAM BROYLES, JR. DIRECTED BY ROBERT ZEMECKIS SPECIAL VISUAL EFFECTS SONY PICTURES IMAGEWORKS INC

DOLBY IN SELECTED THEATRES

DREAMWORKS PICTURES

www.castawaymovie.com

TM & © 2000 DreamWorks LLC and Twentieth Century Fox Film Corporation

CINEMAS NATIONWID

the spirit of the Bill and voted against self-regulation but in favour of the second option.

The vast majority of Labour MPs voted for a ban, which was carried by 387 to 174, a majority of 213. The only Labour members to vote against a ban were Mr Straw, Jeff Rooker, the Social Security Minister, Kate Hoey, the Sports Minister, Llin Golding and Gwyneth Dunwoody.

Most Conservatives voted for the first option and then the second, although a handful, including Ann Widdecombe, the Shadow Home Secretary, voted for a ban.

The Liberal Democrats split three ways, with Charles Kennedy, the leader, voting for a ban, but others such as Lembit Opik, voting for the middle way, and Colin Breed, the agriculture spokesman, voting for voluntary regulation.

Tony Blair, Peter Mandelson, Gordon Brown and Clare Short were among the Cabinet ministers who did not vote.

With our Flexible Mortgage, if you pay a little more each month you can reduce the mortgage term, saving you thousands of pounds in interest. And if you've made overpayments, you can pay less or nothing at all for a while. The choice is yours.

For more details, contact us through any of the routes below.

0845 303 3000 **alliance-leicester.co.uk** **visit your local branch**

Lines open 8am-8pm Monday-Friday, 9am-5pm Saturday. Quoting ref: A294

Alliance Leicester

Local call rates apply. Example: £52,000 capital and interest loan for 25 years on a property valued at £55,000 at an initial interest rate of 5.24% **8.0% APR** (variable) with the first monthly payment of £529.06 (including accrued interest), followed by 11 monthly payments of £311.31, 287 payments of £389.94 and a final payment of £381.22. Total amount payable is £117,320.97. The total amount payable includes solicitor's mortgage charge (£117.50) (charges may vary in Scotland and Northern Ireland), deeds production charge (£75.00), High Percentage Loan Fee (£806.00) and redemption and sealing charge (£75.00). For the purposes of the example provided, the APR and total amount payable have been calculated assuming the Variable Discounted Rate will apply for the first 12 months and that our Basic Variable Mortgage Rate at the current rate of 7.74% will apply thereafter for the remainder of the term of the mortgage. The APR for your mortgage may be slightly different from that shown in the example if your circumstances differ from the assumptions on which the typical example is based. Mortgages are subject to status and valuation and are only available to new customers or to existing customers moving home. You must be over 18 and a UK resident. Your home will be used as security and must be insured. Written quotations on request. If you redeem this mortgage in full during the first year a repayment fee of 6 months' interest at our Basic Variable Mortgage Rate (currently 7.74%) will be charged. All applicants moving home will receive £250 cashback on completion. Applicants moving their mortgage to us without moving home will receive our Mortgage Transfer Service. Alternatively you may use your own solicitor, however you will be liable for any charges incurred. Our Free Valuation for Mortgage Loan (Option 1) offer is available to all applicants. Alliance & Leicester must choose and instruct the valuer. If a Homebuyer Survey and Valuation (Option 2) is required, the difference must be paid on application. For first time buyers Mortgage Payment Protection Insurance is compulsory for mortgages over 90% of the purchase price/valuation (whichever is the lower). Interest will be charged at a Variable Discounted Rate (currently 5.24%) of 2.5% below our Basic Variable Mortgage Rate for 12 months, then at a variable rate (currently 6.95%) of 0.95% above the Bank of England Base Rate (our Base Rate Tracker Rate) for 10 years and thereafter at our Basic Variable Mortgage Rate. Changes to our Base Rate Tracker Rate will be effected on the 1st of the month following a change to the Bank of England Base Rate (or the 1st of the following month if any change to the Bank of England Base Rate does not occur 7 days before the end of the month). Rates and APRs shown are for residential capital and interest mortgages. The mortgage is restricted to 95% of the purchase price/valuation (whichever is the lower). For mortgages exceeding 90% of the purchase price/valuation (whichever is the lower) a High Percentage Loan Fee will be charged. The value of any underpayments, payment holidays or drawings you select cannot be greater than the accumulated value of any payments you have made which exceed your normal monthly payments. Drawings subject to a £500 minimum. You must, at least seven working days prior to your next monthly payment date, give us notice of your intention to take a payment holiday or to make an under or overpayment of your normal monthly payment. Payment must be made by direct debit and must be available for collection between the first and twenty-fourth day of each month. Subject to you having received an Offer of Loan, we reserve the right to amend/withdraw this mortgage at any time. If, having received an Offer of Loan, you transfer to another of our mortgages, a switching fee will be charged. Details correct at time of going to print. For security/training purposes telephone calls may be recorded/monitored. Alliance & Leicester plc. Registered Office: Carlton Park, Narborough, Leicester LE9 5XX. Company No: 3263713. Registered in England. Authorised as a bank pursuant to the Banking Act 1987. Member of the British Bankers Association.

YOUR HOME IS AT RISK IF YOU DO NOT KEEP UP REPAYMENTS ON A MORTGAGE OR OTHER LOAN SECURED ON IT. A294

HOGG, NORMAN (Cumbernauld and Kilsyth) – Director of Kelvin Central Buses Ltd; Consultant to the Bus and Coach Council
JACKSON, CAROLINE (Wiltshire*) – Director of Peugot Talbot Motor Company
MARSHALL, JOHN (Hendon South) – Consultant to Bus and Coach Council
NORRIS, STEVE (Epping Forest) – Shareholder in Anthony Ince Ltd
RATHBONE, TIM (Lewes) – Consultant to Eurotunnel plc
SIMPSON, BRIAN (Cheshire East*) – Director of Coachlines of Warrington Ltd, and shareholder in Great Central Railway plc
SMITH, SIR DUDLEY (Warwick and Leamington) – Consultant to Volvo UK Ltd
SNAPE, PETER (West Bromwich East) – Director of West Midlands Travel plc
SPEED, SIR KEITH (Ashford) – Consultant to the Inner City Division of British Rail
SUMBERG, DAVID (Bury South) – Consultant to Peninsula Bus Services Ltd
TWINN, IAN (Edmonton) – Consultant to TNT
TYLER, PAUL (North Cornwall) – Shareholder of Bodmin and Wenford Railway plc
WALKER, BILL (North Tayside) – Director of Stagecoach International Services Ltd; Director of Stagecoach Malawi Ltd
WATTS, JOHN (Slough) – Consultant to British Bus plc

* MEPs

Index of Companies and Organisations

Excludes City and County Councils, and Trade Unions mentioned only as sponsors under the Hastings Agreement.

Entries are arranged alphabetically, as if there were no spaces between words. Prepositions, conjunctions and initial numbers are ignored
eg Able Bakers
A & B Ltd
5 Amber Street Ltd
A. M. Brown
Columns are indicated by a or b after the page number.

Index of UK Constituencies

Index of Euro-Constituencies